T0318198

PRIMITIVE CAPITAL ACCUMULATION
IN THE SUDAN

PRIMITIVE CAPITAL ACCUMULATION IN THE SUDAN

Abbas Abdelkarim

LONDON AND NEW YORK

First published 1992 by
FRANK CASS & CO. LTD.

Published 2004 by Routledge
2 Park Square, Milton Park, Abingdon, Oxon OX14 4RN
605 Third Avenue, New York, NY 10017

Routledge is an imprint of the Taylor & Francis Group,
an informa business

British Library Cataloguing in Publication Data
Abdelkarim, Abbas *1950–*
Primitive capital accumulation in the Sudan.
1. Sudan. Economic conditions
I. Title
330.9624

Library of Congress Cataloging-in Publication Data
Abdelkarim, Abbas, 1950–
Primitive capital accumulation in the Sudan / Abbas Abdelkarim.
p.   cm.
Includes bibliographical references (p.   ) and index.
ISBN 0–7146–3324–0
1. Saving and investment—Sudan. 2. Agriculture—Economic
aspects—Sudan. I. Title.
HC835.Z9S32 1991
339.4'3'09624—dc20
91–2589
CIP

ISBN 13: 978-0-7146-3324-4 (pbk)

Typeset by Selectmove Ltd, London

CONTENTS

PREFACE
AND ACKNOWLEDGEMENTS

Primitive capital accumulation is understood in this work as the historical stage in which the capitalist and non-capitalist modes of production articulate and wherein capital has not yet established its domination. I say 'yet', as this implies that the capitalist mode of production has the capacity to transform the specified socio-economic formation towards the establishment of its domination.

The book attempts to analyse the main tendencies and forces in the development of the Sudanese socio-economic formation after the systematic penetration of the capitalist mode of production. Its primary aim is to provide a class analysis and thus expose the main tensions encountered by the present stage of development – an analysis that may be useful for the development of a progressive political strategy in Sudan. The book also endeavours to contribute to a methodological approach that could be of wider relevance to studies of the political economy of transition to capitalism.

Data resources used in the book are contemporary case studies, small sample surveys and interviews as well as appropriate published and unpublished materials. That the overwhelming majority of the population in Sudan live in rural areas justifies the heavier emphasis of this book on the rural population.

The research upon which this book rests was undertaken at the School of Development Studies, University of East Anglia, Norwich (England). Finance for this study was provided by the Overseas Development Administration (through the British Council) and by the University of Juba, Sudan. A small grant has also been made available by the Economic and Social Research Council in Khartoum.

During the course of my research I have been assisted by many individuals to whom I am personally, politically and intellectually greatly indebted. I am in no position to mention all names.

Agricultural workers in Gezira, industrial workers in different towns in Sudan, Gedaref farmers and household producers, as well as other individuals in different places have educated me patiently about their situation and about Sudan. What I have learned about Sudan in my field work (which took about a year) definitely exceeds in depth all that I have learned about it during the rest of my life. Elfatih Shaaeldein has been a source of continuous help, encouragement and advice during my field work. Omer Tamim, a long-standing friend, offered me hospitality and provided me with transport in Gezira. Wagdi Mirghani and Hashim Khalid made my stay comfortable in Gedaref and helped me to learn a great deal about Gedaref farmers and farming. Not least, members of my extended family and many other friends in Khartoum have been, as usual, a great help in many ways.

My lifelong friends Anwar Ali and Amna Mohammed offered me a warm welcome in Britain (in a country where, on my arrival, I hardly knew anyone else). In Norwich, Tony Barnett and John Cameron, who were my supervisors in UEA, offered me unfailing guidance, encouragement and friendliness, without which this work would have been very difficult to undertake. Abdalla Elhassan, my friend and colleague, has been a source of continuous encouragement, help and stimulating ideas. Norma Meecham has not only typed and retyped this and other works many times, but she has also helped a great deal in editing of the draft. My wife Samia has patiently tolerated my ups and downs while writing this work and also helped me in processing some of the data.

To all these individuals and institutions I am greatly indebted.

A.A.

CHAPTER ONE

Primitive Capital Accumulation: A Theoretical Framework

I. THE NOTION OF PRIMITIVE CAPITAL ACCUMULATION

The notion of primitive capital accumulation first found expression in Adam Smith's *The Wealth of Nations*. Adam Smith presupposes an accumulation of 'stock' that must precede the division of labour; 'as the accumulation of stock is previously necessary for carrying on this great improvement in the productive power of labour, so that accumulation naturally leads to this improvement' (Smith, 1976: 277).

Marx came to conceptualise Smith's 'previous accumulation' from his own historical materialist method. The capitalist mode of production, according to Marx, presupposes the transformation of money into capital and the 'double freeing' of wage labourers ('free' from access to the means of production and 'free' in their persons to dispose of their labour power commodity). For him, then, the process of primitive capital accumulation 'is a process which operates two transformations, whereby the social means of subsistence and production are turned into capital, and the immediate producers are turned into wage labourers' (Marx, 1976: 874).

Marx argues that the expropriation of land from the agricultural direct producers is the basis of the whole process. However, 'the history of this expropriation assumes different aspects in different countries, and runs through its various phases in a different order of succession, and at different historical epochs' (*Ibid*: 875). Conceiving that histories of expropriation are conditioned by different factors in different places and times leads Marx to a study of the process of primitive capital accumulation within the particular historical context of one country – England.

After Marx, both at the theoretical and empirical levels, the study of the process of primitive capital accumulation has been the subject of little attention by Marxian scholars. This is no surprise. For decades after Lenin and Kautsky, and still largely at present, class formation and class relations have been removed from the centre of analysis of socio-economic formation.

1

It may be worth mentioning that some Marxian scholars used the concept of 'primitive capital accumulation' accidentally and/or in a limited, narrower sense, a sense closer to Adam Smith's 'previous accumulation'. Rosa Luxemburg in her book *The Accumulation of Capital* written in 1912 (Luxemburg, 1963) characterises the non-capitalist socio-economic formations as sources of 'primitive capital accumulation' (narrowly understood as sources of surplus appropriated by 'primitive', non-capitalist methods which is to be transformed into capital elsewhere). Preobrazhensky, in his book *The New Economics* (1967), written in the 1920s, was mainly concerned with the study of some theoretical economic aspects of the transition to socialism. He uses the concept of primitive capital accumulation in a comparative, narrow sense. He attempts to draw an analogy between the role and method of merchant capital and the capitalist state as the two main forces in the process of primitive capital accumulation, and the role of the Soviet state in what he calls the process of primitive socialist accumulation.[1] Banaji (1973) uses the concept of primitive capital accumulation within his conceptualisation of the 'colonial modes of production':

> We can thus define the colonial modes of production as the historical effects of a worldwide process of subordination of pre-capitalist modes of production to capitalism, that is, of an epoch of primitive accumulation, but where subordination itself least assumed the simple aspects of destruction. (*Ibid*: 396)

Banaji's understanding of primitive capital accumulation is apparently different from that of Marx, and he never puts it explicitly. Primitive capital accumulation for him is not exactly the pre-history of capital. Those 'colonies or semi-colonies' are not 'non-capitalist' 'as the laws which govern their reproduction derived from their subordination to imperialism' (*Ibid*: 396). Although those colonies or semi-colonies are subordinated to capitalism (he also characterises them as 'backward capitalism'), nevertheless, their development along capitalist lines is blocked (*Ibid*: 401). Difficulties with understanding Banaji arise from his inconsistency and misconception of the dialectics of subordination–domination of the capitalist mode of production – a characteristic of many 'dependency' theorists. I shall return later to the problem of the relations of subordination–domination. However, for a discussion of Banaji's general method and critique of his ideas, see Harriss (1979) and Wolpe (1980).

A common element in many post-Marx users of the concept of primitive capital accumulation is that they have failed to conceive it as essentially concerned with a process of internal class formation. The process of primitive capital accumulation is essentially the process whereby capital is transforming the socio-economic formation. It is the process of class formation in its initial stages, wherein the majority of the producers have not yet been transformed into 'double free' wage labourers and where capital has not yet established its domination over the socio-economic formation though transforming it towards that end.

The process of primitive capital accumulation can be conceived as essentially a situation of 'articulation of modes of production'. Issues of conceptualisation of modes of production, socio-economic formation and articulation of modes of production have been among the most controversial issues in the Marxist literature in the 1970s, and remain so today.

II. MODE OF PRODUCTION AND SOCIO-ECONOMIC FORMATION

Oscar Lange (1963; published much earlier in Eastern European languages) was among the first, if not the first, Marxist political economist to elaborate definitions for 'mode of production' and 'socio-economic formation'. (This appears to have been rarely, if ever, acknowledged by reviewers of the modes of production literature.) Lange's conceptions of mode of production and socio-economic formation can be illustrated in the figure below:

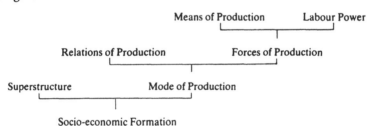

Lange conceives of mode of production as a combination of forces and relations of production. Hence he may be called the founder of the 'economistic conception' of mode of production. This conception, still largely predominant in Marxist literature, although expressed in somewhat different variations, is one which reduces mode of production to its economic level and which investigates the juridical, political and ideological levels only at the level of the socio-economic formation. Among many other advocates of such a view, Laclau gives the following definition:

> We therefore designate as a mode of production the logical and mutually co-ordinated articulation of 1 – a determinate type of ownership of the means of production, 2 – a determinate form of

3

appropriation of the economic surplus, 3 – a determinate degree of development of division of labour, 4 – a determinate level of development of the productive forces. (Laclau, 1971: 33)

Wolpe (1980), following Balibar, makes a distinction between two different conceptions of mode of production, both of which are 'economistic', although he does not describe them as such. The first, which he refers to as a 'restricted' conception, conceives of mode of production as a combination of forces and relations of production. The second, which he calls the 'extended' conception, understands mode of production as 'the combination of the relations and forces of production together with the mechanism of reproduction or laws of motion derived from these relations and forces of production' (*Ibid*: 7).

The concept of mode of production has been rejected completely by some scholars. After accepting it and offering, to borrow Wolpe's terminology, a 'restricted' conception, Hindess and Hirst came to replace it with 'relations of production' (see *Ibid*: 19–27). Friedmann offers an alternative concept, 'reproduction totality', which encompasses 'relations of exploitation, appropriation plus relations of realisation, circulation plus forces of production as the significant theoretical totality' (cited in Harriss, 1979: 52). Foster-Carter (1978), finding difficulties with the economistic conception of mode of production, has come to reject completely the need of the concept itself. He says: 'Some studies tend to treat modes of production as an entity occupying the totality of explanatory space – either omitting the political level (or juridical or ideological) or relegating them to a minor place. This is not only economism but reification'; and further – 'as modes of production are not the subject of history, so neither should they be the subject of a sentence' (*Ibid*: 55).

Presenting himself as the advocate of an anti-'economist' interpretation of 'mode of production', Alavi (1975) has not gone as far as to construct an alternative. He asserts: 'What we do wish to emphasise here is the inadequacy of any conception of the "mode of production" that is premised narrowly on sets of relationships that are arbitrarily assigned to the "structure", ignoring the totality' (*Ibid*: 182). What will immediately appear from this argument is that by 'totality' Alavi means both the economic base (or structure as he calls it) and the superstructure; indeed in his article, just before the above quotation, he mentions relations of 'structure–superstructure'. However, it seems that either Alavi's definitions of the 'structure' and the superstructure are different from those commonly understood in Marxist literature or that he has been inconsistent in pursuing his argument. Apparently

Alavi identifies the structure with the relations of production and he takes the latter as different from the relationships of appropriation. He comes to offer a total conceptualisation of the 'mode of production' as 'a theoretical construct that defines a coherent and historically defined set of relations of production and appropriation' (*Ibid*: 182). Alavi's thrust has been to stand against attempts at reducing the concept of mode of production to the production relation (such attempts apparently he takes as 'economism'); however, his attempt to 'emphasise the complex, dialectical unity of the whole and the necessity to consider all the aspects of that unity for an adequate conceptualisation of the mode of production' (*Ibid*: 182) has not produced an alternative to the economistic conception of the mode of production. 'Relations of appropriation' are still directly related to the economic level, although they need to be legalised, protected politically and founded ideologically. And here comes the crux of the difficulty with the economistic conception. By not including the juridical, political and ideological levels or aspects explicitly, we remain without a construct wide and abstract enough to grasp the social entities in their totality – their laws of motion, and the dialectical relationship between their different aspects and between each of the latter and the whole. The linkages, dialectical relations of determinations and counter-determinations that exist between the economic base and the superstructure, and the different factors and conditions that secure uninterrupted (but not repetitive) reproduction of, and cause change (transformation) in, the totality cannot be conceived at the theoretical level without such a wide abstract concept, from which further theoretical concepts can be derived.

The primacy of the economic aspect, determining the direction of the motion of the totality in the last instance, obviously does not mean that other aspects are deduced from it or determined by it directly, or that they do not in their turn determine the direction of change.

The concept of socio-economic formation is not an alternative for such a wide abstract concept (be it mode of production or another new concept). The concept of socio-economic formations is applied to concrete societal entities, while we still need to construct abstract dialectical relationships between the economic base and the superstructure. (Lange's schema provides this link only at the concrete level.)

Scholars also disagree on the definition of 'socio-economic formation', although generally this generates less controversial discussion. Banaji (1977) does not see any necessity of distinguishing between the two concepts, as he considers such a distinction 'to obscure the mechanism of modes of production'. In fact he sees the world economy as composed of different modes of production (rather than countries) at different levels of hierarchy and relations of subordination (Banaji, 1973). Bettelheim (cited in Wolpe, 1980) identifies socio-economic formation with national economy. Harriss (1979) seems to conceive of it as not limited only to one level (i.e. a national economy). He usefully points out that 'As a concept, mode of production is clearly *not* spatially restricted, and it may be employed in the analysis of concrete societal entities at various levels' (*Ibid*: 51).

The dilemma of the debate focuses more strongly when the concept of 'articulation of modes of production' comes under inspection. What follows is not intended to be a complete review of the debate. (Foster-Carter, 1978; Harriss, 1979; and Wolpe, 1980 provide excellent reviews of the debate on mode of production.) A central issue that has come out of the debate and which is at the same time one of the main concerns of this work is how to comprehend relations of subordination, domination and transformation in a situation where the capitalist mode of production is articulating with other modes of production. Or to put it another way, for those who are not sympathetic to the use of the concept of 'articulation': how can we determine whether or not the capitalist mode of production has become dominant in a specified socio-economic formation?

III. THE CAPITALIST MODE OF PRODUCTION: DIALECTICS OF SUBORDINATION–DOMINATION AND TRANSFORMATION

Wolpe (1980: 36–41; all quotations below are from these pages) sums up the debate on mode of production (m.o.p.) and socio-economic formation (s.e.f) with three possible definitions. The first conceives of s.e.f 'as comprising a combination of modes of production restrictively defined' (see section II above for Wolpe's definition of 'restricted' and 'extended' concepts of m.o.p.). For Wolpe, this way of conceptualising s.e.f. would lead to the construction of a linking mechanism between m.o.p.'s – if at all possible – at the level of a specified s.e.f. and necessarily on an arbitrary basis. This would deny any significance to the concept of m.o.p. The second possible definition of s.e.f. is one that sees it 'as being constituted by a combination of extended modes of production'. Wolpe points out that this conception is objected to because some writers think 'it is not possible to conceive of a social formation in which a dominant mode of production does not constitute the principle of unity'. Against this objection, Wolpe suggests that at least in transition, a concrete s.e.f. may be seen as constituted by extended m.o.p.'s none of which is dominant. He adds that the analysis of s.e.f. in this fashion has not received much attention in the literature of articulation.

The third possible definition of s.e.f., which Wolpe himself seems to agree with, sees it as one 'which is constituted by the co-existence of an interrelationship between a dominant extended mode and subordinated restricted modes of production'. According to Wolpe, in an s.e.f. where the capitalist mode of production is dominant, its abstract laws of motion constitute the unity of this s.e.f.: 'the relationship between the units or enterprises is entirely dependent upon the movement of the capitalist mode of production'. He argues that there is no necessary connection between the reproduction of m.o.p.'s restrictively defined and the existence of the laws of motion belonging to them. In this sense, 'there is no necessary reason why capitalist enterprises (restrictively defined) should not arise and be reproduced in social formations in which the laws of motion of capitalist mode of production are absent'. The converse is also true for Wolpe: non-capitalist m.o.p.'s restrictively defined can persist in an s.e.f. where laws of motion of capitalist m.o.p.'s have already displaced those of the non-capitalist m.o.p.'s.

Wolpe has directed criticism at Hindess and Hirst's *Precapitalist Modes of Production* in which they suggest separation of forces and relations of production from the reproductive mechanism. What he has suggested, namely that 'subordinated' m.o.p.'s could exist without the laws of motion 'belonging' to them, is exactly the same as the view he has attempted to criticise. Wolpe does not seem to offer any clear definition of the 'laws of motion' or the 'mechanism of reproduction', and how they are essentially different and could be neatly separated from production relations and forces of production.

However, the major difficulty with Wolpe's favoured conception of articulation is that it does not include a theory of transition. According to him, laws of motion in an s.e.f. are those of the dominant m.o.p. Other subordinated m.o.p.'s are not effective at the level of reproduction. How is it possible then for a capitalist m.o.p. in a subordinate position and not effective at the level of reproduction to establish its domination over the s.e.f.? Wolpe does not seem to give any answer. And again, if the non-capitalist 'enterprises' or m.o.p.'s are reproduced through the laws of motion of capitalist m.o.p. (when the latter is dominant) what, then, makes it necessary for them to change, to be transformed or to vanish?

Towards the end of his work Wolpe asserts that 'relations of articulation are themselves relations of struggle'. However, all through his work Wolpe, unfortunately, has not given any ground for struggle to be comprehended as the driving force behind development.

An entire line of Marxian theorists has failed to conceive of domination –subordination relations in s.e.f. as essentially relations between classes. 'Dependency' or 'world systems' theorists (or neo-Smithian Marxists,

7

as Brenner, 1977, calls them) have replaced social classes by 'systems' – domination–subordination relations are between 'world systems' and their components. Their methods have greatly influenced 'the articulation theory' or at least the 'Anglo' version of it. Definitions of articulation given by Wolpe and by many others (again see Foster-Carter, 1978; Harriss, 1979 and Wolpe, 1980 for a review of different conceptions of articulation) have failed to break from the limitations of the 'world systems' theory. However, Rey's conception of articulation has definitely broken away from the 'world systems' theory. His conception of articulation, for me, is much more in line with Marx's historical materialist method. For Rey,

> the articulation of two modes of production, one of which established its domination over the other not as static given, but as a process, that is to say a combat between the two modes of production, with the *confrontation and alliances* which such a combat implies: confrontation and alliances essentially between *the classes* which these modes of production define. (My emphasis, cited in Foster-Carter, 1978: 56)

Rey brings the articulation to the level of classes that constitute the different modes of production – an articulation that is characterised by confrontation and alliances (this is definitely better than Bettelheim's 'dissolution/conservation' concept, which not only sounds functional but is also appropriate for domination–subordination relations that characterise 'systems' rather than classes).

Domination of the capitalist mode of production over other modes of production is to be conceived as necessarily domination of the capitalist class. Domination of the capitalist class necessarily entails the transformation of the production process into a capitalist one (i.e. it becomes the process of surplus value production), and the transformation of the legal, political and ideological systems and forms of consciousness into predominantly capitalist ones.

Domination of the capitalist m.o.p. is established through a process of confrontation and alliances, or 'conflict' and 'unity', between the capitalist and the non-capitalist classes. The dialectic of confrontation and alliances implies that development is not a linear process. Development of the capitalist m.o.p. may go through relative stagnation, relative rest or even falling back, depending on the concrete outcomes of class struggle. The relative rest or stagnation in the development of capitalist m.o.p. in specific areas over a number of years or decades has led an entire line of Marxian scholars to conclude that the development of the capitalist m.o.p. in the 'periphery' is 'blocked' and that Marx's thesis, put forward

8

in the *Manifesto*, of the inevitability of the destruction and transformation of the non-capitalist m.o.p.'s into the capitalist m.o.p. has not proved to be accurate. A critique of such ideas or theories is to be found elsewhere (most notably in Brenner, 1977). However, those observations often lack detailed empirical evidence. They have not shown that classes in the 'periphery' are not forming along capitalist lines, no matter how slow the pace of that formation.

A confusion of the usage of the concepts domination and transformation seems to be quite common in the 'development–underdevelopment' (which includes 'modes of production') debate. If a capitalist m.o.p. has been penetrating and transforming an s.e.f. it is immediately looked upon as being the 'dominant' m.o.p. in that s.e.f. In fact, transformation starts from a subordinate position. The fact that some of the forces that may initiate the process of transformation (e.g. a colonial power, private capital and the transitional local state) in a specific s.e.f. (e.g. colonies) are dominant elsewhere (i.e. in the home country) does not mean that the capitalist m.o.p. is immediately going to establish its domination over the colonial s.e.f.'s. Domination is essentially domination of allied classes within the specific s.e.f. However, the capitalist m.o.p. can be subordinated in a specific s.e.f. while also transforming that s.e.f. It can transform the s.e.f. towards establishing its own domination because it produces and reproduces the conditions of that transformation, i.e. it produces a capitalist class that in its thrust for accumulation and survival (extended reproduction via innovation) will use all means available to it and will struggle against all social and natural forces that may stand as an obstacle.

It is this stage, in which capitalist m.o.p. is in a subordinate position while also transforming the s.e.f., that I claim Marx means by 'primitive capital accumulation'. The practical question that arises is: when do we start talking about 'capital accumulation' rather than 'primitive capital accumulation'? – or in other words: when do we conceive of the capitalist m.o.p. moving from subordination to domination? As has been mentioned, the capitalist m.o.p. establishes its domination at the economic aspect or level of an s.e.f. by transforming the production process into a valorisation process (i.e. the production of surplus value). At the superstructural level the domain is complete only after transforming the different forms of consciousness into predominantly capitalist forms, in other words, after the freeing of both classes in the capitalist m.o.p., capitalist and wage labour, from the non-capitalist forms of consciousness. The capitalist m.o.p. cannot be conceived as a dominant m.o.p. in a specific s.e.f. unless its domination is established over all the different levels.

It is suggested here that the essential first condition to establish the dominance of capitalist m.o.p. in an s.e.f. is the transformation of the majority of the producers into free wage labourers in a double sense – as free individuals who can dispose of their power as their commodity, and as free from all objects needed for the realisation of their labour power (see Marx, 1976: 272–3). This argument needs a little more elaboration.

As an indication of the development of capitalism, the contribution of the so-called 'modern sector' in the national income is often contrasted with the contribution of the so-called 'traditional sector'. Leave aside now the controversy about usage of such terms. Even were it possible to quantify the total value of commodities and services produced under capitalist production relations, still such an indicator alone would be inadequate for assessing the development even of the economic aspect of the capitalist m.o.p. Such an indicator would show that countries such as the Arab oil-producing ones, since the discovery of oil, have become predominantly capitalist, as the major share of the national income is produced under capitalist relations, and indeed using the highest level of technology! Change and transformation is necessarily about people, rather than their products. The transformation of the majority of the producers into wage labourers indicates that the large part of the production process is capitalist and that the large proportion of the population are living under capitalist production relations. Moreover, the double-freeing of the wage labourers also means that they are free from the non-market relations that might hinder their standing on a footing of equality as commodity owners with the purchasers of the labour power commodity. In other words, the double-free wage labourers are not only free from access to the means of production, but also forced to become free from non-capitalist forms of consciousness that might not allow their transformation into 'free individuals', that is, 'free' in the capitalist sense.

IV. PRIMITIVE CAPITAL ACCUMULATION AND THE DOMINANCE OF MERCHANT CAPITAL

Dominance of merchant capital is not as Kay (1975) argues 'the cause of underdevelopment' but, rather, it represents a specific (lower) stage of development of capitalism, i.e. the stage of primitive capital accumulation. In the history of capitalism, merchant capital has always been the first and, for a time, the dominant form of capital. While productive capital appropriates surplus from the capitalist production process (wage workers), merchant capital appropriates surplus from both wage workers (the capitalist production process) and household producers (the household production process). In the stage of primitive capitalist accumulation the capitalist production process is not the dominant one.

Hence the material base for merchant/circulation capital, which also appropriates surplus from the household producers, is wider.

The 'double' role of circulation capital has been well demonstrated in *Capital*, Vol. Two (and also in Kay, 1975). While widening the frontiers of the process of commoditisation in non-capitalist sectors and hence opening up doors for capitalist development, circulation capital withdraws a proportion of the surplus value from capitalist production and keeps it locked in circulation and hence closes some other doors in the face of the process of expanded reproduction.

Kay rightly points out that the 'merchants do not make their profits by revolutionising production but by controlling markets, and the greater the control they are able to exercise the higher their rate of profit' (*Ibid*: 96). In the stage of primitive capital accumulation, when merchant capital enjoys a wider material base, it is in a position to tighten control of markets as it is definitely able to concentrate and centralise its capital faster than productive capital can. However, not all fractions of merchant capital are in this position or capitalist production would never come into existence; this is one thing among others that Kay's analysis fails to note. If all fractions of merchant capital were able to control the market in such a way that they could always attain a higher rate of profit than productive capital, we could not assume that productive capital would ever come into existence. But productive capital does exist in the 'periphery' (though its size and rate of development will vary widely at different times and at different places), contrary to Kay's assumption that merchant capital is the only form of capital that exists in the underdeveloped countries (see, for example, *Ibid*: 100).

Kay's method not only fails to go much beyond the dependency thesis of underdevelopment, which is that it has tried to transcend 'exploitation of the periphery by the centre'; it also fails to offer an alternative guide to revolutionary practice (which is the whole objective of the theory of value in which Kay attempts to seek an explanation of relative development). By considering merchant capital in the periphery as the 'agent' or 'aspect' of developed industrial capital (e.g. *Ibid*: 100, 105) for which it is losing profits and by which it is dominated (*Ibid*: 123), Kay holds the same 'dependency' view. Class struggle is still not on the agenda. The immediate enemy or the immediate tasks are outside the immediate socio-economic formation.

Capital in general cannot be the dominant force in a society if capital has not become the owner of the production process, i.e. become productive capital. However, the dominant position of certain fractions of circulation capital, if existing, could hinder the achievement of that objective. Productive capital, and probably also other less privileged fractions of circulation capital, whose interests may be affected by the relative stagnation of the market, in order to maintain rates of profit need to enter into an overall struggle against the privileged fractions of circulation capital. This is a struggle in which productive capital may need to mobilise non-capitalist classes at the level of the political whilst resisting their demands at the level of the economic. This struggle is essentially internal, within the immediate socio-economic formation, although the wider (regional or world) socio-economic formations may also influence it. Foreign capital or its 'agents', when they exist, can be treated as part of the classes internal to the immediate socio-economic formation.

CHAPTER TWO

Some Aspects of Commoditisation and their Impact on the Household Producers

This chapter provides a background and an introduction to the major case studies of this book – the Gezira and Gedaref. It attempts to expose some processes that are less discussed in the following chapters and which are nevertheless essential for our understanding of the changes and transformations that are taking place in rural Sudan.

Thus it does not claim to be comprehensive in its treatment of the themes selected. Where more details are to be found in other chapters or other sources the reader will be immediately referred to these.

I. COMMODITISATION OF THE MEANS OF PRODUCTION AND CONSUMPTION AND THE ROLE OF CIRCULATION CAPITAL

Trade and the Commoditisation of the Means of Production and Consumption

Trade centres and trade routes connecting some parts of the Sudan to each other and connecting the country to the outside world via the western, eastern and northern borders and later via Suakin (an old now deserted harbour on the Red Sea) had been in existence for many centuries before the coming of the British army and are relatively well documented (see Amin, 1970; Elhassan, 1985). Although exchange of products in local markets between farming and pastoralist communities seems to have existed in many places for basic goods, external trade served mainly the consumption needs of the elite of those communities. The relative intensification of the commoditisation of the means of consumption and production, which has been developing at different paces and affecting the different communities in a variety of ways, is a matter of recent origin, commencing at the beginning of this century. British rule opened the way for a systematic and wider linking of Sudan with the world market by initiating some material conditions for the creation (where previously non-existent) and intensification of money–commodity relations.

Following the British flag, British and other companies and individuals moved into the country. Large companies like Gellatly, Hankey and Company, Sudan Mercantile and Mitchell Cotts, soon dominated the export–import market. Export traffic started to increase (see Table 2,1), with the country's main export items in the first three decades of British rule (before the Gezira's cotton) being gum arabic, groundnuts, sesame and livestock. These products had been produced by household producers. Incentives for increased production could only follow from an increase in cash needs. Those big companies, helped by their network of agents (of both foreign and local traders – see Chapter 7) within a few decades had flooded the market with new consumer goods, thus starting

TABLE 2,1

Expansion of Sudan's total exports and imports 1907–1925 in £S millions
(before the Gezira Scheme)

Year	Total Exports	Total Imports
1907	0.4	1.6
1910	1.0	1.9
1915	1.6	1.7
1920	4.7	7.0
1925	3.8	5.4

Source: Beshai: 1976, p.336.

TABLE 2,2

Quantities of some selected principal imports into Sudan in the first three decades of
British rule
(in thousand tons)

Year	Sugar	Coffee	Tea	Soap
1907	6.7	0.6	0.1	0.4
1910	10.8	1.1	0.4	0.9
1915	10.8	1.7	0.4	0.9
1920	14.8	4.2	1.1	1.1
1925	13.7	4.2	1.4	2.1
1930	31.2	6.3	2.2	2.6

Source: Beshai: 1976, p.312.

to create new tastes, enlarging the circle of needs of the household producers.

Table 2,1 shows clearly how much produce for the external market had multiplied within two and a half decades of the start of the systematic incorporation of increasing numbers of household producers into commodity production. From 1907 (the earliest data available) to 1925, that is in less than two decades, the total exports of Sudan (which up to that time were exclusively produced by household producers without any intervention in the production process by foreign or indigenous capital) had multiplied almost tenfold. An increase in cashcropping had been accompanied, as is clear from the total number and quantity of imports, shown in Tables 2,1 and 2,2, by an increase in consumption, in the area of mass consumption by household producers. (Total imports exceeded total exports in that period obviously as a result of the immediate needs of the Colonial Administration to establish and consolidate its rule.) These changes in a few decades had reached even the most remote, self-contained communities in the country (see, for example, the case of Dinka in Lako, 1983 and Western Savannah in Elhassan, 1985). When some local communities resisted the penetration of some of the merchandise goods, which was occurring to the detriment of their own local industries (e.g., the textile industry, which had been known in the country at least since the last century, see A. Abdel Rahim, 1963: 8) the state came to the aid of merchant capital by effectively banning those industries (see the case of banning cotton cultivation and the local textile industry in the Rahad area in central Sudan referred to by O'Brien, 1980: 166). However, the statement above should not be too strongly emphasised, as the type of capitalist goods which arrived in the markets had for the most part been either unknown before to the local communities (e.g. sugar, tea, flashlights) or had been able to compete with and replace the local industries (textiles, shoes, cooking oil).

With the expansion of what constitutes the reproduction 'needs' of the household producers, commoditisation intensifies and the role of exchange in the reproduction cycle increases. When increased cash-cropping is possible then this may be a way of meeting the increased level of subsistence needs. In Eligayla village in Western Sudan, for example, the villagers started to grow sesame as a cash crop in the 1920s and, having limited labour resources, they replaced the time-consuming *dukhun* (millet) by *dura* (sorghum) as a food crop (*Ibid*: 454). In fact, sesame, cotton, gum arabic and groundnuts, which are four of the five most important cash crops grown in the country are, up to the present time, mostly produced by household producers. For example, 75% of the 1979/80 sesame output had been grown by household producers (Statistical Abstract, 1981: 92).

When cashcropping or its intensification is not possible, seasonal or permanent migration to local or district employment centres – that is commoditisation of labour power – may be the only means of satisfying the expanded household needs. The relation between cashcropping (or local wage income) and migration as alternatives to meet the increased needs of subsistence is reflected in the fluctuation in the numbers and sources of migrant labourers coming to the large agricultural and urban areas. In Gezira, for example, the fluctuation in the influx of seasonal labourers depends not only on the quantity of labour needed in the Scheme itself but also to a great extent on the conditions of home production of the potential seasonal labourers. Through the Gezira labour recruitment office in Nyala (Western Sudan), for example, in 1973 with the poor rainfall in the region, 18,000 workers went to wage labour in the Gezira Scheme. A year later, and after good rains, only 4,000 went (Haaland, 1980/a: 11).

Increased dependence on the market to obtain the means of production has also been characteristic of many farming communities in the Sudan in this century. Hand tools still remain the only means of production used in most of the agricultural areas in the country. Even in the so-called mechanised farming and other tractorised areas, hand tools remain very significant; weeding and most of the harvesting labour is carried out using hand tools. Hand tools apparently are increasingly bought from the market. This is obvious in agricultural areas like the Gezira and Gedaref where most of the produce is market oriented and where the market generally has become indispensable for the reproduction process. However, it also seems that in communities, where provision of subsistence (and not exchange) constitutes the basic logic of the production process, the means of production are also often bought in the market as opposed to the earlier practice of making them at home (Western Savannah in Elhassan, 1985).

In Sudan in this century two major advantages in the mechanical input into agricultural production can be distinguished: the introduction of water pumps and tractors. These, however, did not represent a mere change in the level of the forces of production introduced from outside. Pumps and tractors appeared and have proliferated as a result of some quantitative changes in a process of primitive capital accumulation, and also, from their side, have contributed considerably to the progress of this process. The socio-economic, as well as the political, context and the physical extent of the expansion of pump irrigation and tractorisation will be discussed in the following chapters. Here, only a few notes on the extent of their use will be given.

Pump irrigation was first used on a commercial scale in the Zeidab project (a foreign, privately owned project – see Gaitskell, 1959) in the northern region. Pump use started to grow rapidly from the late 1940s and its expansion had reached a plateau by the early 1960s (T. Ali, 1983). In the late 1970s land irrigated by pump was estimated to be 1,472,000 feddans. That was about 34% of the total irrigated land, about 8% of all land cultivated in Sudan and producing about 14.5% of the country's total produce.[1]

Tractorisation has been causing a more fundamental change in the level of the forces of production (and in the class structure) in Sudan. Tractors are used in opening up new land for cultivation, ploughing, seeding and also in transport. Tractors can be used in most of the cultivable (i.e. irrigated and rainfed) lands in the Sudan. It was in the Gezira Scheme that machinery was used for the first time in land preparation on a large scale. However, it was with the so-called Mechanised Farming Schemes, which started in the Gedaref region (see Chapter 4), that tractors became widely used. In six decades from the mid-1920s to the early 1980s, use of tractors in cultivation in Sudan rose from virtually nil to covering about 49% of the total land cultivated.[2]

Trade, Finance and Increasing Pressures Towards Commoditisation

As has been mentioned above, household producers in general depend increasingly on the market to meet their subsistence needs. Most of the commodities they buy are processed commodities: sugar, cooking oil, tea, coffee, clothing, tools, etc. In exchanging their own produce for these the household producers seem to face disadvantages. The origin of these disadvantages is twofold: deteriorating terms of trade between agriculture and manufacturing, and the monopoly of the village merchant. Household producers face the consequences over time of deteriorating terms of trade not only at the level of the world's economy, but even within the national economy. As a result of government policies, agricultural products seem to exchange on unequal terms with internally processed goods such as cooking oil, salt, clothing, flashlight batteries, which constitute a considerable part of household needs. Investigating government policies which may influence the effective rate of protection, and based on data for the year 1971, Acharya (1979: 66) concluded that Sudanese industrial products on average had an effective rate of protection of 170% as opposed to −27% attributed on average to agricultural products (which effectively means +27% taxation). If this conclusion, at least as a tendency, is true, it is clear that household producers enter into unequal exchange both when buying internally processed goods and when selling their own crops. (In this case the rural population's unfavourable terms of trade arise from government policies which interfere in the process of exchange value formation.)

Except in rare cases when villages inhabited by household producers lie immediately outside towns, household producers seem to buy their necessities from within the village from a very few resident merchants. In most cases it also seems that they would sell their products to the same merchant or others also residing in the village. However, apparently in a few cases (as for example some household producers in the Gedaref area field-researched by the author in 1983), household producers may rent vehicles to take their products to a town-market, and probably also buy some products from there. Being very few in number, probably one or two in small villages, the village merchants seem to stand in an effective, though not unlimited, monopolistic position which gives them an advantage in their exchange relations with the household producers. Nomads are not subject to the same unfavourable exchange relations, as during their migration they can choose between many merchants and trade centres.

From the foregoing it can be established that amid conditions of increasingly unfavourable terms of exchange, and assuming other things remain the same, the more household producers depend on the market to meet their subsistence needs the more pressure they will feel towards commoditisation, that is, the more households will need to cashcrop and/or sell their labour power as a supplement to previous production if they want to maintain the same level of consumption.

Household producers also face commoditisation pressures to borrow, in money or in kind. There are different forms of money-lending in rural Sudan. Some of these may not involve paying interest (i.e. borrowing from friends and relatives, or in the Gezira and similar projects, from the Scheme's Administration) and are therefore not part of our concern here. The best known, widely used form of interest-bearing money-lending by individuals in rural Sudan is commonly called *shail* (sometimes written *shayl*). The *shail* financiers extend credit to household producers before or during the agricultural season, which is then normally repaid after harvest, together with interest. Either end of the *shail* transaction may take the form of money or kind. However, money–kind and kind–kind forms of transaction seem to have been the more common forms of *shail* transactions in the earlier periods and still are in some places. This is perhaps best explained in terms of ideological factors. As most of the *shail* financiers are Moslems, and as they try to give the impression of being good Moslems, while Islam prohibits interest (but not profit) in commercial transactions they will try to arrange receipt of their repayments in kind form. This makes the whole transaction at the surface level look like 'buying in advance' (though for a price below market price – which, however, is still acceptable by Islam) rather than 'money-lending'.

Shail money-lending seems to be widely spread in different parts of the Sudan (see among others O'Brien, 1980 and Elhassan, 1985). It has been an important means of surplus appropriation (although it is very difficult to estimate the significance of this). *Shail* financiers, who are in many cases merchants (e.g. village shopkeepers) as well, realise relatively high real interest rates. The rate varies according to the length of the period and risk involved, personal relationships, the financial position of the recipient, and expectations of production and prices. In one locality normally few people can afford to extend credit, and in many cases there may be none. In the Gedaref region, as has been reported by some household producers and small farmers, some may need to go to Gedaref town to look for *shail* finance as there may be none available or, if available, it may be below the level of demand in their own villages. Under such circumstances *shail* financiers can charge high interest rates. In Gedaref, the few large farmers who have reported entering into *shail* credit arrangements paid up to 50% interest for periods ranging from 2 to 5 months, while small farmers and subsistence household producers over the same period have reported paying from 50% to 300% interest (see Chapter 4). Gezira seasonal labourers (discussed in Chapter 3) who are also independent producers in their own home areas have reported paying interest rates ranging from 50% to 150%.

Circulation capital seems to feed the process of commoditisation and differentiation from many sides. First, it enlarges the circle of needs of the household producers by introducing new goods. Second, it involves deteriorating conditions of exchange and hence the need for further commoditisation. Third, and as a result of an increasing need for cash, household producers enter into relationships with money-lenders. By intensifying money–commodity relations at levels described above, circulation capital contributes significantly to the disintegration of (1) the household and other forms of non-capitalist social forms of organisation of labour, and (2) the non-capitalist forms of land control.

II. COMMODITISATION OF LAND

It seems appropriate to start this section with a survey of the land tenure system in the Sudan before and immediately after British rule.

Land Tenure

The main source of information in this section is Bolton (1948).

By the time the British colonial administration was set up in the country in 1898, three main forms of land tenure were in existence.

1. Where settled farming had been practised, members of the community had access to the land through their membership of the community and might have been offered their plots by the leaders of the community or might have been using the land with such leaders' explicit consent. Normally, no one would claim rights over land that had been cultivated by others. Land might or might not be inherited and could be changed if exhausted (generally, land was relatively abundant). Land could be offered to other people if it was abandoned temporarily or permanently by the original user. Ties to specific plots were very loose.

2. In some cases in some farming communities, land had been recognised by people as being privately owned. No rights over these lands would be established by others in cases of temporary absence. Land could be inherited, sold or rented. This type of ownership had been established largely over lands which could be cultivated continuously for long periods, for instance, in the riverain lands of central and northern Sudan, in Tokar and Gash Delta lands irrigated by floodwater, and in *wadi* (watercourse) lands in several parts of the Sudan, but also in the rainlands of the Gezira (where documents of title dating from the Funj kings were produced by the natives for the authorities in the early stages of land settlement), in Nuba mountains and probably in other areas.

3. In the case of pastoralist communities, land had normally been communally used by the community (tribe, sub-tribe, camp) as a whole. Organisation of land use among different segments of the tribe (e.g. long migration routes) has been and still is vested by the members of the community in the hands of the leaders (see Asad, 1971 for Kababish, and Leinhardt, 1967 for Dinka).

By a series of land settlement ordinances (see also Gaitskell, 1959: 42–48) from as early as 1899, the British administration attempted to 'regulate' ownership and transfer of ownership of land and to establish itself as the major 'legal' land-owner. According to those ordinances, three forms of ownership were registered (these forms still exist):

1. *Land individually owned.* The criterion for registration of such land was continuous cultivation, but apparently this had not always been adhered to. Riverain land of central and northern Sudan (along the

Nile from Kosti in central Sudan to Halfa in the northern region) and rainland of Gezira which satisfied the criterion of continuous cultivation were registered on the basis of individual ownership. In other places (like Tokar and Gash Delta in eastern Sudan, *wadis*, etc) this right had not been recognised; instead land had either been expropriated (Gash and Tokar) or was registered to be potentially expropriatable by the state.

2. *Government land subject to rights vested in a community* (tribe, village and sometimes individuals). All land not recognised as individually owned or not yet expropriated by the government came into this category. The government thereby established itself as the 'legal' owner of these lands (this continues to be the case at present). Although the right to use the land had been vested in the hands of the customary leaders, this right when the need arose could be lifted. Indeed, this was the case when, for example, land was needed for experimentation of mechanised farming in Gedaref in Eastern Sudan in the 1940s (see Chapter 4). The national governments that succeeded the British rule, using this 'legal right' had also expropriated hundreds of thousands of feddans (1 feddan = 1.038 acres) to be leased to large farmers for the so-called mechanised farming and when establishing schemes on the model of Gezira (see Chapter 3).

3. *Government land subject to no rights.* In this category fall expropriated lands, for example, Tokar and Gash Delta in the first two decades of British rule, basin lands of Karu near Shendi in the northern region in 1938, as well as land incorporated into the government sponsored schemes, e.g. Gezira, or bought by the government from private owners to be used for certain projects.

The paradoxical situation brought about by those land settlement ordinances is that the state formally owns the vast majority of all the agricultural land in the country, while the people, most of whom are in fact ignorant of the formal right the government has given to itself, think and act among themselves according to their own customs with regard to land ownership. Where land has not yet been expropriated, people recognise each other's rights over their land plots. In fact, when lands were expropriated from the original producers by the government to establish 'modern' projects, this had often been resisted, and conflicts in some places continue to exist (see Simpsons, 1978 and AOAD, 1978). In the following sections and throughout this work, when 'land ownership' not recognised by the government is discussed, it should be taken as 'ownership' according to the people's view (although generally the term 'access' will be used).

Commoditisation of Land: Major Steps and Tendencies

The state has been the major force (both positively and negatively) behind the commoditisation of land in Sudan. Obviously, its role is conditioned by the socio-economic and political factors and environment prevailing at the specific time. The role played by the large land-owning classes in many other areas in the process of transition to capitalism is being played in Sudan by the state. The conditions of class struggle that have led the land-owning classes in different countries to relinquish control over land in non-capitalist forms, and/or to develop into agricultural capitalists, have also been pressing the state in the Sudan (as the largest land-owner) in the same direction.

Due to the absence of a landless class during the early period of British rule, and to expected unfavourable political consequences of utilising forced labour in Sudan (a measure that the British administration tried to avoid),[3] appropriation of surplus was thought to be best arranged through sharecropping arrangements. Indeed, this was started first in smaller pump schemes in the northern region (see Chapter 3) and was then transferred to the Gezira which promised to be the most important economic project for the colonial government (and remains such in the post-colonial period as well). The most fertile permanently irrigable lands were selected for that purpose. This was natural. With the relative abundance of lower-quality rainlands in the Sudan, sharecropping arrangements will not be an attractive alternative to the household producers if their returns fall below what they could get from their rainlands.

To establish the Gezira Scheme on lands where private ownership had been prevalent for centuries, the colonial government had to buy out or force owners to leave their lands. This was probably the most significant step in the history of land commoditisation in Sudan. Several hundred thousand feddans of the government's expropriated bought or leased lands were leased to tenants in smallholdings starting in the mid-1920s. (In the first phase of the Scheme over 300,000 feddans were distributed – Gaitskell, 1959.)

The second and third major steps in land commoditisation in Sudan were largely initiated by the rising indigenous capital, in the second as circulation capital and in the third as productive capital.

Private pump schemes developed first in the northern region. Starting from the late 1940s/early 1950s and up to the mid-1960s private pump schemes had been multiplying rapidly, reaching well over one million feddans in total area cultivated (Shaaeldin, 1981). As will be discussed later, it was the relative development of the process of primitive capital accumulation (money wealth accumulating in the hands of some as a result of their activities in circulation, and the development of landless or semi-landless classes that had been prepared to accept entering into sharecropping arrangements as tenants) that had led to the emergence and expansion of those schemes. However, the rising indigenous and foreign capitalists also encouraged the state to acknowledge its 'formal' land ownership and to lease that land to them (which they in turn leased to tenants). Both the colonial and post-colonial governments had an interest in such action. Besides the obvious economic benefits (especially during the early period of the private pump schemes' boom, when cotton prices were escalating and remained high for a time) there were political interests as well. As T. Ali (1982, 1983) and Shaaeldin (1981) have maintained, the colonial government was interested in establishing an economically powerful class ally. This ally came to power in the post-colonial period and its interests have been fully protected by the post-colonial governments.

The third major step in land alienation in Sudan started in the Gedaref region in eastern Sudan. Its preconditions were the development of the process of commoditisation of labour (Chapters 5 and 6) and the accumulation of money capital in the hands of a rising number of Sudanese nationals who were prepared to move to production. The rising national capital pulled the 'land-owner' (the state) in two directions. First, to realise its 'ownership' of parts of the land (which were at that time only its property on paper) by expropriating them from their original 'users' (in the government thinking) or 'owners' (in people's thinking). Second, to lease the land to capitalist producers. This started in the mid-1950s in the Gedaref region and since that time has developed considerably in Gedaref itself and has spread to many other places in Sudan (see Chapter 4).

The expropriation of the lands of household producers on which these 'Mechanised Farming Schemes' had been established and the lease of the land to private capitalists was in itself a great step in land alienation (commoditisation). Later, further steps in commoditisation are to be observed. The government leased land under those schemes on a long-term basis (originally 25 years, but in principle extendable). Transfer of the scheme's leases and sub-renting, as the case study of Gedaref shows, has become common despite the fact that it is considered illegal; the government apparently takes no action – at least this has been the practice up to the present. In fact, the scheme leaseholders consider themselves land-owners rather than tenants; to the extent to which they cultivate the land it is theirs, to be inherited (the transfer to a son or immediate relative can even be made 'legal'), sold, or rented.

There is no fear that the original land-owner (as may be the case of a private land-owner who leaves his land) may find a better lease offer and enforce the end of contract with the current leaseholder. While the government's rent from those schemes is non-differential, the rent and the price for the transfer of the scheme asked for by the schemes' owners are differentiated. During late 1982 and early 1983 the author observed that the selling price of schemes (of 1,000–1,500 feddans in size) ranged from 40,000 to 200,000 Sudanese pounds, and the rent per year ranged from 2,000 to 12,000 Sudanese pounds. These differentials were based on type of soil and location, in terms of rainfall and proximity to main roads and market centres.

The development of land commoditisation in Gedaref and other Mechanised Farming Schemes is in great contrast to the large Gezira Scheme. Land purchasing or renting with a view to establishing larger farms is very limited, if taking place at all. The government stands as the obstacle to the development of land commoditisation. Private capital, being unable to produce on an expanded scale in the Gezira because of the strong hand of the government on the Scheme (which is considered as one of the government's main sources of revenue), has moved largely to off-farming activities and to outside the region. With the freezing of further commoditisation of the land in the Gezira, apparently a process of decommoditisation of labour power is taking place. Increasing numbers of settled wage labourers who at times depended almost solely on selling their labour power have been entering into sharecropping arrangements with the tenants, and providing their own households' labour in the sharecropped plots (see Chapter 3).

Alienation of land in other places is even lower. In the Dongola area a large part of the land is freehold. Nevertheless, sale and purchase of the land is very restricted. Freehold land-ownership, no matter how small, in Dongola brings a social prestige which is desirable (Omer, 1979). As a result, landholdings are continuously being divided among heirs according to Islamic traditions and law until land-owners are unable to subsist off their small plots and may be compelled to migrate. The normal situation in that area is that the land-owners (many of whom may be absentees) enter into sharecropping arrangements. The major form of labour is the household labour of the sharecroppers.

In the case of Western Savannah some commoditisation of land seems to be developing, although currently at an early stage. In one of the villages which is most affected by the nearby development of mechanised farms, 4.7% of the people acquired their land through purchase and a similar percentage through rent. There is no landless class there, but the majority of the producers also engage in wage labouring in the nearby mechanised farms and on each other's plots in peak periods (Elhassan, 1985).

In the case of the Dinka in the sample surveyed by Lako (1983), 3% have reported acquiring their land through purchase and 5% have resorted to wage labour to assist in land preparation. Similarly in Dinka there is no landless class.

What can be observed from the different cases referred to above is that there is a strong correlation between the processes of commoditisation of land and of labour power in Sudan. Where a clearly distinct landless class has developed and where wage labour is almost the only form of labour used (i.e. Gedaref and other Mechanised Farming Schemes) the commoditisation of land has reached its relatively highest level. Where an initial step of land alienation was undertaken as in the Gezira (and where wage labour had developed as a main social form of labour for the first time in Sudan), but where the position of the state hindered the further development of commoditisation of land and labour, a process of decommoditisation of labour started to prevail and expand. A similar analogy between degrees of commoditisation of labour power and of land can be observed in the other cases as well. However, it is also important to note that as in the case of other social relations a positive relationship between the development of the processes of commoditisation of labour power and land can be seen only as a tendency and not inevitable. At any specific place and time, a number of other variables may also play a role and may influence these processes in different directions.

III. COMMODITISATION PRESSURES AND CHANGES IN THE GENDER DIVISION OF LABOUR

Depending on the source of livelihood (whether it is cultivation or pastoralism or a combination of the two) and the cultural position of women (mainly whether a more rigid form of Islam is ideologically dominant leading to the seclusion of women), different forms of household division of labour can be seen in different communities. Also within different households in the same community the gender division will vary, depending upon different conditions and attitudes (for example, the age and sex structure and the number of members in the household, the attitude to the 'ideal' of women's seclusion, the economic situation of the household).

By contrast, division of labour based on age is similar in different communities. Generally, children below the age of 12 and elderly people are assigned only a minor role in the production process, if at all. Children may give a hand irregularly in some farming activities, providing services for the working adults by fetching drinking water, bringing food and tea from home, giving a hand in domestic work and rearing home-based animals. At this age young girls even in communities which practise women's seclusion may be allowed to perform these minor tasks and mix with other people (Um Fila in O'Brien, 1980).

Regarding the varying division of labour based on gender, there are still some common features among different communities in the Sudan. Women, even if undertaking a full role in the production process, are still assigned the domestic labour (the case of non-Arab cultivators in Southern Darfur, Haaland, 1980/b, and the case of Eligayla village in Northern Kordofan, O'Brien, 1980). Among nomadic and semi-nomadic pastoralist communities, regardless of whether or not they are Moslems, generally both young boys and girls may engage in rearing home-based animals, and both men and women may milk, but other tasks associated with animal rearing, which may include seasonal migration and travelling distances away from villages or camps, are generally assigned to men (see the cases of the Baggara tribe (Cunnison, 1966), Kababish (Asad, 1970) and Dinka (Lako, 1983)).

In the Kababish pastoralist-nomadic tribe, the woman performs all tasks associated with the household, including spinning wool and weaving for making tents, as well as making beds and decorations (and the finished products belong to her). In the Baggara pastoralist tribe, the woman carries out all domestic labour and also erects, dismantles and moves the tents as the camp-site changes (and she also owns the tent). In both cases, women also process milk products (prepare clarified butter called *samin*), sell the surplus of this, and may help in milking and in other 'men's' work.

In some farming communities women participate fully in the farming activities. Where there is no, or less, seclusion of women, they may be able to own and cultivate their own lands. In some of the farming communities it has been observed that women have separate fields where they exercise full command over the land and the produce grown (Haaland, 1980/b:72 and O'Brien, 1980:442).

In some of the places where seclusion of women is exercised, it is women's participation in public work that is objected to, rather than their participation in agricultural work as such, as O'Brien (1980: 359) observes in his study of Um Fila. In fact, to a great extent, O'Brien's argument may be generalised to some other communities. In Um Fila, women cultivate small plots within their *hosh* (home area). Mustafa (1980: 112) also observes the same thing in the Radom area (in Southern Darfur in the western region). Shaw (1961) argues that in the Gezira, women's participation in agricultural work in earlier times was apparently higher than later, when wage workers coming from outside the region started to settle and to form a major proportion of the total labour force. Where women are secluded, and where they cannot cultivate in private because of the conditions of production or for other reasons, their work, in principle, may be confined to home. However, this does not mean they will not be engaged in productive work, as they may be engaged in household production. For example, the married women amongst the poorer section of the community in Maiuro produce cooked foodstuffs and craft goods (Duffield, 1981: 107).

The ideal of women not participating in 'public' or in agricultural work as such is no longer held by many households in an increasing number of communities. To mention but a few cases, in three villages surveyed in the Gedaref region – where women's seclusion is still advocated, women are not supposed to work in the fields, and women are denied the right to inherit land – it was found that in three classified income groups of people, 'rich', 'medium' and 'poor', the percentage of women engaged in income-generating activities in 1982 was 16%, 30% and 50% respectively (ILO/UNHCR, 1984: 42). However, household heads in those villages, as was mentioned in the study, would still largely deny this. In Um Fila changes regarding the ideal of women not participating in 'public' agricultural activities can also be observed. O'Brien (1980: 326) mentions the case of the merchant-farmer whose mother and two wives work in the fields. Duffield (1981) also found that among West African migrants in Sudan, who seemed to be one of the strictest communities in respect of women's seclusion, the practice has been relaxed.

What we can conclude from the above is that the development of capitalist commodity production is causing some changes in the household division of labour based on gender in many communities in rural Sudan, especially where the ideal of women's separation from agricultural work as such, or from public agricultural work, has been dominant. The increasing pressure on the standards of living of agricultural producers has led some poorer households to relax their ideals and pushed female members to work in the fields, either alongside the male members of the household, or to replace the men in maintaining the household production base while they are away working as migrant wage labourers. And even among richer households the desire to keep their relatively higher level of consumption or even to increase it or to accumulate has led to the same position. These changes in the household division of labour have led to an increased burden on women, as they still have to bear the responsibility of all the domestic work in which men generally do not participate.

CHAPTER THREE

The Gezira: The Transitional Pattern of Sudanese Agriculture

INTRODUCTION

In the development of the economic aspect of the capitalist mode of production in rural Sudan we can identify three broad stages or patterns existing at the same time (in the early 1980s) in different communities and areas. These are: (1) household production, (2) the transitional pattern, and (3) the capitalist pattern. Although a wider variety of production relations may exist within those categories, in our classification here only the dominant production relations are emphasised.

The first, 'household production', is characterised by being in a relatively earlier stage of transition to capitalism. The logic of production of the majority of the households in this type is towards simple reproduction of the production unit (the household); that is, accumulation is not yet the motive or necessity behind the process of production and reproduction. The main social form of organisation of labour is the household itself, although extra household labour, communal voluntary (*nafir*) or wage labour, may be needed at certain periods during the production cycle. Some household members may also need to supplement their household income from their own produce by selling their own labour power to other households within the same community (often implying monetisation of *nafir*), in some other agricultural areas or in urban areas (seasonal migration). We find almost no landless classes settling as wage labourers in those communities.

However, a trend of labour power release shown in permanent migration to settle elsewhere (in large agricultural production or in urban areas) as wage labourers seems to be occurring in some of those communities. This is probably because the village economy may not be in a position to absorb excess labour power or may hinder the freeing of wage labour in the sense of being free proprietors of their own labour power.

Surplus is appropriated mainly in trade. Involvement in trade as buyers and sellers varies from one community to another depending on the profile of own produce compared to subsistence needs. For example, in Kababish, dependence on the market to buy subsistence needs is higher

28

than in Dinka. The two communities are mainly pastoralists, but while the latter also practises cultivation and thus secures a large part of staple food (sorghum or millet), the former does not. In other communities, e.g. Western Savannah, the means of production (e.g. hand tools) are increasingly bought from the market and in some villages which lie in the vicinity of Mechanised Farming areas, a trend of hiring tractors is also observed among some household members.

Access to land in those communities is largely secured through membership of the community. In the case of pastoralist communities, land is used by the whole community (with some possible internal divisions). In communities practising cultivation, land is under private control as far as members of the community are concerned. The ultimate 'legal' owner of the land in both cases is the state (according to land ordinances enforced during the early period of colonial rule). However, those communities seem to be largely unaware of this fact.

Land alienation is low, except when the state realises its legal ownership and confiscates land from the household producers, establishing large private farms as in Gedaref or small tenancy schemes as in Gezira and New Halfa. In pastoralist communities apparently no land is sold, purchased or rented. In cultivating communities a very limited transfer of land title does occur, for example in Western Savannah and in Eligayla. From information available at present it is difficult to suggest specific trends in this respect.

Under this relatively earlier stage of transition to capitalism, which I called here predominantly 'household production', live the majority of the rural people in Sudan. In this category come among others the following Sudanese studies: Baggara (Cunnison, 1966), Kababish (Asad, 1970), Dongola (Omer, 1979), Um Fila and Eligayla (O'Brien, 1980), Dinka (Lako, 1983) and Western Savannah (Elhassan, 1985).

The second stage of the development of the economic aspect of capitalism in rural Sudan is called here the 'transitional pattern'. This is not to suggest that transition is absent in the first category of communities discussed above, but only to indicate that transition is more heavily marked than in some other communities in Sudan.

I. ORIGIN AND DEVELOPMENT OF THE TRANSITIONAL PATTERN

Very little is known to us at present about the economic history of the pre-British colonial period in Sudan. Whether the relations between circulation capital and the producers were such that the former financed part of the production process supervised by the latter could not be adequately investigated from the available sources. In such circumstances it seems logical to consider such relations from the time some documentation is available.

The transitional pattern was first noted in the Zeidab project in northern Sudan in 1907. The Sudan Plantation Syndicate (SPS), a British private company, later to take up the management of the Gezira Scheme, acquired land of about 11,000 feddans (one feddan is 1.034 acres) through a concession from the colonial government.[1] Land was distributed among small producers (tenants) in holdings of 10 or 15 feddans of cotton as well as small areas in which to grow their own subsistence crops. The SPS provided land and irrigation as well as ploughing. For the first two, land rent and water rates were paid for in the form of half of the cotton produce. For ploughing, tenants paid separately. Their duty was to provide labour in their own tenancies. The company undertook the ginning of cotton in its own factory and also its marketing (Tracey, 1948: 760–1).

The state also established seven similar projects (six of which varied from 2,000 to 4,000 feddans), during and immediately after the First World War, in northern Sudan. Hewison (1948: 749) states that the primary intention of those pump schemes was to meet fodder needs of the British armed forces then stationed in Egypt as well as to increase local crop production. Later some foreigners acquired pump schemes (which had to close down during the depression between the wars).

Indigenous entrepreneurs then took the lead. By 1937 and 1943 the number of private pump schemes in northern Sudan was 77 and 147 respectively (*Ibid*: 759). Hewison attributes this relatively large increase to the high wartime price of food crops, which attracted many merchants to invest in agriculture. From this period, as Omer (1979) shows us, private as well as cooperative, and to a lesser extent, government schemes, increased in number and in total land cultivated. In the late 1970s, total land under pump irrigation, which is almost without exception under more or less the same production relations, covered an area of about 235,000 feddans (World Bank Report, Vol II, 1979: 105).

Although the transitional pattern started in northern Sudan, its further expansion took place mainly in central Sudan (where suitable land is relatively more abundant). The first private pump scheme was established in 1925 (called Gondal, later abandoned and taken over by the government). However, this scheme apparently was not run following the same relations as those involved in other pump schemes.[2] The first government pump scheme was established in 1927. This was followed by others called 'Alternative Livelihood Schemes', the official intention of which was to provide a means of living for those displaced from their lands as a result of the building of Jebal Aulia dam on the White Nile. By 1943 there were 10 private schemes totalling 48,000 feddans in area (see Mackinnon, 1948:

790–803). Since that time and until the mid-1960s, the number and area cultivated by private entrepreneurs under these relations had increased dramatically. A survey of pump schemes undertaken in 1964/65 (cited in Shaaeldin, 1981: 109–10) shows that, in central Sudan, land registered for pump schemes (most of which were run by private entrepreneurs) totalled 888,509 feddans. (The ratio of licensed to actually cultivated land in that year for the pump schemes as a whole in Sudan was 10:7.) For the whole of Sudan, according to the Pump Schemes Survey of 1964/65, there were 2,283 schemes cultivating 1.2 million feddans (and controlling 1.7 million feddans). Since 77% of the land was government land, private scheme leaseholders had to get licences from the government to use it. The schemes employed about 90,000 tenants.

Compared to private pump schemes, the state-owned ones constituted only a small fraction until the 1960s. From the latter half of the 1960s, an increasing number of private schemes were transferred to the state with the leaseholders' consent, in fact coming to their rescue. By 1979 a total area of about 770,000 feddans was taken over by the state (with the consent of its owners). Schemes run by private entrepreneurs in the late 1970s totalled only about 298,000 feddans (World Bank Report, Vol II, 1979: 105).

The state's largest investment in schemes similar, in terms of production relations, to those described above, was in Gezira in central Sudan. After the Managil Extension to Gezira, land cultivated totalled over two million feddans and was distributed among 100,000 tenants.

Long after Gezira, some other state-sponsored schemes were established. New Halfa (or Khasm el Girba as it is also called, starting in 1964) in eastern Sudan extends over an area of 390,000 feddans. The Es Suki Scheme in central Sudan (established in 1973) covers an area of 85,000 feddans. The Rahad Scheme, also in central Sudan, started its first phase of over 150,000 feddans in 1977, and increased to 300,000 feddans in the second phase. (For details on New Halfa, see Sorbo, 1977; on Rahad and Es Suki, see O'Brien, 1980.)

The private, cooperative and government pump schemes, and other large government schemes, which are to be categorised as being in the stage of transition to capitalism, extended over a land area of about 4,250,000 feddans in the early 1980s. This constituted about 20.5% of the total cultivated land in the country, producing about 32% of the total produce and accommodating roughly 250,000 tenant households.[3] Privately owned schemes amounted to only 7% of the total land cultivated by all schemes under the transitional pattern (World Bank, Vol II, 1979: 105), while in the mid-1960s they had accounted for over half. This sharp decrease was due to the government's taking over of

31

some privately owned schemes, in an effort to rescue them following the sharp decline in the world cotton price (see T. Ali, 1982 and Shaaeldin, 1981).

Production relations in the transitional pattern are more or less as has been described in Zeidab above. Whether the state, companies or individuals run the schemes and whether land is owned by the scheme holder or leased from the government does not make much difference to the role of the scheme management. Normally, irrigation is provided by the scheme leaseholder/manager. Land is subdivided into smallholdings to be offered to tenants. Tenants are to provide labour in their own tenancies. Part of the agricultural labour needed (e.g. ploughing) may be provided by the scheme management. There is either a sharecropping system or fixed rates for land and water are to be paid by the tenants. For other extra duties performed by the management, tenants normally have to pay additional amounts either in cash or, if marketing of the crops (or the main crop, normally cotton) is undertaken by the management, by deduction from the proceeds of those crops. In most cases the main crop is in fact marketed by the management. Money advances are also extended by the management in most cases.

In such conditions the scheme management appropriates surplus as land controller and as circulation capital (financier and merchant). In addition, although only to a marginal extent, the scheme management may appropriate surplus directly in the form of surplus value from directly employed labourers. In most cases the scheme management undertakes the land preparation, generally using its own tractors. For the operation and maintenance of irrigation equipment (in the case of pump schemes) or systems (gravity irrigation) the scheme management employs direct wage labour. In these cases surplus value is being produced by those wage labourers, a part of which is appropriated by the scheme management. However, we should not take capital invested in irrigation and in tractors or other means of production by the scheme management as essentially productive capital. This kind of investment is meant mainly to be hired out and not used directly to produce surplus value. In this sense the scheme management plays the role of a machinery contractor, i.e. essentially a merchant selling the use of the commodity for a certain duration.

This distinction is very important to avoid misconceptions adopted by many political economic studies of Sudan. Mahmoud (1979) and T. Ali (1982) describe the scheme leaseholders as agricultural capitalists. Dealing with capital accumulation, Shaaeldin (1981) describes the transference of the control of most of the private pump schemes to state control in the 1960s and 1970s as a reversal to commerce and finance. Without going into detail, O'Brien (1980) categorises the transitional pattern as capitalist. If the scheme leaseholders (whether private individuals or the state) are agricultural capitalists, this implies that the process of production is the valorisation process and that they are the direct controllers of this process. This would entail showing that the tenants and their households, as well as the large number of labourers employed by them, are in fact employed by the scheme leaseholders/management as wage labourers. Studies referred to above have not attempted to demonstrate that. However, Fonno (1978) has argued that Gezira tenants are de facto wage labourers.

Confusion over the role of the scheme leaseholders and their place in the production process originates from neglecting the analysis of the production process itself. As has been demonstrated above, in those areas categorised here as 'transitional', the scheme leaseholders/management are not the direct purchasers of labour power (except marginally). Nevertheless, they still appropriate surplus labour, although, in their case, not as productive but as circulation capitalists. This situation is characteristic of the stage of primitive capital accumulation.

Since its establishment in 1925/26 the Gezira Scheme has been the most important economic project in the country. It was established by the British colonial rule in the Sudan (1898–1956) with the aim of producing cotton for the British textile industry and also to provide revenue for the administration of the quasi-colony. Gezira's importance in the economy of Sudan derives from the fact that it is the major producer of cotton, the country's largest export crop. The Scheme extends to over 2 million feddans, which is nearly half of the total irrigated land area and about 11% of the total actual cultivated land in the Sudan.

The Scheme was established, according to official terminology, on a 'partnership' basis, the three partners being the Government, which provided land and irrigation (land was either confiscated, bought or leased from the original owners); the Administration of the Scheme (the Sudan Plantation Syndicate, a private British company, replaced in 1950 by the Sudan Gezira Board, a parastatal corporation); and the tenants.

The Gezira Scheme has been the focus of considerable attention in the literature of development in tropical Africa. This is because it is one of the largest agricultural projects initiated by a colonial government. Divergent views are expressed in two of the main works on the Scheme, which describe it as a 'Story of Development' (Gaitskell, 1959) and an 'Illusion of Development' (Barnett, 1977).

II. TENANTS' HOUSEHOLD LABOUR INPUT

As was laid down in the Tenancy Agreement, the provision of labour was considered to be the responsibility of the tenants. It was believed that the bulk of the farm labour would be supplied by the tenants' households. Yet it was also recognised that at certain peak times (e.g. weeding and cotton-picking) they might need extra household labour, and the Tenancy Agreement of 1927 allowed for loans to be extended to the tenants for the provision of wage labour.

Contrary to expectations, the tenants' household labour (thl) has proved not to be the main form of labour in the Scheme. The earliest available documentation for this statement is Culwick's report (1955), where it was established that thl has always been second to wage labour in respect of the proportions of labour input.

In her study based on three villages in 1952/53, Culwick suggests that for a holding of 10 feddans of cotton, 5 feddans of *dura* and 2.5 feddans of lubia – a standard tenancy size at that time – 3.6 'full' person units would be required to meet the demands of all farm labour needed. According to her calculations, only 1.8 person units were available, on average, per tenant household. She also realised that not all the person units available were actually fully involved in farm labour. In two villages the thl contributed only one eighth and a third of the total labour requisite, about a quarter on average (Culwick, 1955: 150–63).

Table 3,1 confirms Culwick's findings. It shows that the contribution of the thl in the total labour required for the production of cotton and dura for three seasons from 1958/59 was relatively low. It is also noticeable that in some blocks the thl was quite low and may even be considered as negligible (those blocks seem to be mostly the ones closer to the urban centres in the northern and eastern parts of the Scheme).

TABLE 3,1

Contribution of thl in the production of cotton and dura crops in percentages in 3 successive years in Gezira

Crop	Season 1958/59	Season 1959/60	Season 1960/61
Cotton	7%	8%	10%
	(1:16)	(2:18)	(2:21)
Dura	14%	16%	16%
	(0:30)	(2:30)	(1:39)

Source: Adapted from Abdelhamid, 1965, Table XXXXV.

TABLE 3,2

Percentage contribution of thl in the different crops from 1976/77 to 1980/81 in Gezira

Season	Cotton	Wheat	Groundnuts	Dura
1976/77	25	48	26	22
1977/78	22	52	37	32
1978/79	28	55	32	22
1979/80	30	45	20	29
1980/81	36	52	29	37
Average Rounded Down	28	50	29	28

Source: Euroconsult Report, 1982, Vol. II, Table B.5.4, p. 154.
(Estimates appear to have been used on Field Crops Economic Surveys of the Sudan Gezira Board.)

A survey based on data collected from 96 tenants randomly selected in Gezira estimates the thl in 1973/74 to be only 16% of the total labour expended in the Scheme (Ahmed, 1977: 99). Another more recent report (Table 3,2) estimates the contribution of thl, with the exception of wheat, as on average for the five seasons less than 30%.

Certain methodological difficulties in the estimates of the above mentioned attempts to calculate the thl contribution may make it inappropriate to establish a time-series based on the results of the different estimates, and difficult to assess the reliability of them.[4]

Notwithstanding their limitations, all the above four estimates, which refer to four different periods, indicate clearly that the thl is secondary compared to other social forms of organisation of labour, i.e. wage labour and household labour of the 'subtenants' (those who have sharecropping arrangements with the tenants and who have risen from the ranks of the wage labourers – see below).

III. TENANTS' NEGATIVE ATTITUDE TOWARDS FARM LABOUR?

The negligible contribution of tenant household labour was a matter for which the Administration of the Scheme and other concerned groups required an explanation. Several attempts have been made, not only to explain the 'tenants' negative attitude towards farm labour' – as has been stated by some scholars – but also to propose measures by which their labour contribution could possibly be increased. What is common among these attempts is that they have all sought explanation of that phenomenon (the 'negative attitude') in the history of Gezira people – a history which has definitely been misread!

In the pre-Scheme era, slavery had been considered by most of the advocates of the 'negative attitude' theory to be the dominant mode of production in the socio-economic formation of which today's Gezira forms a part. A 'slave–master mentality' continued, so it was maintained, after the official abolition of slavery during British rule. One of the advocates of this view, Culwick, writes: 'since its association with slavery makes fieldwork a despised occupation, there has always been a strong tendency to depend on outside labour to the maximum extent possible, i.e. to the maximum that the tenants' pocket and social position could command' (Culwick, 1955: 10). Finding some difficulty with this sort of explanation, as slave owners could only constitute a fraction of the people, but still loyal to the 'negative attitude' theory, Shaw (1961: 10) puts it this way: 'Rich men used slaves for work, the poorer ones cultivated the land with their own family labour, but probably did less than 100 working days in a year and hence were not used to the relatively heavy demands of an irrigated scheme with rigid timetable for almost the whole year'.

Al-Arifi (1975: 11–12), besides acknowledging the 'slave–master mentality' as the first factor, adds some others. These are mainly: the poor diet of the tenants; high temperatures in the Gezira, which affect tenants' ability to work for long hours; tenancies too large for the tenant households to cultivate properly; the development of towns, which according to him has increased the dependence on hired labour.

Shaw also has some post-Scheme factors to suggest. While in the pre-Scheme era women used to work in the fields alongside male relatives, after the Scheme and with the existence of outside hired labour it has been considered improper for women to work in the fields. Shaw also refers to 'wrong' educational policies which put little emphasis on agriculture and the result of which is that 'once a son acquired a little education, he would look for employment outside the Scheme or loaf' (Shaw, 1961: 13).

While disagreeing with the 'slave–master mentality' theory, O'Brien (1980: 513–16) still asserts that 'many Gezira tenants have an aversion to manual labour in agriculture'. He seeks explanation for this mainly in the following two ways. First, in the influence of the 'pastoral ideal'. For O'Brien many Gezira tenants are under the influence of an ideology which associates agriculture with poverty and animal-owning with wealth. This for him is probably more the case with the population of the northern and western areas of the Gezira. Second, in the eastern areas of the Gezira, the source of the 'negative attitude towards farm labour' is to be sought in the model of non-working land-owners to which many aspire – in these areas, according to O'Brien, important religious and political figures used their influence to draw people to work for them, often without pay.

Before attempting to discuss factors that in my view influence the contribution to farming of tenants' household labour, a few initial remarks are needed on the ideas put forward by some of the scholars mentioned above.

Referring to some sources, O'Brien contends that slaves in Gezira worked to supplement the family labour of the slave-owning families rather than to substitute for it. Slaves, he states, were primarily used as domestic servants in the richer families and as drivers of the waterwheels (*sagiyas*) in order to free family labour for farm work. O'Brien also, rightly, asks why, if it were a slave–master mentality that made Gezira tenants withhold their family labour, do we find the same tendency among tenants who were not previously land-owners, many of whom, especially tenants of Managil Extension, had themselves been wage labourers in the Scheme for some 30 years?

It is true that extensive studies and material on the history of the region are scarce; however, the few which are available do not suggest any grounds for the slave–master mentality theory (see Spaulding, 1979; O'Fahey and Spaulding, 1974; and Elhassan, 1985). Taking the relatively low level of productivity in the pre-Scheme rainlands of the Gezira, in comparison to the post-Scheme experience, one would expect to find the larger proportion of the people to have been slaves producing surplus to maintain a smaller proportion, if the notion that slave labour was the main form of labour is to be upheld. If this were true, then by the establishment of the Scheme the larger part of the population must have been slaves or ex-slaves. Available evidence does not suggest this; most of the Gezira people were of (or claimed to have) Arab origin, and, as is well known, enslavement in Sudan among Arabs was rare.

If we accept that some of those who became tenants had been originally nomadic or semi-nomadic pastoralists who for one reason or another settled in the Gezira, the questions one would then pose are: first, why do we still find 'prejudice to the pastoralist life' and 'aversion to manual labour in agriculture' (O'Brien, 1980) among the third generation of settled tenants who had never known the pastoralist life themselves? Second, why do not those tenants who have been able to accumulate some financial wealth from their farming activities become pastoralists by buying herds, instead of becoming merchants and other types of entrepreneurs?

Other reasons proposed to explain the alleged negative attitude of the tenants towards manual labour in agriculture (wrong educational policies, poor diet, withdrawal of women's labour for social reasons, laziness, etc.) are no more convincing. However, the aim of this section is not a critique of the 'negative attitude' theory, but rather a study of some of the problems and tendencies of capitalist development in the region.

I shall discuss factors influencing the contribution of thl in manual farming labour in Gezira under three headings: (1) the effects of technical factors; (2) the effects of the non-capitalist logic of the production process; and (3) the effects of the unstable low income from farming, the possibilities of off-farming activities and the process of differentiation among the tenant population.

(1) Effects of technical factors (size of tenancy, cyclical development of the household, fluctuations in production and changes in the social composition of tenants)

For many years, it has been clear that even if tenant households worked to their fullest capacity, they would still require additional labour, at least during the peak seasons. Since the inception of the Scheme, the size of a standard tenancy and of the crop rotation (and hence the labour requirement) have undergone significant changes.

Four different systems of crop rotation can be distinguished. In the first (1925–31), tenancy size was 30 feddans; 10 were cultivated to cotton and the rest was left fallow. *Dura* and a little *lubia* for fodder were allowed outside the rotation area. In the second system (1931–33), tenancy size was 34.4 feddans, of which 10 were allocated to cotton and 4.4 to *dura* (which only then entered into the rotation pattern) and the rest was left fallow. From 1933 the standard tenancy size increased to 40 feddans in Gezira Main, of which 10 were allocated to cotton, 5 to *dura*, 1–2 to *lubia* and 23–4 were left fallow. In the fourth system of crop rotation, adopted in 1961, new crops were introduced, notably wheat and groundnuts. Cropping was intensified in the 1974/75 season. In the fourfold rotation areas (in Gezira Main), 10 feddans were allocated to cotton, 10 to wheat and 10 to groundnuts and *dura*. In the threefold rotation areas, mainly in the Managil Extension, 5 feddans have been allocated to cotton cultivation and a similar area to groundnuts and *dura*. Vegetable growing has also been allowed in both the fourfold and threefold rotation areas. In the past 20 years, fallow lands have been considerably reduced, especially in the Managil Extension.

With the increase in the average size of a tenancy and the intensification of cropping, and if other things remain the same, on average a greater quantity of labour will be needed. In other words, if we assume thl to remain constant, as a result of these changes, on average more non-thl will be required on each tenancy.

Yet with the development of the Scheme other counter-tendencies have also been showing up. There has been subdivision of holdings among heirs of tenancy holders, a reduction of the tenancy size to 15 feddans in Managil Extension, and also, in its new allocation policy, the Scheme's Administration has been offering half standard tenancies in Gezira Main as the number of people demanding tenancies has been growing. Table 3,3 shows that the tendency in Gezira, even during that nine-year period, has clearly been towards smaller holdings. In the category of tenants with less than 10 feddans of cotton (a standard tenancy), as the same source points out, the majority have 5-feddan cotton holdings. Thus if other things remain the same, the greater the tendency towards smaller holdings in Gezira, the less is the need for extra-tenant household labour.

The number of economically active persons is naturally not identical in every tenant family. According to Culwick's estimate mentioned above, a standard tenancy in the early 1950s required 3.6 full person units, and hence families of two economically active persons, even if working fully, would still need 1.6 units from outside. So, at certain periods in their cyclical development, some Gezira tenant households would be in need of outside labour even if the economically active members of the household worked fully. The effect of this factor, if we take the Scheme as a whole (that is the aggregate and not the individual supply curves of thl) and if other things remain the same, will be constant.

TABLE 3,3

Tenants percentage distribution according to size of cotton holding in seasons 1972/73 and 1980/81

Percentage of Tenants with Holding

Season	Less than 10 feddans cotton	10–15 feddans cotton	15–20 feddans cotton	More than 20 feddans cotton
1972/73	74.9	21	3.7	0.4
1980/81	83.3	15.4	0.8	0.5

Source: SGB Economic Survey, 1981, Ch. V, Table 2, p.53.

Note: A 10-feddan cotton tenancy equals a standard tenancy (which with other crops + fallow equals 40 feddans); a 5-feddan cotton holding equals half a standard tenancy.

Even if the number of economically active person units available to the tenant household remains constant, as does the size of holding, still the quantity of extra-thl can fluctuate above and below the norm according to possible fluctuations in different crop yields (and therefore fluctuations in labour requisite in harvesting) and in labour requirements in other operations (e.g. heavier weeding).

The last among what I call technical factors affecting the thl input (and the demand for extra thl) is the change in the social composition of tenants in connection with the distribution of tenancies. During the early stages of the Scheme, when the policy was to give priority in allocation of tenancies to land-owners, significant areas were allocated to so-called rightholders (i.e. those who own lands). For example, in 1923 (at the beginning of the first phase when tenancies were first distributed), of the 1,154 tenancies distributed in Wad al Nau in the south of the Gezira, 52% were allocated to rightholders and 20% went to their nominees, as land-owners were given the right to nominate people to be offered tenancies if the land they owned exceeded the maximum number of tenancies to be offered to one person (Culwick, 1955: 9). Having many tenancies in hand (either directly or through nominations), and being offered land rent for their land in addition, meant that many rightholders were able and were indeed compelled to resort to non-thl (which mostly took the form of wage labour in the early stages of the Scheme). The composition of tenants, between rightholders and non-rightholders, later changed considerably, with the incorporation of more and more government-owned land in the Scheme, allocation of which went mainly to non-rightholders. The proportion of rightholders (with large holdings and financial resources in the form of rent) among the tenants became less and less. If other things remain the same, with the decrease in the proportion of rightholders among the tenant population of the Scheme, a tendency towards less dependence on outside labour will prevail.

(2) Effects of the non-capitalist logic of the production process

The capitalist mode of production (cmp) did not begin its development in a social vacuum in the Gezira. It has been developing in articulation (unity and struggle and transformation) with other non-capitalist modes of production (non-cmp). The law of motion of all the non-cmp is that while production is meant to satisfy needs, reproduction does not assume an extended scale. Since accumulation is not the driving force behind the reproduction process, surpluses that may arise are ultimately consumed and changes in the level of needs and forces of production tend to be very slow. Satisfaction of needs in non-capitalist socio-economic formations is meant to be attained, naturally, with the least possible effort – the least labour input.

The establishment of the Scheme brought about a new, higher technical level of production in the region. The new irrigation network (building of the Sennar dam and the channelisation system), the use of machinery in land preparation, use of fertilisers, controlling of pests and diseases and use of other modern agronomic (e.g. the rotation system, production schedules, etc.) and management techniques which have featured in the Gezira since the start of the Scheme, have resulted in the production of relatively larger amounts of surplus. The colonial government and the Sudan Plantation Syndicate – the private company which administered the Scheme during the colonial period – followed by the national governments and the Sudan Gezira Board – a parastatal corporation responsible for the administration of the Scheme – had attempted to appropriate the larger part of the surpluses produced. Nevertheless, at least some of the tenants, especially those land-owners who had been compelled to lease their lands to the government and who had also been receiving a land rent of 10 pt (one Sudanese pound = 100 pt) per feddan, which was not an insignificant sum during the early period of the Scheme, had been receiving an income higher than the then relatively limited level of their needs. (One assumes that in the early stages of the Scheme changes in the level of needs had been somewhat lagging behind the 'sudden' change brought from outside in the level of the forces of production and the income rise that may have followed from this.)

By the terms of their Tenancy Agreement, Gezira tenants are obliged to produce cotton and other crops every year, up to the standard set by the Administration of the Scheme. Producing surpluses above the level of their limited needs, and not having a choice in whether or not to engage in production in the following season, some Gezira tenants may have decided to make other people (the wage labourers, who in the early stages of the Scheme's development were mainly 'Westerners' coming from West Africa and Western Sudan) do the farming labour or part of it on their behalf. They do not do so because they are 'lazy' or because of their 'negative attitudes towards farm labour', but because production for accumulation is not their motive (although it may be the motive of their 'partner', the government).

It can be established that the effects of the non-capitalist logic of the production process in the Gezira were stronger during the early stages of development of the Scheme and did not affect all the tenants equally. Not all the tenants had been receiving land rent, the quantity of surplus attained varied from one tenant to another and from one year to another (depending on variations in crop yield) and so did the level of needs.

(3) Effects of the low and unstable farming income from farming, the possibilities of off-farming activities and the process of differentiation among the tenants

Hitherto, attempts to calculate the thl input in Gezira have concentrated on the aggregate side of it, and on only one aspect of this, namely, the total thl input compared with the total labour requisite in the production of one or all of the crops. Hence, studies on Gezira thl and on Gezira generally have not been able to grasp adequately the reasons behind the apparently low level of thl contribution and to expose at least some of the aspects of differentiation between Gezira tenants.

The average age of household heads in Gezira seems to be quite high. Among the Gezira tenant population 72% of the household heads are 45 years old or more (Barnett, 1983: 29). This does not reflect the distribution of the age structure in the region or in the country. We are then left with two possible explanations. Either the younger generation has no easy access to tenancies or they do not want to stay to look after the tenancies. As will be seen below, the latter is the more probable.

The average potential labour units per household in Gezira according to Barnett (*ibid*: 32) is 6.5. From information given elsewhere it can be estimated that in 1979/80 (2–3 years after Barnett's estimate of potential labour units per household given above) only 0.63 full labour unit per household was fully engaged in farming labour in Gezira.[5] If we assume the average potential labour units per household to be the same (or nearly the same) in 1979/80 as in 1982, we can conclude that not even the tenants themselves, let alone their households' members, were fully engaged in farm labour in 1979/80. In other words, only about 10% of the Gezira tenant household's economically effective labour force were fully engaged in farming labour. About 90% were engaged either in domestic labour, or in other off-farming activities, or were under- or unemployed, or were not available in the Scheme (i.e. had migrated).

Table 3,4 shows us that in the Gezira in 1981/82 only about 8% of the tenants depended fully or mainly on their household labour to meet requirements of manual labour in their tenancies. On the other hand, 92% resorted entirely or mainly to non-thl, that is, to wage labour and sharecropping arrangements. It should be noted that in category II of tenants (i.e. those depending mainly on non-thl), which is the largest category, comprising about 80% of all the tenants, over half (about 44% of the total sample) have reported contributing to watering labour only. Watering labour has been estimated to amount to less than 5% of the total labour required in all operations, that is, about 23 person days a year.[7] It is obvious that the contribution of those tenants undertaking watering labour only is marginal. Therefore, while 13% of Gezira tenant households contributed no manual labour, 57% undertook less than 5% of the manual labour in their tenancies. Category I (contributing nothing in terms of manual labour) is composed of tenants who have departed from, or probably never contributed to farming labour. However, some of them may still supervise the tenancy, while others may run their tenancy through a *wakeel* (agent).

Category I of the tenants, and those in category II who only contribute to watering labour (together amounting to 57%) are, in theory, in a position to devote most of their time (or all of it as may be the case of some tenants in category I who do not even undertake supervision) to non-farming activities. Apparently most of this group does so. In a survey conducted in 1982, Barnett found that 36% of Gezira tenants have other occupations (Barnett, 1983: 77). We are then left with at least 21% of Gezira tenants who contribute no or very little manual labour (about 23 full working days a year). This group may be composed mainly of elderly, female or 'minor' tenants and other tenants who are 'content' with the level of income attained from their tenancy without becoming involved themselves to any great extent in farming labour, and those who decide so because they can supplement tenancy income from remittances. In 1974, 11% of the total income received by Gezira tenants came from social transfers, mainly remittances, as Table 3, 5 shows.

Table 3,5 shows how much Gezira tenants are in fact dependent on activities and sources of income other than from their tenancies. Farming provides only 39% of the total income of all Gezira tenants. Ahmed divides the off-farming business activities of the tenants into

TABLE 3,4

Distribution of tenants according to their major source of manual labour in the season 1981/82

Labour Source	Number of Tenants	% of the total
I Non-thl entirely	5	12.8
II Non-thl mainly	31/17 watering labour only	79.5/43.4 watering labour only
III Thl mainly	2	5.1
IV Thl entirely	1	2.6
Total	39	100

Source: Adapted from Appendix III, Barnett, 1983.[6]

Note: 'Entirely' means 100%, 'mainly' means 50 − <100%

TABLE 3,5

Percentage and sources of income of Gezira tenants in 1974

Sources	Percentage of total income
Income from social transfers (remittances mainly + gifts in social ceremonies, etc)	11%
Farming	39%
Farming allied activities (wage labouring, *samad*, *Khafir* permanent jobs)[8]	3%
Non-farming activities	47%

Source: Ahmed, 1977: 118.

two groups: (1) small businesses, which he takes to include handicrafts, collection of wood, repairing bicycles, self-employment in building, and driving lorries; (2) big businesses, which include shopkeeping, trading in crops and livestock, money-lending, hiring of agricultural machinery (tractors and harvesters) and transport facilities. One can also distinguish three other groups of tenants in relation to off-farming activities: a small group of salaried tenants such as *Khafirs* and *Samads* employed by the Sudan Gezira Board, and *Imams* of local mosques employed by the Department of Religious and Social Affairs; a group of tenants who need to wage labour to supplement their farm income; and a third group, the members of which are not engaged in any off-farm activities. This latter group may be fully engaged in farm activities (manual labour as well as supervision) although this is not necessarily the case. Some members of this group may also be in receipt of money remittances sent by members of their household working in other places or in salaried or other jobs within the area of the Scheme. Members of other tenant groups may, of course, also be receiving contributions from other members of their households working outside the tenancy. In fact, differentiation among Gezira tenants seems to occur mainly outside of farming activities. A sample of 96 tenants studied by Ahmed (Table 3,6, 1977) which was randomly selected and could be considered as representative of the Scheme, shows clearly that in the Gezira there is no significant stratification of tenants according to tenancy size if compared to other regions in the Sudan, such as Gedaref (Chapter 4 below). The tendency towards smaller landholding has already been shown in Table 3,3. However, what makes some of the Gezira tenants who have been able to accumulate some financial wealth from their farms unable or unwilling to extend their farming activities in Gezira, but rather to seek investments in off-farm business, and what for other tenants constitutes a need to supplement the tenancy income by other sources or even by abandoning farming altogether, can only be understood by a closer look at the specific conditions amid which the Gezira Scheme has been developed, at other conditions and factors related to developments outside the Gezira, and at the tenants' responses to those specific conditions and factors.

As is already known, the decision on what to grow in the Gezira, and largely on how to grow it, is centralised in the hands of the Scheme's administration (the SGB at present). Cotton has been the major crop grown, although after the diversification policy in 1974/75, apart from dura, other new crops such as wheat and groundnuts, when taken together, have become more representative in terms of area than cotton. The high fluctuations of crop yields and especially cotton prices have made the cash income of the tenants fluctuate considerably (in 1974 the cash expenses compared to total expenses of Gezira tenants were between 76% and 86%. See Ahmed, 1977: 185).

TABLE 3,6.

Percentage distribution of tenants in Gezira according to size of tenancy in 1974

Size of Tenancy (in feddans)	Percentage of Tenants
< 23	62
23 < 33	32
33 < 43	3
44 < 53	2
> 53	1

Source: S.A. Ahmed, 1977: 118.

Tables 3,7 and 3,8 both manifest clearly the great fluctuations in the tenants' cash income. During some of the years of the Great Depression the tenants' cash income from cotton was virtually nil, and until 1947 it remained below the cash income of 1929 (in money terms). The years 1948 to 1950 witnessed an unprecedented and unsurpassed high price for cotton. In the 1960s and early 1970s another depression in tenant income is apparent in Table 3,8, especially if we take two additional factors into consideration: the first is that income cited is for 10 feddans of cotton (a standard tenancy), whereas the average size of holding had been showing a decline in the Gezira, especially after the Managil Extension in the 1960s when 5-feddan tenancies were distributed, and the second is that the value of money over the years in Sudan had been showing a continuous decline. Another observation from Table 3,8 is that up to the season 1964/65 the government share per 10-feddan holding was higher than that of the tenants. After that season the balance clearly changed, thanks to the October revolt of 1964, which overthrew the first military rule in Sudan. In that revolt the Gezira Tenants' Union played an effective role, and its president was appointed as a minister in the first government that superseded Aboud's military regime. Nevertheless, Gezira tenants' incomes from their tenancies, as has been pointed out by many other studies (for example, IBRD, 1982; Barnett, 1983; SGB Economic Survey, 1981), has remained relatively low and subject to fluctuations.

These fluctuating, low incomes have led many tenants to get into a state of chronic debt and many others to seek other occupations for themselves or other members of their household. Many tenants and members of their households have been leaving the Scheme to seek outside jobs. Between 1929 and 1934, during the Great Depression, 10% of the tenants left their tenancies (Shaw, 1961: 35). In 1943, with a relative improvement in tenancy income, 6% of the tenants were also reported to have resigned, as apparently they 'were taking the opportunity of a good year to get out' (*Ibid*). The SGB Economic Survey of 1980/81 (1981: 54) notes that 'due to low yields and insufficient tenancy income which has characterised crop production in the Gezira Scheme during recent years, most young people prefer to work in other sectors of the economy or migrate to oil producing countries'. Again, this external

TABLE 3,7

The economic return to the tenants from cotton per standard tenancy from 1926 to 1950

Year	Tenants Net Returns £E	Year	Tenants Net Returns £E	Year	Tenants Net Returns £E
1925–6	67	1935	17	1944	28
1927	84	1936	16	1945	54
1928	58	1937	24	1946	49
1929	55	1938	11	1947	96
1930	Nil	1939	11	1948	204
1931	Nil	1940	17	1949	221
1932	12	1941	21	1950	281
1933	Nil	1942	23		
1934	5	1943	33		

Source: Gaitskell, 1959, Table 4, p. 270.

TABLE 3,8

The economic returns to the government, the SGB and the tenants per 10 feddans of cotton (a standard tenancy) from 1961/62 to 1973/74

Year	Returns in £S per 10 feddans of cotton			Year	Returns in £S per 10 feddans of cotton		
	Government	SGB	Tenants		Government	SGB	Tenants
1961/62	240	33	163	1968/69	119	3	190
1962/63	136	− 3	94	1969/70	100	−11	168
1963/64	43	−13	19	1970/71	107	− 5	133
1964/65	110	− 5	87	1971/72	88	−12	112
1965/66	70	−14	97	1972/73	80	−13	79
1966/67	101	− 1	138	1973/74	205	24	251
1967/68	71	−16	92				

Source: Hakem, 1976, Table 6, p. 87.
Note: 1£S during those years was more or less equal to 1.25£E.

migration has also been noted by Barnett (1983: 123), who found that in Neuila village, out of about 442 men, about 100 had left to seek jobs elsewhere.

The tenant households' response to low, fluctuating farm income is clear: (1) the tenant household head may choose to engage in off-farm activities besides keeping the tenancy (as has been seen in 36% of cases); (2) tenant household members may remain in the Gezira but practise mainly off-farm activities; (3) household members may migrate in search of jobs outside the region and send remittances to maintain the economic viability of the household; or (4) tenants and their households may decide to leave their tenancies and move elsewhere.

Notwithstanding the general low level of income compared to needs, some tenants have been able to accumulate surpluses from their tenancies (especially those holding many tenancies) and from other resources. These other resources include land rent of 10 pt per feddan, received by landowners who had been compelled to lease their landholdings to the government, an amount which was significant only during the early stages of the Scheme, as it remained unimproved throughout the history of the Scheme. Some tenants would also probably have utilised part of the income they obtained in 'good years' in petty businesses (trade, money-lending, craftsmanship etc). Latterly some tenants, through their access to the leadership of the Tenants Union, have been able to obtain credit facilities from the Agricultural Bank and use that credit to acquire agricultural machinery (tractors and/or harvesters) which they then rent to other tenants. In a survey referred to by Adam (1978: 37) it was found that 43.6% of owners of agricultural machinery had obtained their machinery through loans from the Agricultural Bank under the guarantee of the Tenants Union (then dominated by 'rich' tenants).

From data in Tables 3,3 and 3,6, it is clear that surpluses appropriated by tenants are not reinvested in the Scheme's farming in order to extend its scale, but are directed outside to off-farming activities both within and outside of the Scheme. Even the renting out of agricultural machinery is to be considered an off-farming activity as, in fact, owners of agricultural machinery, even if tenants themselves, by renting out this machinery are assuming the role of machinery contractors. Machinery hire is the main motive behind their purchase, as even the largest landholdings in the Gezira are still too small to justify their economic use solely on the tenant's own farm. Reasons for abstaining from significant investment in farming in the Scheme are to be sought in the production relations of the Scheme. In the Gezira, the Administration is the only decision-maker on what to grow and how to grow it. Purchase or rent of tenancies with a view to establishing large production units is difficult and undesirable amid such conditions as those prevailing in the Gezira.

Apart from the reasons explained above which may compel Gezira tenant household heads and members to seek other sources to supplement their farm incomes, to migrate and, for some, to invest surpluses in off-farming activities either inside or outside the Gezira, there are other reasons which may also encourage Gezira people to adopt these attitudes.

Compared to many other people in other regions in the Sudan, Gezira people are generally in a privileged position regarding access to more desirable jobs (better wages, better working conditions, more profitable businesses etc). This privileged position is derived from many factors: the geographical location of the region, level of education and general social sophistication and also cultural and racial affiliation. The Gezira region has been accommodating or in the immediate vicinity of centres of economic, social and political activities in the country since the Funj Sultanate (from the beginning of the sixteenth century). In recent history, the Scheme being the most important economic project in the country since 1926, the Gezira has enjoyed many more facilities than other regions, in infrastructure, services, and education. With the exception of Port Sudan, most of the urban trade and employment centres of the country lie within the region or close to it. What adds to Gezira people's privileged position is their racial and cultural background (being 'Arab-Moslem'), which is advantageous not only in the urban areas of the Sudan, which are dominated by Arab-Moslem culture, but also in the oil-producing Arab countries to which the number of Sudanese immigrants has been multiplying rapidly since the early 1970s.

When Gezira people leave the Scheme or engage in off-farming activities, and therefore contribute less to the manual farming activities in the Gezira, they do so because the latter is financially less rewarding, less desirable compared with advantages available elsewhere, and not because of 'negative attitudes towards farm labour' based on ideological norms. Less advantaged segments of Sudanese people (e.g. Westerners), being driven by need from their home areas, and being unable to compete with Gezira people elsewhere under the present racial, cultural and social balance of power in the country, will come, as indeed they do, to replace the labour force of the original people in the Scheme.

Sharecropping Arrangements and their Spread in the Gezira

The conflict between tenants' farming and off-farming activities has led (among other reasons as shown elsewhere – Abdelkarim, 1985/a) to the appearance of and the spread of sharecropping arrangements between tenants and subtenants (originally wage labourers).

Sharecropping in the Gezira Scheme is an unofficial agreement, not recognised by the Scheme's Administration. It is usually a verbal contract between a tenant and a wage-worker in the Scheme. The tenant agrees to abandon for a season his or her right to use the land, although in principle such arrangements are renewable. The wage-worker then becomes a subtenant, and obliged to meet all the labour requirements of the holding and to cultivate it in accordance with the crop rotation laid down by the SGB. The subtenant further agrees to share the produce with the tenant at the end of the season.

In a small survey, among 25 subtenants, carried out by the author within a survey of non-tenant labour in the Gezira in 1983 (see Chapter 5) it was found that these subtenants were almost entirely Westerners living in the labour camps of the Gezira. About 78% of the camp labourers reported entering into sharecropping agreements in that season. The typical subtenant – accounting for 85% of the sample of subtenants – is aged between 20 and 50 years. Half are actually under 35 years. Given that the tenants' average age is higher (see Barnett, 1984: 91) one must conclude that the subtenants are in a more favourable position to do the manual work of the tenancy, being generally younger. On average, each household taking a subtenancy has about four members engaged in farming activities in the Scheme. This makes it possible for subtenants to depend mainly on their own household labour, provided that the household forms one production unit, which is apparently the case with most of the households, and thus to provide the bulk of the labour required in their sharecropped holdings. More than half of the subtenants do not require extra-household labour at any stage, while the remainder need it only very occasionally. It should be noted that the average size of a sharecropped farm will usually be smaller than the average tenancy. On occasions when extra-household labour is required, it is for weeding, harvesting of dura and pulling and threshing of groundnuts. Extra-household labour is normally provided by wage labourers, who can be other subtenants or other camp labourers who have no sharecropping agreement. In a few cases, it was reported that some of the extra-household labour had been provided by traditional voluntary labour (*nafir*).

With the exception of some minor variations, the terms of all share-cropping agreements are similar. In most cases, tenants are required to prepare the land and to provide seeds and fertilisers (mainly nitrates) although, in fact, this latter arrangement often only applies in the first year of the agreement.

About half of the subtenants interviewed reported entering into credit arrangements some time during the year. Credit is needed in order to pay wages where wage labour has been contracted for certain operations, as well as to meet everyday subsistence costs when cash and other resources dry up. In some cases it was reported that these loans were provided by the tenant-sharecroppers. In a few cases, loan recipients repay the loan by working for their creditors, but in most cases repayments are in cash or kind, with a relatively high interest rate. The availability of financial resources such as cash savings, money appropriated from petty trade and money-lending, together with paid jobs in the Scheme, means that half of the subtenants are in no need of any credit during the agricultural season.

Most of the subtenants work for wages in addition to working in their sharecropped holdings; only 5 out of 25 reported that they never worked for wages. Most of this minority were in the northern part of the Gezira where, perhaps because of proximity to Khartoum, the tenant household labour input is apparently considerably below the average (see Abdelhamid, 1965) and the tenants mostly depend on sharecropping agreements and on wage labour. It also seems that subtenants in that area may in fact have larger than average subtenancies.

Sharecropping started first in groundnuts and has spread to a consid-erable extent in that crop. Groundnuts are second only to cotton, in their demand for labour. Up to 1980/81, when the government sharecropped cotton with the tenants under the so-called 'partnership' system, sharecropping in cotton would have been very difficult to arrange. In fact the Westerners, from whom almost all the subtenants come, have developed special skills in the cultivation of groundnuts, it being among the most popular crops in their areas of origin. In some earlier reports of the Scheme's Administration, groundnuts are referred to as the only crop in which sharecropping agreements are made. Only in Tamim (1980) is it mentioned that they also occur in dura and additionally, but rarely, in wheat and vegetables. The 1983 survey suggests that such agreements have in fact spread to all crops in the Scheme.

Table 3,9 shows that it is not only in groundnuts that the subtenants are active, but also in *dura*. It is also clear that in the Gezira in 1982/83 no crop was free of crop-sharing, not even cotton! From 1981/82, with the abolition of the cotton sharecropping system between the government and the tenants and its replacement by a land and water charge system for all crops, it has become possible to sharecrop in cotton too, and this may become more widespread in the future.

Tamim estimates that in 1979/80, the percentages of camp labourers who sharecropped in groundnuts and in *dura* were 39.1 and 25.8 respectively (Tamim, 1980: 42). Results from the 1983 survey are 71.4% and 60%. Assuming that the two surveys are comparable, it is quite clear that between the seasons 1979/80 and 1982/83, a sharp upward trend in sharecropping had occurred. Additional evidence for this trend comes from another source. In 1974/75 it was estimated that 32.3% of the tenants sharecropped in groundnuts (Tamim, 1980: 42), while in 1980/81 the comparable figure was 70% (SGB Economic Survey, 1981: 41). The specific reason for this rapid spread of sharecropping agreements remains to be explored.

TABLE 3,9

Percentage of subtenants according to the crops in which they sharecropped in 1982/83

Crop	Percentage of subtenants sharecropping
Groundnuts	100
Dura	85
Cotton	15
Lubia	15
Vegetables	15
Wheat	8

Source: 1983 Own Survey

IV. CLASS POSITION OF THE TENANTS AND LIMITATION TO CAPITALIST DEVELOPMENT

In the relatively extensive literature on the Gezira Scheme, differentiation among the tenants, and their position (or that of their different segments) in the class structure, have been treated in a very inadequate manner, and apparently inappropriate criteria have been applied. Among others, Kursany (1982) uses the terms 'rich', 'middle' and 'poor' to describe different categories of Gezira tenants. His categorisation is based on size of land. In themselves, however, these terms are not political economic concepts. Used alone, without qualification, they do not show any essential differences among the differently categorised groups in terms of their place in the production process. Moreover, size of land could be a quite misleading criterion in class differentiation in the conditions of the Gezira, as will be shown below.

Our concern in this section is to see how far we can talk about an agrarian capitalist class (either in formation or already existing), and why the Gezira is classified in this work as being in the transition to capitalism.

The connection between land size and 'richness' and 'poorness' that Kursany (1982) among others attempts to draw, seems not to hold. The concepts 'rich' and 'poor' refer to wealth, total income rather than income derived from one source. Table 3,10 shows that the highest total income group of tenants attains the second lowest average farm income (which may be taken to indicate the size of land available to them if other things remain the same). Table 3,11 also shows that the difference in farm income between groups I and II, the latter's being 3.9 times that of the former, is reduced considerably (to 1.5 times) if we take into account the total income. However, figures in Table 3,11 should not lead us to conclude that Gezira tenants in terms of total income attained are a more or less homogeneous group. Table 3,10 shows that the highest total income group in 1973/74 attained an income equivalent to 12.4 times the lowest one. Interestingly enough, these two groups attained the lowest farm income among the seven groups identified. The real differentiation among Gezira tenants seems to take place outside the farming activities.

It is apparent from both Tables 3,10 and 3,11 that the majority of Gezira tenants depend heavily for their total income on off-farm resources. Table 3,10, for example, shows that Gezira tenants on average obtain only 39% of their income from farming activities.

If we compare income from farming earned by Group I in Table 3,11, which is £S550, to the minimum wage level determined by labour

TABLE 3,10

Distribution of Gezira tenants according to farm groups, contribution of household labour and size and source of incomes for 1973/74

Farm Group	(1) Number	(2) % of the total	(3) Household labour to total %	(4) Non-thl (sharecropping and wage labour) to total %	(5) Farm Income per tenant (in £S)	(6) % of (5) in total	(7) Non-farm Income per tenant in £S	(8) % of (7) in total	(9) Total Income (in £S)
I	48	53.3	24	76	101.90	58	73.38	42	175.28
II	10	11.1	9	91	189.49	49	193.79	51	383.28
III	5	5.6	7	93	133.79	32	423.23	68	557.02
IV	4	4.4	6	94	132.76	6	2072.50	94	2205.26
V	17	18.9	15	85	225.17	72	85.98	28	311.15
VI	3	3.3	7	93	278.16	89	77.00	11	355.16
VII	3	3.3	4	96	275.81	19	1147.07	81	1422.88
Total	90	99.9	16	84	149.73	39	233.34	61	383.07

Source: Ahmed, 1977: 99 and 204

Note: Farm groups have been identified by interrelating three variables; involvement in vegetable production (which the author found to be a source of high income), asset endowment (categorized in three levels) and involvement with relatively big business (trade, transport, mill ownership etc).

TABLE 3,11

Distribution of Gezira tenants according to mean agricultural and total household income for the year 1981/82

Tenancy Size	(1) Mean Agricultural Income in £S	(2) Mean Total Household Income in £S	Percentage of (1) over (2)
I Less than 6 feddans cotton	550	1829	30%
II 10–20 feddans cotton	2129	2765	77%

Source: Barnett, 1983: 54 and 55.

Notes: (1) 10 feddans cotton tenancy is equivalent to one standard tenancy (totalling 40 feddans) in Gezira Main.

(2) Tenants with over 20 feddans cotton constitute 0.5% of the total; 10–20 feddans make up 16.2%, while those with less than 6 feddans are the majority of the tenants (see Chapter 3, Table 3,3).

legislation for the whole country in the same year (1981/82), which was £S504, and to the wage paid by the Sudan Gezira Board for its wage labourers, ranging from £S600 to £S1,625 (Barnett, 1983: 52), off-farm resources seem to be a necessity for the household. In fact, off-farm resources equal 70% of the total household income of this group (which constitutes the majority of Gezira tenants). These off-farm resources come mainly from jobs undertaken (on a part-time or full-time basis) by the tenants themselves (36% of them, according to *ibid*: 77) or by their household members who live with them, and from remittances. As has been discussed earlier, for the majority of the tenants and their household members, off-farming activities include selling their labour power, largely outside the region, where they can earn more. They prefer to employ the socially and ethnic-culturally less advantaged segment of the population ('Westerners') in their own tenancies and benefit from the difference in wage levels between what they can earn and what they offer.

It can be asserted then that notwithstanding that most Gezira tenants seem to resort to wage labour more than to their own household labour, the majority of them are not petty agrarian capitalists. Both the intention behind and the result of purchase of labour power of others is not accumulation. This peculiar situation (of buying labour power to substitute their own, while selling their own elsewhere) is the result of the present imperfect labour markets in the Sudan.

Whereas the above may be true for most Gezira tenants, it does not hold for them all. For some (for example, those in categories IV and VII in Table 3,10) the tenancy may be only part of their business profile. (The equivalents of those tenants are probably in both categories I and II in Table 3,11.) Members of this group may not be selling their labour power elsewhere as the others discussed above may do. However, the size of their capital involved in farming and surplus appropriated thereof cannot allow us to categorise the majority of them as agrarian capitalists. For a person to become an agrarian capitalist, it is not enough to be the owner of a farm on which wage labourers are employed. Surplus value appropriated must also be enough to maintain the position of that person outside the production process merely as the owner of it. We can of course also talk about 'petty' agrarian capitalists whose appropriated surplus is not yet enough to free them completely from expending their own labour power in the farm while also purchasing labour power of others systematically with the intention of producing on an expanding scale. The farm income of categories IV and VII in Table 3,10 is £S133 and £S276 respectively (which constitutes respectively 6% and 19% of their total income). If we compare these figures to the minimum wage level (as set by legislation) in the same year which was £S504, we can see that surplus derived from the farm (and also amount of capital invested in it) is insufficient for those tenants to be called agrarian capitalists. The same is true even if we take into account farm income of tenants in category II in Table 3,11, which was £S2,129. This level of income is not unusual among skilled industrial labourers. However, the fact that some tenants are able to appropriate surplus from off-farming activities which is enough to secure a living and to accumulate (like perhaps some members of categories IV and VII in Table 3,10) makes them 'off-farming' capitalists.

The category of tenants that cultivate over 20 feddans (only 0.5% of the tenants) has not been classified in Table 3,11. Hence we have no data on their income.

A final note on a category of tenants who may be appropriating surplus but who have not so far been discussed. This is the group of tenants who sharecrop out. Their position is clear. Surplus appropriated comes from their position as land controllers and not as direct producers. Thus this kind of surplus is land rent and not surplus value.

It can be concluded that in the Gezira (and in similar areas) we can hardly talk about an agrarian capitalist class. Although all factors for capitalist production seem to be present (as least in Gezira), still they fall short of transforming the production process into that. The main obstacle to capitalist transformation in areas categorised as of transitional pattern is the land tenure system, which makes investment in farming with the intention to expand both difficult and undesirable.

CHAPTER FOUR

Gedaref: Mechanisation and the Development of an Agrarian Capitalist Class in the Sudan

INTRODUCTION

In the Gedaref Region, which lies in the central eastern part of Sudan, the so-called Mechanised Farming Schemes (MFS) were brought into being for the first time in Sudan. The MFS are rainfed, relatively large-scale, the production process is relatively mechanised, and wage labour is almost the only form of labour. The MFS largely constitute what may be called the 'capitalist' pattern of Sudanese agriculture (indicating that capitalist production relations are already dominating). Rainfed and relatively mechanised agriculture was introduced as an experiment in the Gedaref area in 1944/5 during British colonial rule. It started to spread widely and was opened up for Sudanese indigenous private capital from the year 1954/5. Soon after that the region became one of the most prominent agricultural regions in the country. After a few years, the type of farming and relations of production started in it found their way out to some other areas in the Sudan (e.g. Damazine in the Central region, Habila in the western region, Upper Nile in the southern region etc. – for more details on those areas see Elhassan, 1985).

The main crop grown in the MFS is *dura* followed by sesame. Cotton may also be sown in some areas. However, land sown to cotton is a negligible proportion of the total land cultivated in the MFS. The contribution of the MFS and especially those of Gedaref in the production of *dura* (the main food grain in the country, and also in the late 1970s and early 1980s becoming important as an export crop) and sesame (one of the major export crops) in the country is quite significant as Table 4,1 shows.

This chapter attempts to give a historical account of the development of the MFS in Gedaref and to expose their impact on the social structure and on the forces of production, that is, their significance in the development of capitalism, not only at the level of the Gedaref region, but also nationally (since the MFS have found their way to other regions in Sudan).

TABLE 4,1

Percentage contribution of all the MFS and those of Gedaref region in the total production of dura *and sesame in the Sudan for the years 1977/8, 1978/9, 1979/80*

Agricultural season	1977/78		1978/79		1979/80	
	Dura	Sesame	Dura	Sesame	Dura	Sesame
All MFS	46.4	31.0	46.3	16.8	56.0	27.3
MFS of Gedaref	27.5	18.7	30.1	10.3	38.7	19.1

Source: Statistical Abstract 1981, different tables.

In comparison with the relatively extensive literature and data on the Gezira Scheme (in central Sudan), neglect of Gedaref is quite surprising. In terms of total exchange value produced, the Gedaref region is a very close second to the Gezira, if not running neck and neck with it. In terms of the development of capitalism, Gedaref is the leading region in rural Sudan. In fact, Gedaref is probably one of the most interesting cases of the development of indigenous capitalism in Africa.

A large survey on agricultural labour and Gedaref agriculture was undertaken by the International Labour Office and United Nations High Commission for Refugees in 1982. (This survey will be referred to here as Dey et al, 1983.) Besides this survey, to the author's knowledge, there has been no significant study of Gedaref MFS other than Abdel Aziz (1976). Aziz deals with the political economy of the region only marginally.

Reliable data and statistics on surplus (in the form of different types of income) and labour requirements is very scarce, if available at all. Some estimates of the area under cultivation and total production have been made by some parastatal agencies, some of which have been published (but, however, not without discrepancies and inconsistencies in the same and between different sources).

This chapter has been mainly based on findings of a field trip to Gedaref during the *dura* harvest of the 1982/83 season. Lengthy interviews were held with 47 farmers (covering the 3 categories I identify below: small, large and 'super-large' farmers) and 20 household producers, in addition to bank managers and some other officials associated with agriculture as well as many leaders of the Farmers' Associations. Other people with long experience in Gedaref – elderly farmers, the first Sudanese agricultural inspector of Gedaref, two members of the Abu Sin family (the traditional leadership of the area), were interviewed mainly as sources of history. In addition, many informal interviews were held with people from different sections of the Gedaref population. These informal interviews were of great value. Gedaref people in their private lives always talk about different aspects of farming; this seems to be the only common theme for the majority, as in terms of ethnic and cultural background Gedaref people come from diverse origins. The purpose of the field survey was not to establish statistically significant data on the subject of the study, but rather to try to conceive and expose the main relations and trends that have prevailed and developed as a result of the development of the MFS.

I. THE EVOLUTION OF AGRICULTURE IN THE GEDAREF REGION FROM 1900

The economic history of Gedaref before the MFS has not been recorded anywhere to the author's knowledge. The following section has been based mainly on oral history recorded by the author during his field trip to Gedaref.

The Period Prior to the Establishment of MFS (1900–1944)

Different forms of labour existed in the region before the establishment of the MFS. Besides household labour (both peasant and pastoralist), which was apparently the main form of organisation of labour, there existed forced labour, wage labour and voluntary labour. Slave labour did not finish immediately with the anti-slavery decrees and the anti-slavery campaign announced during the late period of Turko-Egyptian rule (1821–81). It seems that wage labour had been in existence from as early as the beginning of the twentieth century, but had especially flourished in the late 1920s after the building of the railway and after taking effective measures to free slaves.[1] Voluntary labour performed by household producers existed in two forms. In the first form no reciprocal relations existed, as voluntary labour was performed for traditional leaders (sheikhs and paramount sheikhs) and for respected religious people. In the second form some reciprocity was entailed. Work was performed by and for 'equal' members of the community at times of need (nafir). In Gedaref, as in the larger part of the country, land has been government property since the early 1900s. Land use rights had been vested in the communities through their traditional leaders and also later through local government authorities (Chapter 2). Up to that period land in itself had not yet developed into a commodity.

A number of nomadic tribes (or subtribes) existed (and still exist) in the region, migrating from the northern part during autumn down south to Butana land in central Sudan to avoid swarms of harmful flies which attack their animals in that season, and also to benefit from the different varieties of pastures that exist in Butana. After the rainy season they migrate back to the northern part of the region. Animals bred by nomads include camels, cattle, goats and sheep.

Settlers, living in scattered villages, practised land cultivation and also raised animals (goats and cattle were more common as they need relatively less care). Two types of land were cultivated and sometimes for different purposes. *Bildat* lands, which lie just round the villages, were meant to produce subsistence for cultivating households. *Harig* lands were normally at a considerable distance from villages – many hours or sometimes even days distant; they were partly meant to meet subsistence needs, but were also meant to produce for the market. Rights to the use of *bildat* or *harig* lands were normally obtained from either *nazirs* (paramount sheikhs) or sheikhs, and later also from local government councillors. The difference between the two types of land, besides location and probably nature of production (being mainly subsistence or market-oriented), is as follows. *Bildat* land, once allotted to a people or to households, would continue to be theirs for as long as they lived in, or maintained relations with, the community, and could be inherited. *Harig* land, on the other hand, might not entail these rights, and individuals might not necessarily cultivate the same pieces of land every time. Special permission was needed for *harig* cultivation, which was normally offered by *nazirs*, sheikhs or local government councillors. The permission-holder would go to set fire (which is the literal meaning of *harig*) over a large piece of land. A representative of the *nazir* or sheikh would go afterwards with that person to identify his/her entitlement and also to distribute the remaining land, if any. (The fire might spread over a large area of land, normally more than an individual could afford to cultivate in those times.) The remaining land would be distributed among other villagers applying for *harig*, priority being given to relatives of the permission-holder. The fire was meant to get rid of weeds that grow after the first rains, and thus reduce the amount of labour needed in weeding. Apparently this was necessary because of the relative scarcity of labour force in those days.

Production for the market was normally undertaken by well-off people (*nazirs*, sheikhs, merchants and religious leaders) who could afford to pay for wage labour and/or had access to labour free of charge. As a result of the increasing influx of wage labourers coming to the region encouraged by the spread of *harig* cultivation and especially persuaded by those *harig* cultivators who had no access to other forms of labour, free-of-charge labour became less and less significant.

The wage labourers came from western Sudan and also from West Africa. In Gedaref, cultivable lands were not scarce for local people. Apparently this resulted in a relatively slow rate of free labour formation in the region prior to the establishment and development of large-scale mechanised farming. Migrant workers either had no access to land, as they were not considered members of the local communities, or could not afford, at least for a time, to become independent producers. These people had no alternative but to sell their labour power. Some of these migrants settled and formed a permanent wage labour force but apparently the majority came only for a period, perhaps an agricultural season (4–5 months a year). Wages in these earlier periods were mostly fixed on a daily or monthly basis. In the latter case, the actual payment might not have taken place before harvest, as a contract was normally made for the whole season. During the contracted period food was also provided by the farmers.

Commodities produced (*dura*, sesame, animals, gum arabic, as well as sesame oil) were normally taken to the local markets (generally on Thursdays in different locations in the region). Oil was produced from sesame using primitive oil presses worked by camels – an industry known in the country for a long time. Part of these commodities were then transported by camel and after 1927 by train also, to Khartoum, where they might then be redistributed to other areas. Direct trade with Ethiopia as well as Egypt had also been going on since earlier periods. *Dura*, sesame and oil were bartered mainly for coffee, lentils and ginger in Ethiopia.

Harig cultivation began to flourish after 1927 when Gedaref town was connected by railway to Wad Meddani, the main town in Gezira, which had already been connected to Khartoum. (The Gezira Scheme had already been established and migration of wage labourers to it had already become a regular feature.)

During the Second World War crop prices rose sharply; an *ardebb* of *dura* (178 kilos) rose from £3 to £7 and more. This instigated market-oriented production in Gedaref. It also probably made the government think seriously about establishing large-scale production in the area, as its enormous possibilities were well known. *Harig* cultivation persisted in the region up to the 1960s, when as a result of the expansion of MFS it was banned.

The Development of MFS from 1944 to 1955

The first attempt to explore the practicalities of mechanised farming was made in 1944/5 in an area near Wad el Huri in Gedaref. In the same season an area of approximately 300,000 feddans (one feddan is 1.034 acres), of which 275,000 feddans were found to be cultivable, in the western part of the Gedaref region called Ghadambaliyia was earmarked 'and the few existing rights were expropriated' (Laing, 1953: 2). Laing (*ibid*, 6–10), our source for the period 1944–52, went on to say that experimentation had been carried out from seasons 1945/6 to 1947/8 cultivating land of different sizes and in widely separated areas in the Scheme. Although cultivation was difficult, yields were satisfactory. From these first experimental years, it became clear that *dura* could not be fully mechanised as the available types of *dura* grown could not be harvested mechanically. In 1948/9 an area of about 7,600 feddans was allotted to 'participating cultivators' in holdings of 28 feddans on a sharecropping basis. The Scheme management prepared and sowed the land and also provided machines for threshing, and the participating cultivators did the rest. Yields were then shared by the management and the cultivators. Of the 7,600 feddans, about 4,200 were allotted through *nazirs* and 3,400 were allotted by the Agricultural Inspectors directly to cultivators. Average yield was 0.29 tons of *dura* per feddan.

A year later, besides 6,500 feddans cropped by participating cultivators, holdings of 240 feddans each were allotted to 'notables' and merchants with the idea of introducing them to mechanised farming. They paid cash for the rent of machinery and had to undertake full responsibility for the production process. They probably used mainly hired labour to carry out the non-mechanised operations and the yield was all theirs. In that year, due to lack of sufficient rain, yield was very low: 0.13 tons/feddan. Despite this, land was increased in the following season, 1950/1, and 27,600 feddans were allotted to participating cultivators and five large holdings of 240 feddans (the same as the previous year) were entrusted to merchants. Average yield on sharecropped areas was 0.47 tons/feddan. Sharecropping arrangements continued up to the season 1951/2. From the government's side, these arrangements were not considered to be 'financially rewarding' and were therefore stopped. Different sized experimental farms were then established in which tractors with different capacities were used for two years. The results of these experiments were encouraging in the eyes of the first Sudanese management that had taken over. This management then decided to open up the area for private Sudanese capital.[2]

In 1954/5 the agricultural management of the area began to allot schemes of 1000 feddans each to private entrepreneurs coming from the Gedaref region and from outside it (mainly from the Northern Province and from Khartoum). Conditions put forward by the Allotment Committee were that the applicants should own, or should have enough financial resources to buy a tractor, a disc and a planter, should have sufficient resources to finance the agricultural operations and also, according to the judgement of the committee, have the entrepreneurial ability and the time to manage a large farm. A maximum of two schemes were to be allotted to one person. These conditions have not always been strictly adhered to by the allotting committees. Also, some farmers have been able to overcome the law by applying in other names (brothers, sons etc.). Besides the 1,000 feddans schemes, some smaller holdings of 100, 300 and 500 feddans were allotted to some less financially 'able' local farmers. The management hired machinery for them and they paid only after harvest. (Some of the largest farmers in Gedaref at present originate from among these small farmers.)

Since the region was opened up for private investors in 1954/5 total land cultivated has increased considerably, as Table 4, 2 shows (we shall return to this table in Section V below).

Some studies, tackling the history of the development of mechanised farming in Gedaref (although only within the context of their particular area of study), point out that the failure of sharecropping arrangements between government and participating cultivators that were made experimentally in Gedaref in the 1940s, is to be sought in a number of factors. These include mainly the unsuitability of machinery used and weak infrastructure. 'Inefficiency of participating cultivators' was also cited by some of these studies (see Zein al Abdin, 1977; Simpsons, 1978; O'Brien, 1980; Affan, 1982).

Although inadequacy of machinery used in any project would negatively influence the yields (production), one could not take that as a major factor in the 'failure' of the early experiments of sharecropping in Gedaref, as a solution could easily have been reached by changing the type of machinery (a thing which was actually done in the different sized experimental farms in 1952–54). Between the year 1951/2 (when the sharecropping arrangements were stopped) and the year 1954/5 (when the area was opened up for private capital investment) very little was done to improve the level of infrastructure in the area. Failure of sharecropping cannot, then, be attributed to poor level of services, as, with this same 'poor' level, private large-scale farms were established in 1954. Claims of 'inefficiency of participating cultivators' are not justified, nor are they well documented. Affan (1982: 23), for example, says that 'it should, however, be mentioned that tenants were ill-prepared for sedentary life because of their nomadic attributes'. Participating cultivators (or tenants) were partly selected by traditional leaders of the area and partly by the agricultural management of the experimental project as has been mentioned earlier. Settled agriculture and even production for the market were well known in the area. Nothing can justify (and nothing documents) the selection of the participating cultivators from among the nomads rather than from among *bildat* and *harig* cultivators, who were apparently available in large numbers, especially as the Ghadambaliyia area, where those experiments were undertaken, was one of the main areas of *harig* cultivation.

TABLE 4,2

Changes in average areas cultivated and average yield of dura *and sesame in Gedaref*

Seasons	Dura		Sesame		
	Av. annual area in feddans	Av. annual yield/ton/ feddan	Av. annual area in feddans	Av. annual yield Kantar/ feddan	Total area under cultivation of sesame and dura
1954/55–1958/59	526,114	0.514	151,465	3.19	677,579
1959/60–1963/64	773,374	0.465	109,498	3.35	882,872
1964/65–1968/69	1,058,396	0.343	200,211	3.04	1,258,607
1969/70–1973/74	1,285,751	0.272	310,325	3.92	1,596,076
1974/75–1978/79	1,879,751	0.314	312,550	2.40	2,192,301
1979/80–1982/83*	2,610,808	0.283	275,465	3.00	2,886,273
Average of 1954/55–1982/83	1,355,699	0.365	226,586	3.15	1,582,285

* The interval in this category is four seasons. Data for sesame production for the year 1980/81 was not available, the average yield was therefore calculated from the other three years.

Sources: 1954/55 – 1974/75: Agricultural Research Council's Report, 1975
1975/76 – 1977/78: Department of Agricultural Economics (1979)
1978/79 & 1979/80: Statistical Abstract 1981 - Tables (1)B, (2)B, (7)B
1980/81:   Agricultural Bank, Gedaref Office
1981/82 & 1982/83: Mechanised Farming Corporation, Gedaref Office

Problems that faced the government in its early experiments in mechanised farming in the Gedaref area, and which resulted in the financial non-viability of the project (at least from the side of the government), are to be sought mainly, in my opinion, in the attempt to transfer the Gezira Scheme's experiences (in a somewhat modified way) to Gedaref, notwithstanding the difference between the economic-historical conditions in the two areas.

Unlike pre-Scheme Gezira, in the Gedaref region, and particularly in Ghadamaliyia area before 1944, capital–wage labour relations had been developing only slowly, but eventually became the major production relations in the area. Sharecropping arrangements with the government and in such small pieces of land (28 feddans each) could not have been an attractive proposition for *harig* cultivators. Household producers of Gedaref, even those who were compelled to leave their lands in Ghadamaliyia, were not compelled to accept sharecropping arrangements as the only way to secure subsistence. Land in the region was in relative abundance and the government had only assumed control over a part of it. In Gezira the government assumed control over most of the cultivable land, and most of the local people, therefore, had no other alternative than to stay and accept the new arrangements. Moreover, the Gezira experiment was not attractive to Gedaref people, as many Gezira tenants during the recession of the 1930s and also in the 1940s had been abandoning their tenancies in large numbers (Shaw, 1961: 35). Apparently some of these came to settle in Gedaref afterwards.[3]

The economic and political conditions in the 1940s and especially in the 1950s in Sudan and particularly in Gedaref were favourable to the development of capitalist agriculture.

II. PRECONDITIONS OF CAPITALIST DEVELOPMENT IN SUDANESE AGRICULTURE

It is argued here that a class of indigenous agrarian capitalists in Sudan emerged and has steadily started to develop essentially only since 1954 with the establishment of large-scale farming in Gedaref. The MFS could not have developed as they did, had it not been for the development of some essential socio-economic and political preconditions. Researchers so far seem to have emphasised the role of the state in the creation of MFS. There is no doubt that the state played an effective role in the initiation of the MFS. However, what lay behind this initiative, and what were the other essential preconditions that made it materialise, have not so far been investigated.

Before turning to that subject it may be appropriate to note here that the agrarian capitalist class in Sudan is essentially indigenous. The only relatively substantial private foreign capital involvement in Sudanese agriculture during the colonial period was that associated with the Sudan Plantation Syndicate (SPS) (first in Zeidab and later on in the Gezira, though in the latter the SPS's capital investment is relatively small). However, even this involvement was restricted to circulation (hire of the means of production and land). In the post-colonial period, the situation has not changed. Despite the series of foreign investment acts that aimed to encourage foreign capital (especially Arab capital) to invest in agriculture, and the advocating of Sudan as the Middle East's (and sometimes the whole world's) bread-basket, there has been little actual response (see Yassin, 1983). Productive capital in Sudanese agriculture in the 1980s still remains essentially indigenous.

By 1954, as a result of the development of the process of primitive

65

capital accumulation, the following preconditions of capitalist agriculture in Sudan were in evidence:

1. The reproduction cycle of household production, after over five decades of systematic capitalist penetration, started to break. Monetisation had already developed to a considerable extent. The two active forces in this were (and still remain) merchant capital and the state. The former had been active in introducing new consumer goods and organising the purchase of the products of the household producers (Chapter 2), and the latter by intervening in the classical forms of imposition of taxes and court fines. The process of commoditisation and its impact seems to have started first and developed relatively faster in western Sudan (see Chapters 5 and 6). Cash crops had already been grown in western Sudan prior to British colonialism. Livestock trade and trade in oil seeds had long been in existence with Egypt and other bordering countries. Circulation capital during the colonial period came to enhance and expand a process already in existence (contrary to other places, e.g. larger parts of southern Sudan, where it had first to introduce cash crops). Appropriation of surplus and the enlarging of the size of subsistence desires had made an increasing number of Westerners go in search of wage labour. Indeed, the Westerners were among Sudan's first labour power sellers. In Gedaref prior to 1954, during *harig* cultivation, the migration of Westerners to Gedaref was not uncommon. In conclusion, the essential precondition for capitalist development, prior to the establishment of the MFS – the process of free wage labour formation – had started to develop.

2. As a result of the development of the process of commoditisation, surplus appropriated by circulation capital and under the logic and the influence of the new penetrating capitalist mode of production started to be accumulated rather than being all spent to increase consumption. In the colonial period, indigenous circulation capital was mostly limited to finance and trade distribution at local levels (see Chapter 7). Export–import had been dominated largely by foreign firms. By 1954 apparently part of the indigenous circulation capital had been searching for new investment areas outside its customary ones. Indeed during the early 1950s private pump schemes started to multiply rapidly (Chapter 3). Gedaref's potential was revealed during the experimental stage of mechanisation, 1945–52. The cotton price boom after the Second World War, and the rise of the *dura* price during the War, had made investment in agriculture look an attractive venture.

3.   Indigenous capital had been waiting for the right political atmosphere as the colonial government had not been showing a real interest in its development. The Graduates General Congress established in 1938 was, among other organisations, a representative of the interests of the expanding urban elite. In a memorandum of twelve demands presented in 1942, the first was for the right of self-determination. Among the others, two demanded the right of Sudanese to be appointed to 'posts of political responsibility in all main branches of government' and 'imposing on companies and commercial firms the obligation of reserving a reasonable proportion of their posts for Sudanese.' A third demand was: 'The Sudanese to be enabled to exploit the commercial, agricultural and industrial resources of the country' (cited in T. Ali, 1982: 94). Clearly Sudanese indigenous capital was seeking the state's support for its further development. There is a clear indication that the colonial state was not promoting the interest of indigenous capital. However, not much more than a decade later the appropriate moment seemed to have arrived when Sudan's political independence was agreed on. It is during the transitional period (1953–55) in which Sudanese were effectively ruling themselves that Gedaref MFS were opened for Sudanese (and only Sudanese) private capital.

These, in my opinion, were the three main preconditions for the emergence and development of a Sudanese agrarian capitalist class. This stands in contrast with the widely accepted (among both Marxist and non-Marxist students of Sudanese agriculture) idea of seeing the rise of the agrarian capitalists and the MFS merely as a function of the state's initiative.

III. THE LANDED CLASSES AND THEIR ORIGINS

Those who have access to land in Gedaref can be divided into three groups according to the forms of labour used (including degree of mechanisation of the production process), position in the production process, object of production and size of land (as a rough indicator of size of surplus) and other income-generating activities.

Large Farmers

Large farmers normally cultivate one scheme (usually of 1,000 feddans, but this was increased to 1,500 feddans in the Sem Sem and Um Sinat Schemes) or more. They resort to wage labour completely to conduct all agricultural operations and their produce is almost wholly sold in

67

the market. In most cases they employ agents (called *wakeels*) residing in the Scheme during the agricultural season. Those who do not have *wakeels* may either do the job themselves or entrust it to a member of the family. The role of large farmers in the production process is one of general supervision. Everyday farm supervision is normally undertaken by *wakeels*, who may also recruit part of the labour force. Large farmers organise the provision of materials needed in production, including food for the workers. Some of the materials needed, especially fuel, are not always easy to obtain and their provision may require considerable effort. Large farmers also recruit most of the labourers, mostly through labour contractors, and undertake the marketing of the crops. They normally own most of the machinery needed. A tractor and a wide disc harrow are probably the minimum. It is also not uncommon for them to own their own lorry (for transport of workers and crops) and a harvester. Small huts are built on site for use by *wakeels* (or the farmer when on site) and workers. Machinery is normally used in land preparation, sowing, *dura* threshing and transporting of crops. Those large farmers who do not own all the machinery needed will rent it from other large farmers or, very occasionally, from machinery contractors.

The social origins of this group may be largely (but not exclusively) traced as the following:

1. *Harig* cultivators and wealthy pastoralists originally from the Gedaref area who, after accumulating some money, have turned to large-scale mechanised farming;
2. Merchants residing in Gedaref who, seeing the considerable size of surplus which can be appropriated from agriculture, have invested part of their accumulated capital in agriculture;
3. Bureaucrats (including former military officers and teachers), small businesspersons and farmers coming from outside the region, from the northern, central and eastern regions. These might have a small amount of capital in hand when coming to Gedaref, but have mainly depended on substantial loans from the Sudan Agricultural Bank (SAB), which is a state bank, and the Mechanised Farming Corporation (MFC). (The MFC was set up mainly by finance from the World Bank, whose loans helped in the development of MFS in Sem Sem and Um Sinat in the southern part of Gedaref region.)

What can be concluded from the above is that many large farmers had accumulated, or obtained through loans, their initial capital from activity outside 'mechanised' agriculture. However, they have established themselves as large mechanised farmers and are now accumulating capital mainly from farming. Moreover, a substantial number of the large farmers seem to have grown from within the indigenous social structure of the region (small farmers, pastoralists and merchants).

At least at the initial stages a considerable number of the large farmers were assisted by loans or free grants from the state. Machinery loans were provided at some time during the early stages of mechanised farming by the Ministry of Finance and later by the SAB, and during the establishment of Sem Sem and Um Sinat extensions, from the late 1960s to the mid-1970s, by the MFC. Loans to finance agricultural operations have been offered by the SAB since its establishment almost exclusively to large farmers, as is the case with machinery loans. The state also financed the demarcation and clearing of nearly half the area cultivated at present, mostly without requiring repayments from farmers, in the initial phases of MFS. In the Sem Sem Extension (developed in the late 1960s) farmers had to pay the cost of clearing in instalments extending over a period of 25 years, while in the Um Sinat Extension (developed in the early 1970s) farmers had to undertake clearing of land themselves. Land was offered at only a nominal rent to large farmers.

Although at the outset the role of the state was significant (it is probably less significant now), it could not be claimed that its financial assistance to large-scale production in Gedaref was crucial, as privately arranged initial investments were also considerable and more may have been available. The state has only contributed to the acceleration of the pace of development of large-scale capitalist agriculture, rather than being fully responsible for its development.

Despite the lack of official records, it may nevertheless be estimated that land cultivated by large farmers in Gedaref probably amounts to roughly 70% of the total land cultivated in the region in the 1982/83 season.[4] For this reason, Gedaref agriculture can be truly called (by Sudanese standards) large-scale capitalist farming.

Lands cultivated by the group of large farmers have been either allotted by the state (under lease arrangements) or occupied by 'laying on of the hand', mostly on pastoralists' land or on land used by peasants who happened to be absent for a year or two or who had been leaving it fallow. Land could also be obtained through rent arrangements with other large farmers who had been given a lease (or who had occupied it by 'laying on of the hand') but who had been either unable or unwilling to cultivate it.

It seems that a substantial number of large farmers also have other businesses in which they are engaged, ranging from wholesale and retail consumer goods trade, crop trade, services (rent of machinery and transport vehicles, maintenance workshops, small hotels, bakeries, restaurants, rent of storerooms etc.) and animal breeding (normally by farmers who were originally animal raisers, like, for example, 'Arabs' of the Rawashda and Um Shadara areas). Some of them consider the 'other businesses' to be their primary ones.

Small Farmers

The second group that also has access to land in Gedaref will be labelled here as 'small farmers'. Small farmers use wage labour mainly, but they may contribute (together with their family members) in agricultural labour. Normally they do not own the agricultural machinery needed in production. Machinery is normally rented from large farmers, but probably also from Ethiopian refugees who came with their tractors and have no land to cultivate. Some machinery is also brought from outside Gedaref (from the adjacent areas of Gezira and Khasm el Girba) to be hired when it is not needed in the original areas. Small farmers produce mainly for the market, but part of the produce (*dura*) may be directed to satisfy their own needs.

The main social origins of this group may be considered as the following:

1. *Harig* and *bildat* cultivators and small animal breeders, originally living in the Gedaref region.
2. Agricultural workers (who probably used to cultivate some *bildat* lands as well) originally from outside the region. Those coming from outside the region, mainly Westerners, are probably greater in number. (In Gedaref, particularly in the southern part, there are some villages inhabited almost exclusively by Westerners.)
3. People residing at present in the region (but not necessarily originally from it) who have other jobs besides farming, for example, lorry drivers, teachers, employees, small retail traders, *wakeels* etc. Some of these are employed full-time and may supervise (and probably contribute labour) mainly in their spare time and with the assistance of other household members. Some others engage in their other occupations mainly during and after harvest (e.g. small itinerant sellers who sell mainly during harvest when thousands of workers come; lorry drivers transporting crops; crop brokers who are called locally *samasra*, *wakeels* working with large farmers etc).

A considerable number of small farmers from subgroups (1) and (2) above may also raise animals. In fact, most of the households in Gedaref villages do own some animals. Small farmers keep animals for milk and also as a form of keeping wealth, probably to finance agriculture and to provide their livelihood in 'bad' years.

Land cultivated by small farmers is normally not rented. It may have been allotted by the agricultural management of the region in varying sizes of 100, 300 or 500 feddans, or obtained by 'laying on the hand'; or farmers may have been offered the right to use it by traditional leaders before the advent of mechanised farming.

From among the ranks of small farmers, some large farmers have emerged; particularly from among those who were offered land by the state (100, 300 or 500 feddans) during the early stages of land allotment.

Bildat *Cultivators*

The number of *bildat* cultivators is far greater than that of the first two groups (large and small farmers), but the total amount of land available for them is much less. Although *bildat* cultivators depend largely on their household labour, with the expansion of the use of machinery an increasing number are apparently using rented tractors for land preparation and sowing, and a smaller number rent harvesters for threshing (Dey et al, 1983: 212). It has also been reported that some *bildat* cultivators use wage labour as well (*Ibid*: 215). Average size of land available to them frequently does not exceed 20–30 feddans.

What distinguishes *bildat* cultivators from small and large farmers, besides being mainly dependent on household labour to meet agricultural labour needs, is that they also mostly sell their labour power at times when it is not needed on their own land in order to secure subsistence.

Bildat cultivators are normally of peasant or pastoralist origin, being either local people from Gedaref or immigrants – mainly Westerners, Eritreans and Ethiopians – who have come to settle on lands where no rights have been claimed by indigenous people.

From among *bildat* cultivators apparently increasing numbers have been compelled to leave their lands and turn into wage workers. Large-scale agriculture has been expanding on their lands after being expropriated by the state or taken away through some other means by large farmers. *Bildat* lands and most of the land of small farmers not being 'officially' leased from the state are always in danger of being expropriated to be offered to large farmers when new lands are demarcated.

There are no rigid demarcation lines between the small farmer and the larger ones on the one hand or between the small farmer and *bildat* cultivator on the other. In cultivation practices and forms of labour used, some small farmers may be exactly in the same situation as the large farmers as described in their general features above. Some other small farmers may be in the same position as *bildat* cultivators. Differences between the three groups, and their general features, as discussed above, relate to typical situations rather than individual cases.

IV. THE EXPANSION OF PRIVATE CAPITALIST AGRICULTURE

Large-scale capitalist farming, as has been mentioned, has been increasing mainly on lands expropriated from small-scale producers (small farmers, and *bildat* cultivators) and pastoralists who are mainly nomads of the Shukriya tribe. Its expansion over expropriated lands has been going on since the experimental stage, as has been mentioned earlier, but increasingly from the mid-1970s. The state played a central role in the expansion of large-scale agricultural production by directly expropriating lands (in the demarcated areas) or assisting large farmers in some way to do this (in non-demarcated areas). In some of the cases of expropriation of lands of small-scale crop producers in the demarcated areas, some sort of indemnification has been offered, by allotting a number of expropriated local villagers one scheme (1,000 or 1,500 feddans) to be distributed in small plots among themselves. It has been up to the government to decide whether or not to offer indemnification, and this was not based on size of lands previously held, but rather on what the government thought proper. In the case of expropriation of lands used by nomads no indemnification or planning for alternative routes and areas has been considered. A hostile attitude from the side of the authorities towards nomadic life and nomads has often been expressed not only in Gedaref but in the country as a whole (see AOAD, 1978; Shaaeldin, 1981).

Cases of disputes, even reaching a level of bloody confrontation, between large farmers and small-scale crop producers, and especially nomadic pastoralists, have quite frequently been brought to the Gedaref courts (Dey et al, 1983), and stories of clashes are also often heard in Gedaref town. The same thing has been reported to take place in other areas of MFS (see Simpsons, 1978). Not having an official land lease from the state (the only owner of land) means that cases brought in front of Gedaref civil courts by *bildat* cultivators and small farmers stand little chance of success. Obtaining an official lease to use the land is a relatively recent phenomenon in Gedaref. (In the past, permission used to be obtained from *nazirs*, sheikhs and local government councils.) According to the present 'modern' legal system, to cultivate land in non-demarcated areas, which include most of the lands cultivated by small farmers and *bildat* cultivators, is considered illegal. However, no legal actions have been pursued against those using these lands. The danger is that when demarcation comes, those lands may be expropriated. No demarcation, or official distribution of lands has taken place since the mid-1970s, since the last stage of Um Sinat extension. Since that time a large increase in mechanised farming has taken place on non-demarcated areas. Large farmers, fearing the consequences of cultivating non-demarcated lands (because of possible future expropriation), persuaded the authorities to offer them official leases on the lands they cultivate. Consistently with previous policy, the authorities only offered leases for areas equivalent to a standard scheme (1,000 feddans) or more. However, some large farmers are reported to have acquired lease certificates without actually having lands, as these certificates were often offered without proper investigation. These leaseholders would wait for the temporary absence of local cultivators, who had either left the land fallow, or did not have enough financial resources to cultivate in that year, and then claim (official) rights over their lands.

Standard scheme leases could only be offered at the expense of *bildat* and forest lands. Officially further clearing of forests has been banned. The right to use *bildat* land (as explained earlier) comes from the community and is non-official in terms of modern legislation. *Bildat* users, fearing the expansion of standard schemes into their lands, wanted to legalise their access to this land, and to this end asked for official government leases. Unwilling to agree to this, and at the same time not wanting to face them, at least for a time, the government decided to stop offering any new leases!

The resistance of small farmers and household producers to the expansion of mechanised farms had until recently remained on the whole at the level of individual families and smaller communities. In the last few years the situation has begun to change.

When the first Farmers Association (FA) was formed in 1962 (North West Gedaref Farmers Association) it comprised both large and small farmers and so did the other FAs that followed. In 1976 legislation by the National People's Assembly banned small farmers from membership of the then existing FAs, without defining 'small farmers'. However it did not say that small farmers could not have their own FAs. This was a clear expression of the consequences of the ongoing process of polarisation – large farmers wanted to have their own separate class organisations.

By the time of the second conference of the General Regional Union of Farmers Associations (GRUFA) in 1979, there was only one registered Small Farmers Association (SFA). Since 1980–81 a movement to organise small farmers and *bildat* cultivators in the region (under the umbrella of SFAs) has begun to intensify. In 1983 with the registration of 12 SFAs, the membership of the GRUFA rose to 138,000, from only 9,180 farmers in 1979. Large Farmers Associations (LFA) officials claim that the membership of SFAs has been exaggerated. In collaboration with the authorities (the Regional Minister of Agriculture, the Sudanese Socialist Union – the then only 'legal' political party – and other official bodies), the president of GRUFA refused registration to some 17 further SFAs, alleging that 'small farmers' had not been adequately defined and that investigations were needed into the actual membership of those Associations. The third conference of the GRUFA, which was due to be held in April 1983, was postponed indefinitely. LFAs, which dominate the leadership of GRUFA, were fearful of the growing voting power of the SFAs.

One of the main demands of the SFAs is the protection of their rights to use land by being offered official lease certificates or through other means. The refusal to issue lease certificates to small farmers is a clear expression of the future intentions of the authorities. Another demand that has been raised by SFAs is that they receive a share of the local government distributed quota of petrol products and some essential consumer goods at 'official' market prices (otherwise they are difficult to obtain, except on the black market). The distribution of these products has been limited mainly to large farmers. Small farmers also demand the provision of easy-term loans. The state-owned specialised agricultural bank (SAB) at present requires fulfilment of conditions of creditworthiness when offering credit. Large farmers holding official leases therefore have an advantage.

During the author's field trip to Gedaref in 1982/83, LFAs and SFAs were actively preparing for the forthcoming GRUFA elections. The author had the chance to meet officials and active members representing most of the Gedaref Farmers' Associations. It was quite apparent that the leadership of the SFAs had been dominated by a relatively better-off stratum of small farmers (those cultivating relatively larger plots of 300 or 500 feddans or more, who might also have some other business (trade services) or paid job – (teacher, employee). There is less class homogeneity in the SFAs than in the LFAs. In the former, both small capitalist farmers and household producers (*bildat* cultivators) coexist. It has been quite apparent from both formal and informal interviews that the small capitalist farmers are more class-conscious than the *bildat* cultivators. For them, the battle with LFAs is one which may determine their move into large-scale farming. In a meeting organised by the secretary of the Sudan Socialist Union in Gedaref in January 1983, many SFA leaders showed their tendency to compromise with the authorities and large farmers if their own stratum's interests (that is of the well-off small farmers rather than the rest of the movement) could be somehow

TABLE 4,3

Estimates of numbers of super-large farmers and the proportion of total land available to them

(1) Year	(2) Estimate of the number of super-large farmers	(3) Estimate of the percentage of land cultivated by them compared to total land cultivated	(4) Total area of land cultivated
1969/70	10	11.9%	1,590,520
1979/80– 1982/83 (on average)	28	19.3%	2,898,797

Source: Columns (2) and (3) see footnote (5)
Column (4) as in Table 4,2

promoted. Opportunist tendencies of some leaders of the SFAs had also been clear from the informal interviews.

From information the author obtained a year later, after the field trip,[5] the third conference of GRUFA was held in early 1984. The former president of GRUFA (himself a 'super-large' farmer and militant representative of 'super-large' agricultural and large merchant capital) was not re-elected. In terms of voting power, the SFAs were in a far better position than the LFAs. However, they elected as president a large farmer (president of the North West Gedaref LFA, and since 1962 deputy president of the first Farmers' Association in Gedaref). He was interviewed by the author in 1983. He can be categorised as a non-'super-large' farmer and a middle merchant.

Concentration of Land: the 'Super-large' Farmers

The possibility of expansion in non-demarcated areas has considerably assisted the growth of large land-holders in Gedaref. In contrast to the demarcated areas, here there is no upper limit on the number of schemes which may be held. However, even in the demarcated areas the principle of limiting the number of schemes which can be obtained by a single individual is not strictly adhered to. Land is also accessible by renting in from other official lease-holders who are unable to afford to cultivate the land themselves. Unofficial transfers of leases also take place. In fact, land leases are sold (over £S100,000 has been offered in some cases). Evidence of concentration of land in Gedaref is difficult to obtain as schemes are officially registered under the names of the legal holders. Records may not show transfers of leases by purchase or rent and sharing arrangements. Moreover, no records are available about non-lease-holdings in non-demarcated lands. However, I have been able to collect some information on the category of farmers I call 'super-large' farmers; those who cultivate over 10,000 feddans.[6]

Table 4,3 shows that the number of 'super-large' farmers had increased by 180% in 10–13 years, while the total land cultivated had increased during the same period by about 88%. It appears that the average amount of land cultivated by each 'super-large' farmer also changed during this period, although unfortunately no comparable information for the year 1969/70 was available. On average in 1979/80 to 1982/83 'super-large' farmers have each been estimated to cultivate 20,000 feddans – just under ⅓ of the total cultivated land.

In contrast to the process of concentration of land and agricultural capital, the process of centralisation is not growing fast. In 1982/83, with the exception of four large farms, among them one owned by the state, all the others were owned by individuals (or probably families). The three registered shareholding companies have not emerged as a result of unification of smaller holdings (centralisation), but have been established on 'new' areas mainly by people who were not previously farmers.

Private capital has resisted the growth of state agricultural capital in the area. A state farm was established from a fund provided by the IBRD mainly meant to finance the expansion of the demarcated area by 500,000 feddans (the Sem Sem and Um Sinat schemes). The state farm was initially formed to be mainly an experimental farm. A plan to turn it into a large productive unit of 76,000 feddans was resisted by private capital, which won the support of the IBRD. In 1982/83 the state farm cultivated only about 13,000 feddans (MFC, Gedaref).

V. CONCLUSION: THE EXTENT OF MECHANISATION AND CAPITALIST DEVELOPMENT

Capital–wage labour relations on a limited scale emerged in Gedaref during *harig* cultivation. *Harig* farmers had only taken over an existing labour process without altering its real nature significantly. What had changed was the situation of the various agents of production, in particular the free peasant or slave became a wage labourer (and probably the intensity of work and/or the length of the working day also increased).

The situation had not begun to signal a change until 1944/5 when the mechanised farming experimental stage began. Experiments in mechanisation were limited to relatively small areas, affecting a very small proportion of the population of the region. It is from 1954/55 that mechanisation really began to spread in the region.

In most of the lands cultivated in the region, the parts of the production process that have been mechanised are land preparation and sowing (using tractors, wide discs and planters), *dura* threshing (using harvesters) and transportation of crops to the market (using motor vehicles). However, the old techniques, employing hand tools, are still being used in weeding, reaping and picking.

The introduction of this partial mechanisation meant a partial revolution in the labour process. For the first time capital was able to adopt what Marx termed the extraction of relative surplus value by considerably increasing the productivity of a segment of the wage workers. The adoption of this partial mechanisation of the labour process in new areas in the region means a horizontal spread of the methods of production of relative surplus value. Indeed, this expansion has not limited itself to large-scale farms (or 'schemes') only, where it started, but at present has to a great extent altered the profile of cultivation practices in the whole region down even to small *bildat* land, though not yet to the same extent as in large farms (see Dey et al, 1983).

The extraction of relative surplus value and the development of a specifically capitalist mode of production in the Gedaref region however should not be exaggerated. Wage workers operating and assisting operators of machinery have been estimated to comprise around two and a half percent of the number of casual manual workers,[7] although their average productivity is of course much higher.

The expansion of mechanisation in the Gedaref region over the last 30 years, since the opening up of the area for private capital investment, has been limited to the horizontal level (new areas being incorporated at the existing level of mechanised farming), and has not developed vertically (more agricultural operations being mechanised) (ARC, 1975; Zein-al-Abdin, 1977 and more recently Elhassan, 1985). The reasons for this are as follows:

(1) Until recently, land has been readily available for large farmers, either in the form of uncultivated lands (e.g. forest lands) or in the form of expropriated lands.

(2) Labour has been in plentiful supply and cheap, especially since the mid-1970s with the coming of tens of thousands of Eritrean and Ethiopian refugees.

(3) Mechanisation of other agricultural operations is either expensive or has not yet become possible technically. Using chemicals or other methods for weeding is apparently more costly than the still cheap labour. The kinds of *dura* grown – varieties which grow to different levels – cannot be harvested by the existing combine harvesters. The only kind of *dura* that can be reaped mechanically is unpopular with consumers. Consumers' preferences would certainly change if the mechanically reapable kind of *dura* proved to be much cheaper, but this is not yet the case. Efforts to mechanise the sesame harvest have also proved to be difficult technically, as machines will not differentiate between sesame stalks and weeds.

Farming in Gedaref, however, has been facing difficulties. Table 4,2 demonstrates that the average yield of *dura* has been declining steadily. Farmers attribute this to ecological changes causing changes in the period and quantity of rains, to the extensive use of land without fertilisers, to the deterioration in services and lack of agricultural extension. Agricultural experts add to these reasons the non-diversified cropping system that has been adopted, soil erosion and other factors associated with cultivation practices, e.g. one-level ploughing (Zein-al-Abdin, 1977).

With the decline in yields, and as labour becomes scarce (not yet true for Gedaref) and with scarcity of new cultivable lands (as probably has begun to prevail in Gedaref though not in Sudan generally) there will be objective reasons to resort to methods of increasing profits through mechanisation if individual capital is to continue attaining profits. However, this may not be the case in the near future in Gedaref.

CHAPTER FIVE

Rural Labour Markets: Formation, Internal Mechanisms and Segmentation

The Gezira and Gedaref, as we have seen in the previous two chapters, represent two different patterns or stages of capitalist development in rural Sudan. Besides being representative in this way they are also the two main rural labour markets in Sudan.

I. THE GEZIRA

Settled Wage Labourers and their Changing Origin

Wage labour was relatively limited in the Sudan at the time the Scheme was started. The colonial administration had been at pains to encourage West African migrants (mainly of Nigerian and French Equatorial origin) to settle in the Sudan generally and particularly in the Gezira. In the opinion of the colonial administration 'the influx of West African tribes will materially benefit the labour market as these people, unlike most of the Sudanese, are anxious to make money' (quoted in Duffield, 1983: 48). West African migrants and, to a lesser extent, Sudanese coming from the western part of the country (who together are commonly called Westerners), before the establishment of the Gezira, worked as wage labourers in different places in the Sudan (the Funj area, Nuba mountains, Gash Delta, Gedaref etc.) and where land was accessible, cultivated their own smallholdings (Hassoun, 1952). Very few of them settled in the Gezira before the year 1924 as Table 5,1 shows.

During the period in which Gezira land was being prepared for large-scale cultivation and the first batch of tenancies (300,000 feddans) was being distributed, Westerners were encouraged to come and settle in Gezira. In 1924, before the actual commencement of Phase I of the Scheme, their number rose to 4,000. Three years after the start of the Scheme there were 6,000 Westerners residing there, while 9,000 came as seasonal wage labourers. (Another source estimated the latter figure

TABLE 5,1

An estimate of the number of settled Westerners in Gezira (both of Sudanese and West African origin)

Year	Total number of all Westerner wage labourers	Settled	Seasonal
1919	300	–	–
1924	4,000	–	–
1929	15,000	6,000	9,000
1936	28,257	8,257	20,000
1946	55,268	18,268	37,000

Source: Hassoun, 1952

as 16,000, half of whom came from West Sudan – see Tamim, 1980: 6.) Between 1929 and 1946 the number of settled labourers tripled, while that of the seasonal labourers multiplied fourfold. From 1954 to 1980 the number of settlers in Gezira labour camps rose from 59,000 to 169,992 (*Ibid*: 7, 31).

During the early period of colonial rule in the Sudan the process by which household producers were separated from the means of production, fully or partially (and hence the development of the capitalist mode of production), was relatively slow, whereas in some other countries, e.g. Nigeria and French Equatorial Africa, it was apparently faster. The colonial government saw these immigrant Westerners as a potential wage labour army, since when they came they had very few alternatives, if any, to selling their labour power in order to subsist. West Africans as well as some Sudanese Westerners during the earlier periods of the Scheme were encouraged to settle in scattered villages within the boundaries of the Scheme, and some were offered smallholdings outside the rotation area of the Scheme to cultivate *dura*. Some of their sheikhs, as well as other (probably influential) individuals, were even given tenancies to attract more people to come and settle around them and form the nucleus of labour villages (see Hassoun, 1952 and Culwick, 1955).

The policy of stimulating labour settlement in the Scheme by offering smallholdings to some of the labourers, to cultivate *dura* during the periods when their labour power was not needed in the Scheme itself, and also by offering tenancies to others, seems to have been successful. During the 1930s and 1940s, particularly as a result of many local tenants abandoning their tenancies because of the depressed price of cotton on world markets, many Westerners were offered tenancies. In the year 1933–34 there were about 2,000 Westerner tenants; by 1944–45 this had risen to 3,000 (Culwick, 1955: 12). On the other hand, between

1929 and 1936 a yearly average of 322 new Westerners were seeking settlement in Gezira annually, as Table 5,1 shows. This big rise in the number of Westerners settling in the Scheme is probably attributable to the large increase in the number of Westerners acquiring tenancies during the same period.

From the late 1940s the policy of encouraging West Africans to settle in the Gezira (and in Sudan generally) was gradually reversed. The Nationality Law of 1948 stated that only Sudanese citizens were eligible for salaried appointments in government services and for access to land. Before the introduction of this law some people of West African origin had been allotted tenancies in Gezira. Tenancies were not confiscated from them immediately after the introduction of this law. However, a rule prohibiting the *transfer* of tenancies to non-Sudanese was introduced in the Gezira. This means that sons and daughters of those 'non-Sudanese' tenants cannot become heirs to their parents' tenancies, despite the fact that most of those sons and daughters have never known any other home area than Sudan. As a result the proportion of tenants of West African origin started to drop significantly and eventually they disappeared as tenants.

In the early stages of the Scheme's development, the proportion of Westerners of West African origin was higher than that of Sudanese Westerners in the labour camps of Gezira. In a report presented in 1929 (cited in Tamim, 1980: 6), the number of Western Sudanese settling in Gezira was estimated to be only 145, while the number of West Africans was 5,229. Since this period, many more peasants and pastoralists in West Sudan have lost their means of production, resulting in a fresh influx of Western Sudanese. This large alternative labour force was one reason for the new policy against the settlement of West Africans in Gezira. Both the tenants and the State, in their struggle against settled waged labour, had an interest in the creation of an alternative labour source as rivals to the labourers of West African origin. During their stay in Gezira, West African wage labourers had developed great bargaining skills and a high level of solidarity among themselves (on an ethnic rather than a class basis, and obviously as a result of living in an alien and hostile environment).

As a result, the policy was developed of encouraging the influx of Sudanese Westerners (both as settled and as seasonal labourers) and of Arabs of the Blue and White Nile (who mainly come as seasonal labourers only). Offices for labour recruitment from those areas were opened, and tenants organised recruitment trips, particularly during the cotton-picking season. This latter form of recruitment has gone on since the establishment of the Scheme itself, but probably intensified as a result of the strategy of finding alternative labour sources. Some tenants built houses in the labour camps to offer to the labourers willing to settle (personal communication from Albaz and Barnett).[1] Three different estimates of the number of people settling in the Scheme's labour camps according to their origin show that the proportion of Western Sudanese to West African settlers has changed from 0.028:1 in 1929 to 1:1 in 1955–56 to 2.125:1 in 1983. There is no doubt that the proportion of Western Sudanese settling in Gezira labour camps has increased considerably, but these figures, especially the last two, should be treated with some caution.[2]

Hardly any non-Westerners have settled in the Gezira as agricultural casual workers. Arabs of the two Niles (Blue and White) do not settle in the Gezira although they come in large numbers as seasonal workers during peak seasons (mainly during the cotton-picking season). This may possibly be attributed partly to their better assets in land and animal wealth as compared to Westerners, and partly to the better chances they have of employment outside the Scheme, which they may find preferable. A considerable number of former wage labourers from the two Niles (especially from the White Nile) were offered tenancies when the Managil Extension was established in the 1960s.

The following two subsections [(b) and (c)] are largely based on a survey undertaken in 1983 during the peak cotton-picking period of that season (the most labour-demanding operation in the Scheme). The aim of the survey was to provide data on non-tenant household labour. This area has been surprisingly neglected in the relatively wide literature on the Gezira. Gezira tenants and the labour required by different crops have been the major focus of surveys and studies. In the rare cases where wage labour is dealt with, it refers mainly to its major sources and input compared to that of the tenants' households. The survey comprised a total sample of 87, 40 seasonal labourers and 47 settled wage labourers. In fact, five of the latter group reported entering into sharecropping arrangements with tenants and not selling their labour power directly in that agricultural season. The sample was selected from 20 different locations in the Gezira: from work sites and camps in northern, central and southern areas of Gezira Main and the Managil Extension. In addition to the sample survey, background information was gathered from many officials and others in the Scheme by means of informal interviews. This also helped in formulating the subject of the interviews with the wage workers. The size of the sample was not fixed prior to the fieldwork. It had been left relatively open-ended until some definite trend became apparent. Results of interviews were observed on a day-to-day basis.

Towards the last third of the sample, it was noted that information being collected was only confirming already established trends. However, as this survey was probably the first of its kind in the Gezira dealing specifically with non-tenant household forms of social organisation of labour, its aim was to expose some of the main tendencies and relations, rather than to provide statistically sound data. Therefore, the proportions and percentages given here are to be taken as suggestive rather than assertive. Thus different relations and tendencies discussed below should not be taken as being conclusive. Although statistically sound data are still to be collected from larger surveys, the present ones, in my view, clearly indicate directions and paths for such surveys.

The Gezira labour market may be divided for our purposes here into two sections: a settled and a seasonal labour market.

Settled Wage Labourers and the Local Labour Market

Settled wage labour in the Gezira, both from indigenous and labour camp villages, may be divided into two categories according to the type of contract. These categories are:

1. 'Permanent' labour: those labourers who have a 'long' contract, the duration of which may or may not be fixed but which in any case can be terminated by either side, after due notice. Permanent labourers are paid on a monthly basis. This type of contract is used mainly by the Scheme's Administration, but also by a small number of tenants.
2. Casual labour: labourers in this category are contracted to carry out specific jobs lasting for part of a day or longer. They may be paid on a daily basis or on piece rate. Casual labourers may work for many employers during one season. Labourers employed by tenants fall mainly into this category. The Administration also employs casual labourers.

Permanent labourers employed by the SGB are contracted to undertake specific tasks in irrigation works (major canals and stations), in workshops (maintenance of cars, tractors, gins, etc.), in the ploughing section and in the Administration offices. Labourers recruited for such tasks are mainly Sudanese residing in the Scheme or in the surrounding areas. According to the Nationality Act of 1948, non-Sudanese may not be employed on a permanent basis by any government department. Some of the non-Sudanese Westerners had to leave their jobs after the implementation of the Act.

Tenants rarely employ full time wage labourers on a monthly basis, although previously it was not uncommon to find monthly paid wage labourers, who were called *zoul shahria* (monthly paid person). Under this type of contract the labourer is contracted to perform all kinds of agricultural work and may also be asked to help in other non-agricultural tasks as well. The tenant assumes control over the labour of *zoul shahria*. The latter may not be allowed to engage in other work without the consent of the employer. Sometimes, if the employer has no work in his/her own tenancy, he/she may require the *zoul shahria* to work in other tenancies, and if this is paid work it is the original employer who receives the payment (personal communication from Albaz). A relation of domination therefore exists between the tenants and these monthly labourers. However, our evidence indicates that this type of contract is dying out. In many parts of the Gezira it is now probably defunct, although in Managil Extension it still exists, but on a limited scale. At present, part-time monthly paid contracts may be made for certain tasks (e.g. watering) and labourers are free to work where they wish after conducting the specific task for which they were employed.

Most casual labourers employed by the SGB are contracted on a daily basis (although actual payment may not be daily) to perform work connected with transportation of cotton from collection centres to the ginning factories, to work in the gins themselves, mainly in non-skilled work, or to undertake *tulba* labour.[3] Most of the casual labourers needed centrally by the Administration are recruited through labour contractors. *Tulba* labour may be contracted directly by field inspectors.

Casual labour employed by tenants is the most important type of wage labour in the Scheme. Casual labourers employed by the Administration to perform *tulba* labour (the extent of which is very limited compared to casual labour employed by tenants) come from the same labour pool as that employed by the tenants. In what follows, we deal mainly with casual labour employed by the tenants in both forms – settled and seasonal. Thus, in this section, the terms 'wage workers' and 'labourers' refer to this type of wage labour.

Settled casual labourers employed by tenants may be divided into two categories or groups according to their class position. The first is that group of people in the Gezira who have access to land either by being direct holders of tenancies or through sharecropping arrangements, or those who have access to riverain lands and *bildat* (rainland outside the rotation area) or to other means of production. They work for wages in the Scheme at times when their labour is not needed on their own holdings or at times when they need cash. These people sell their labour power to meet only part of their reproduction requirements. They cannot be considered as 'free labourers' from the point of view of their access to the means of production. Nevertheless, in the present context, the wage labouring side of their lives is stressed, and therefore they are included in the category of wage labourers.

The second group of wage labourers is composed of those who have no access to the means of production (except marginally, and indirectly in those few non-privately owned areas around the camps or elsewhere where their animals, kept mainly for milk, may seek pasture), and who depend almost entirely on selling their labour power to maintain themselves. In the Gezira at present this group is in a minority. Research undertaken in 1983 showed that 78% of these labour camp labourers had sharecropping arrangements.[4]

From another point of view, settled wage labourers may be divided, as in the preceding discussion, between those labourers who are considered as 'Arabs' (mainly indigenous Gezira people) and who live in the tenant villages, and a second group of those non-Arab wage workers, mainly Westerners, who normally live in the Gezira labour camps. Some among this second group may live in tenant villages, for example some of the *zoul shahria* workers. Workers in each of these two groups may come from either of the types of wage labourers described above, i.e. those who have or do not have access to the means of production. The distribution of the Gezira population between labour and tenant villages is, as previously indicated, based on ethnic rather than on class affiliation. Many tenants of Western origin live in labour camps with their fellow tribespeople.

Recruitment of Settled Workers

Typically, Gezira settled workers (62% of the sample) said they waited for the tenants or their agents to recruit them. Workers searching for jobs as individuals constituted 21% of the sample, while those who searched for jobs in groups (from the same labour camp and mainly with other members of their household) amounted only to 17%.

It is apparently a common practice among wage workers of the same household working together to make contracts in the name of one member of the household, usually the household head. It is also common for newly arrived settlers, who normally come without their families, to look for jobs by themselves, as they have not yet established working relationships with specific tenants, and if they wait for the tenants to make them an offer they may end up with very little work.

Most of the tenants in Gezira recruit their settled workers from within a limited circle. Tenants of a particular Gezira village may have very few labour camps from which to recruit labour as there are no recruitment centres other than the nearby camps. In the Gezira it is uncommon for tenants to go to different labour camps studying the labour market before deciding on their strategy. The more common practice is for tenants to establish working relationships with certain labourers in a nearby labour camp and/or within their own tenant village, to whom they resort most of the time. If those labourers, as groups or individuals, are busy elsewhere or if no agreement is reached, the tenants may resort to other labourers in the same or in another nearby labour camp.

There are about 710 labour camps in Gezira. On average 235 people live in each labour camp with about 96 (41%) being economically active (Tamim, 1980). Thus it can be seen that in the Gezira the settled labour market is for the most part highly localised and fragmented.

The field survey of 1983 confirms observations made in earlier studies (Barnett, 1976; Abdelhamid, 1965; Culwick, 1955) that some tenants extend small loans or give little gifts such as sugar, oil, or tea to their labourers with the intention of tying them. The making of loans and gifts, no matter how small, is normally very much appreciated by labourers who may consider themselves obliged to such 'open-handed' tenants and may accept offers of work without lengthy bargaining. In other cases, wealthy tenants may build small houses in the labour camps with a view to offering them for little or no rent to labourers, who are then obliged to give this tenant priority when he needs wage labour. Abdelhamid (1965) suggested that some tenants have easier access to labour through relationships such as kinship, marriage and friendship, which probably only occur among tenants and wage workers who have the same ethnic origin. They seem to be very rare today.

These relationships and ties between tenants and workers prevent the Gezira settled labour market from being completely open. The extent of such relationships and their effects on the formation of capital–wage labour relations in the Gezira are not easily measured. Their effect is different among different groups of workers, depending upon their historical, social and cultural background, and probably in different localities. Wage workers of West African origin obviously have fewer such ties and relationships with tenants than do the wage workers from the indigenous villages.

Wage Fixing for Settled Workers

Wages for settled workers in the Gezira are paid in a variety of forms. Piece rate arrangements are most common. In a few cases daily wages may be offered. Daily wage contracts include *tulba* labour and some other casual labour employed by the Administration. They also include cases where unrelated workers are involved in the same task for the same employer. Monthly full-time contracts are now very uncommon in the Gezira. However, some monthly part-time contracts do exist. Arrangements are made for workers to perform certain repetitive tasks (e.g. irrigation of holdings, cleaning of small canals and roads between tenancies etc.) and to be paid on a monthly basis for as long as the task lasts. In the case of piece rates the wages are agreed on site. The job is normally based on the whole holding or part of it (e.g. *inqayia, jedwal, rubat*, which are different areal divisions of a standard tenancy). During cotton picking and in tasks associated with *dura* harvesting, wages are normally based on a weight unit; on *guffa* (about 16 kg of seed cotton) in the case of picking, and on *shawal* (about 90 kg) in the case of the *dura* harvest. West African wage workers fix their contracts almost exclusively on piece rates.

Wages are usually fixed after a bargaining process has taken place (74% of the cases in the sample). In most cases, bargaining took place directly between the employer and the wage workers (81%). In the remaining cases (19%) bargaining took place through a representative of the wage workers.

Those who did not enter into bargaining (or whose bargaining was so weak as to be negligible) comprised 26% of the cases. This group consists of women pickers who work mainly during the picking season. Among this group are those workers who have the type of non-market relationship with tenants described above, which affects their bargaining power. The category of non-bargaining wage workers may also include the new settlers who are more prepared to accept anything offered. Not a single West African immigrant has been reported in the 1983 survey to accept a wage without bargaining.

There are many reasons for the relatively strong bargaining power of West African immigrants, which has been confirmed by tenants and officials. Their well-known higher daily output, due to the intensity of work and also probably length of the working day, compared to other categories of wage workers, allows them to finish the particular task or operation relatively faster. This means they are preferred by many tenants who wish to finish a certain task or operation within the strict agricultural schedule. West African immigrants have more limited relationships with tenants, who are mostly themselves Arabs. This probably removes some of their inhibitions about bargaining. The length of time that they have been familiar with Gezira conditions has taught them greater bargaining skills than other workers. It has also been observed that some of the West African immigrants tend to concentrate the bargaining in the hands of one individual (who may be the sheikh of the village or the elder among a certain group) even when the rest of the group is present at the time of bargaining. Being backed by others may place the delegated person in a stronger position, and he may thus try to drive a harder bargain. Achieving this, of course, may strengthen his position socially as a bargaining leader (this may be especially desired by camp shiekhs to maintain their social position).

The nature of the bargaining may differ for different crops, operations and seasons. In cotton picking for example, bargaining may continue until a fixed payment per *guffa* has been reached. After this and for the rest of the season (with the exception of abnormal cases) that rate may be accepted without further renegotiation. In other operations, e.g. weeding, where labour requirements vary considerably, bargaining becomes sharper. This is also the case with groundnut growing, where some wage labourers try to raise wage claims higher than the average, in order to compel tenants to accept sharecropping arrangements, because they see that their camp-mates who sharecrop are able to derive better incomes than they can achieve in the form of wages (see SGB Economic Survey, 1981: 42). During some critical periods, when tenants are in urgent need of labour, e.g. when preparing land and sowing before the rainy season, wage labourers may bargain for and receive wages higher than in normal conditions. West African immigrants have been reported to be able to drive a harder bargain in such conditions.

After reaching an agreement on a job and actually carrying it out disputes may arise. Of the workers interviewed, 42% reported disputes. These arise for two main reasons. Either the employer does not fulfil all or part of the terms of the agreement, not paying the amount agreed on (57% of the cases of disputes); or does not agree with the way the job has been executed and may require its completion to a higher standard. There are two main ways of resolving disputes. The first, which is the most frequent, is to reach a compromise by direct negotiation between the two sides of the dispute (71% of cases); the second (24% of cases) is to turn to voluntary mediators. Bringing the issue to court is very rare (less than 2%). Courts seem to be either unavailable or impractical, particularly as there are no specialised courts responsible for resolving such disputes. Indeed, there is no agricultural labour legislation in the country at all. Unable to reach a solution over their disputes with employers, wage workers may feel compelled to leave without being paid. However this is quite rare in the Gezira (3% of cases).

Tenants seem to hold the stronger position in cases of disagreements with workers. There are, of course, no written contracts between the two sides. The amount of wages agreed on is known only to the two partners. Wages are not paid until the job is agreed to have been adequately performed. Evaluation of the work performance depends mainly on the tenant–employer's own judgement. Any solution arrived at without the consent of the employer is not very viable. Solutions proposed by mediators are not legally binding, though to some extent they may be morally binding.

This does not mean that tenants can always impose their terms. Having a reputation for being unjust may considerably affect a tenant's ability to hire labour, particularly in such a fragmented labour market. This acts as a pressure on the tenants to compromise.

The Seasonal Labourers

Seasonal labour, which comes mainly for cotton-picking in April and May, has always been needed in the Gezira. In the ten years between 1969–70 and 1978–79 their numbers have fluctuated between 261,000 and 365,000 (O'Brien, 1980: 208). Two major sources have always supplied the Scheme with seasonal labour – the Arabs of the Managil, White Nile and Blue Nile areas, whom we will call seasonal labourers of the 'Two Niles area', and Westerners – mainly people of Western Sudanese rather than of West African origin in the last two decades.

In a small survey conducted in 1983 among 40 seasonal wage workers in the Scheme, 37 (92.5%) reported that they held land in their home areas. Seasonal labourers can be divided into two large groups depending on the prevalent economy in their home areas: (i) a 'cultivators' group, who depend more on farming than on animal-raising; and (ii) a 'pastoralist-cultivators' group, composed of those who depend more or less entirely on animal-rearing. Demarcation lines between the two groups are not always easy to draw. The majority of those coming from the Two Niles are 'pastoralist-cultivators'. These may identify themselves as 'pastoralists', especially those who do not cultivate at all – 25% of the sample. Some of the 'pastoralist-cultivators' have permanent villages in which they stay, or to which they return each time they go in search of pastures or wage labour. Others may not have permanent villages, although they may have camping centres to which they return at certain times in the year during their migration cycles. 'Pastoralist-cultivators' bring some of their animals with them to the Gezira. Westerners who come to the Gezira seasonally are mostly 'cultivators' settled in permanent villages outside the Gezira. Here they cultivate their own plots and may raise animals as well, but they do not bring the animals to the Gezira when they come as wage labour migrants.

Recruitment of Seasonal Wage Labourers

Seasonal wage workers are recruited by three methods. The first is self-recruitment, accounting for about one-third of cases. They come as individuals or in groups looking for jobs. Some of them already have long-established working relationships with particular tenants. A representative of a group of seasonal labourers may be sent ahead to explore the possibilities and to arrange for the arrival of the rest. In this case a money advance, probably equivalent to a cash wage of 2–4 days' pay in 1982–83, will be paid to him for each economically active person arriving later. This helps to prepare for their arrival in the Gezira. Sometimes, after learning of the availability of workers through their representatives, tenants may provide transport. Many of those considered as self-recruited had probably come through the other two methods some time before, after establishing relations with particular tenants. Becoming accustomed to returning to the Gezira each year they have then tended to take the initiative and arrive on their own.

The second method is one arranged by tenants, as individuals or in groups, or by their village councils. Representatives of groups of tenants or village councils are sent to recruit labourers from their home areas. Recruitment normally takes place in the areas of the Two Niles and Kordofan, especially northern Kordofan. Tenants' representatives make verbal contracts with individuals or households through the household head directly or through village sheikhs or other influential personalities. A small sum of money, which is called *mal al-diayia* (recruitment money) is normally advanced and in most cases either transport is provided or a small sum of money is given for this purpose. *Mal al-diayia* seems to be appreciated by the seasonal labourers. Its receipt and the 'word' given at that time means for many a strict commitment.

The third method adopted for recruitment is through the Permanent Committee for the Recruitment of Picking Labour (PCRPL), which was formed in December 1962 by the Council of Ministers. Recruiting centres were opened in different places in Kordofan, in the areas of the Two Niles, and also in Darfur. Surveys of different areas which traditionally supply the Gezira with seasonal labour may be made before the picking season to plan recruitment strategies. When agreement has been reached between officials of the PCRPL and seasonal labourers, transport is provided and a small sum of money is often advanced. On their arrival seasonal labourers are then distributed to different areas in the Gezira.

These last two methods for recruiting seasonal labour were found in about two-thirds of the cases in the survey. Although some labourers could not tell whether they were recruited by the PCRPL or the tenants, it would appear that fewer labourers were recruited through the former (this is confirmed by data cited by O'Brien, 1980: 208).

More seasonal wage labourers in Gezira come as family groups than as individuals. This is especially so with the Arabs of the Two Niles (the 'pastoralist-cultivators' group) compared to the Westerners (the 'cultivators' group). Abdelhamid mentions that although a tenant may receive his pickers in a family group it is not necessary for him to hire them all (Abdelhamid, 1965: 26). He also establishes that half of the tenants have preferences regarding the pickers' tribe when selecting them and even more have preferences regarding the gender of the pickers. Most of the tenants have no preferences as to the age of pickers (Abdelhamid: 30–32).

Although seasonal labourers come to the Gezira mainly during the picking season, which may extend from December to April, some may also engage in associated operations, such as pressing and packing of cotton or transporting it to collection centres. After the cotton harvest, many seasonal labourers remain to perform post-harvest operations – pulling out cotton stalks and clearing the fields (by burning and sweeping). In a few cases, mainly among the Arabs of the Two Niles, some remain or come back for sowing (5% of the total sample) and weeding (7.5%). Some seasonal labourers come earlier, before the beginning of cotton-picking, to work in the *dura* harvest (10%). During their stay in the Gezira a few have been reported as working in the provision of services in the tenants' villages – for example building or in some form of craftwork such as shoe making, or in making and selling beer – these latter are usually female Westerners.

Wage Fixing for Seasonal Labourers

The wages of seasonal labourers are normally based on piece rates. Picking is paid for on the basis of *guffa*. Pulling out of stalks, clearing of fields as well as sowing and weeding are paid for on piece rates based on the whole or a part of the tenancy. In most cases wages contain both cash and kind components. In some cases, terms of payment are set by the employers and the seasonal labourers may be unable to demand cash only, but may have to accept a mixture, while in other cases they may be able to choose between the two methods – cash only or cash and kind.

Payment in both cash and kind is normally preferred by the seasonal labourers as most of them do not have enough cash to support themselves until the time of their first payment, which may be delayed depending on the time when cash advances are received from the SGB by the tenants. Having their food – or the major component of it, *dura* – provided before starting work gives them a feeling of security. Moreover, the market places where they would have to go for food are normally quite far away from the temporary huts on the tenancies where they stay. Tenants also prefer to pay in cash and kind. This may help to conceal the differences in the level of wages between the settled labourers (who are paid exclusively in cash) and the seasonal labourers. Tenants try their best to make the seasonal labourers understand that paying in this dual form is a 'favour' as food is both difficult to get and costly.

Wages paid for seasonal labourers are determined in three ways: (1) by the tenant (or representative) alone (40% of the cases in the sample); (2) as a result of 'talking' (probably involving some bargaining) between representatives of seasonal labourers (sheikhs or other individuals) and employers (35%); (3) by the employers and the seasonal labourers directly (25%).

Tenants or their representatives have developed some skills in wage fixing, which include how to please those sheikhs and other representatives of the seasonal labourers who may have some control over the labourers. Labourers recruited from their home villages have no knowledge of prevailing market rates; many among those who are self-recruited may choose the same tenants every year. It is difficult for any seasonal labourers to learn about labour market conditions because there are few places where they can gather together socially, and because of the nature of farm organisation, with only a few labourers working on each plot. Moreover, there is little competition among the tenants for seasonal labour, as the latter seems to be in adequate, or even excessive supply. In any case, competition is not yet the driving force behind production (and reproduction) in the Gezira (Chapter 3).

Delays in paying the cash and especially the kind component of the wages may lead to disputes between the tenants and the seasonal labourers. Those who confirmed the occurrence of disputes (of this kind and/or of another kind) amounted to 33% of the sample, while 20% said disputes occurred very rarely, and 47% asserted that no disputes occurred. Complaints about the amount of wages received were few and were mainly about the adequacy of the kind component.

In most cases, disputes are resolved directly between the parties, while in a few cases some mediation may be needed. This will usually lead to a small compromise on the side of the employers. After agreement has been reached and work has started, seasonal labourers usually continue to work for the same employer even if they realise later that other tenants are offering higher rates. Giving their word to the tenants, being transported by them, accepting *mal al-diayia* and in some cases *mal al-dukhla* (a cash advance paid at the start of the work, normally given to self-recruited labourers who have not received *mal al-diayia*) and having received their first advance of *dura*, and sometimes other food items, is interpreted by the seasonal labourers as a strong moral obligation to hold to the initial terms of the contract. In fact by giving such advances, tenants consciously aim to tie the seasonal labourers to them. From their side, the seasonal labourers, with their pronounced ideology of 'honour' and 'trust', will try to prove that they are worth the trust which the tenants have placed in them. Thus they stick to the original agreement, even if they consider it not entirely fair.

II. GEDAREF

There are no official or other estimates of the number of wage workers (both settled and seasonal) in Gedaref. According to the author's own estimate, as has been mentioned in Chapter 4, in the *dura* harvest of the 1982/83 season, there were roughly 350,000 casual workers and 8,000 machine operators. Wage workers in Gedaref come from different parts of Sudan and also from outside; indeed, it may be considered as the most diversified agricultural labour market in Sudan. As Table 5,2 shows, with the exception of the Northern Region, workers come from all over Sudan, as well as from Ethiopia and Eritrea, and to an insignificant extent, from Chad also. This table demonstrates the large dependence of Gedaref on migrant seasonal labour; only 21% of wage labourers engaged in weeding consider their current home to be Gedaref. This does not mean that the other 79% will be going away after weeding or at the end of the agricultural season, although a proportion of them may do so. Many refugees, who have been driven away from home because of famine, war or for political reasons, and many Westerners also may anticipate going back in the future, and therefore do not regard Eastern Sudan as their current home, although they may have to spend several years there, and indeed the wish to return home may never be realised for some of them.

In 1982/83 among wage workers interviewed in Gedaref it was found that 51% of them had access to land directly or through their households (Dey et al, 1983: 231). As no other significant occupation or wage labour was reported by the rest, it would seem that about half the Gedaref workers depend completely on wage labouring in the region. This leads us to believe that, in fact, at least for the year 1982/83 Gedaref had been the de facto current home for 49%, not 21%, of Gedaref wage workers.

Recruitment, Wages and Bargaining

Wage labourers in Gedaref are recruited in different ways.

1. Recruitment is undertaken in the main recruiting centre of Gedaref town itself or in other much smaller centres in the towns of Dawka and Hawata. Workers either wait in the streets of the town centre for farmers, their agents (*wakeels*) or labour contractors to come with their offers of work, or, less frequently, may pass from one large farmer's office to another searching for jobs.

TABLE 5,2

Percentage distribution of labourers by place of birth and current home in the weeding season of 1982/83 in Gedaref

Place	Place of Birth	Current Home
Eastern Region	11	21
Central Region	7	9
Southern Region	10	10
Western Regions (Kordofan & Darfur)	52	49
Ethiopia & Eritrea	19	11
Chad	1	–
Total	100	100

Source: Dey et al, 1983: Table 4.1, p.229.

2. Farmers or *wakeels* may go to villages and refugee camps in the vicinity of their farms to recruit wage labour. This is especially the case in areas more isolated from Gedaref town (in the southern part in Sem Sem, Um Sinat and Abu Sabika, and in the eastern part in Fashaga and Abu Irwa) and in the rainy season when the roads are difficult to use.

3. Many *bildat* cultivators and some small farmers often depend on recruiting wage labour from within their own villages, especially in slack seasons when wage labourers are not encouraged to go to Gedaref town selling their labour power.

4. Some *wakeels* and farmers, whose farms are close to the main roads, also recruit wage workers passing by on the roads as they make their way from other farms (probably after failing to reach an agreement about wages with other farmers who would have recruited them from elsewhere).

5. It may also happen that wage workers go from farm to farm searching for jobs. When workers are recruited away from the farm, the farmer has to provide transport to the site. Many large farmers have their own lorries. Other farmers may either rent lorries or let the workers find their own way by public transport after paying them the cost. Not having their own transport makes it difficult for small farmers and *bildat* cultivators to recruit labour, as using the inadequate public transport and also probably having to walk long distances afterwards is less attractive to workers who are making a choice in a wide market.

During the 1982/83 agricultural season the overall labour supply in Gedaref seemed to be generally adequate and no serious labour shortages were reported by the farmers. Some labour shortages may occur during the sesame harvest as the period in which it is harvestable is very short (about 10 days) and it is normally ready to be harvested at the same time all over the region. Until the early 1970s, labour contractors used to travel widely, mainly to the west and the south of Sudan recruiting labourers for the farmers. This is no longer the case, notwithstanding that demand for labour, with the continuous increase in total land cultivated, has increased considerably. The influx of Ethiopian and Eritrean refugees has increased substantially, especially since the late 1970s. By the end of 1983 over 110,000 refugees were reported to have settled in agricultural settlements, with many others going to the urban centres of the Eastern and other regions, bringing the total to more than 470,000 (*The Guardian*, 1 Oct. 1984). The need to sell labour power has also increased, and has become so important in those areas in the Sudan where wage labourers normally come from that the people there no longer wait for labour contractors, but make their own way to Gedaref.

Most of the workers arrive in groups composed mainly of people from the same origin (tribe, village). Searching for jobs and carrying out the work in groups strengthens their bargaining power, gives them a feeling of security (which apparently starts to dwindle as they move away from their home areas) and also secures them caring and familiar company. The nature of the work in Gedaref allows them to work in groups, as jobs are offered on piece rates and not on a daily or monthly basis, and as the size of the jobs, on average, is relatively large.

The main peaks for labour demand are weeding and *dura* harvesting; the former is normally conducted in August and September and the latter extends from December to February.

In weeding, large farms (between 1,000 and 1,500 feddans in size) are divided into sections, normally 8, 10 or 12 sections. Each section is then allocated to a group of workers. In the case of workers coming as individuals or in small groups not large enough to undertake a whole job, adequately sized groups will be formed by combining the individuals and the smaller groups. In the case of smaller farms or *bildat* lands, division of the plots may not be necessary, or alternatively they may be divided into smaller sections than suggested above for the large farms, and smaller groups of workers will be allocated for each piece of work.

In weeding, wages are based on a *gowal* system (literally meaning bargaining). In *gowal* the bargaining process takes place between the *wakeel* or the farmer and the worker groups in the presence of all their members. This takes place after the workers have had a look around to evaluate the size of the job. It seems that in many cases no agreement can be reached. Farmers interviewed said that agreement was reached in only a half to a third of cases. If no agreement is reached the farmers do not take the workers back to Gedaref or wherever they were recruited, and consequently workers are then either compelled to walk back long distances probably reaching tens of miles or to go searching for jobs in nearby areas. Even when agreement has been reached and work commenced, disputes often arise. Workers, after commencing the work following agreement, may then demand an increase in wages, claiming that the job is too large for the wage agreed on – it is often difficult to make a proper estimate of the size of the job by just walking around it, and it may happen that due to continuing rains, weeds multiply considerably before the job is finished. Workers also sometimes protest about the quality or quantity of the kind component of their wages (food offered). Farmers or *wakeels* are sometimes dissatisfied with the way the job is executed and may ask for reweeding to be done. This often happens when, due to rains, weeds grow again in already weeded areas. In cases of disputes over wages after the initial agreement, farmers and *wakeels* may agree to make a small increase in the wage, but sometimes they do not. In the latter case, workers may decide to leave the job. In this case some farmers will pay for the work already done, but others will not as no law exists compelling them to pay.

The amount of weeding labour required by the farmers per feddan cultivated depends on the location of the farm and the amount of rain, which determines the quantity of weeds. It also depends on the farmer's forecast of relative costs and returns (e.g. when a farmer expects the yield to be low he may not spend much labour on weeding) and also on the farmer's liquidity position. Farmers interviewed estimated that one feddan required from 1 to 6 person-days of weeding in the season 1982/83. In a unit of 1,000 feddans (normal size of scheme) between 100 and 400 workers may be used at the same time for a period ranging from 10 to 45 days.

Until a few years ago there was only one form of agreement on wages for *dura* harvest, and that was based on the quantity of *dura* harvested, which is normally measured by a unit called *ardebb* (an *ardebb* of *dura* equals 188 kilos). The system itself is called *ardebbia*. In recent years however another form has appeared whereby wages are set (after bargaining) according to the area of *dura* to be harvested, regardless of the quantity. This system is called *gowal* or *mougowala* meaning bargaining. Some farmers associate the appearance of this system with the arrival of Eritrean and Ethiopian refugees. What is evident is that the *gowal* system in *dura* harvesting is generally more lucrative to the workers, particularly in low yield farms where relatively more work would be required to gather the same quantity of *dura*. Under the *gowal* system, the lower the yield on a farm the more the workers may raise their wage claims, and wages are only agreed on when the actual yield of the farm has been inspected by the workers, contrary to the *ardebbia* system where wages are agreed on before going on site. Both systems operate at present; *ardebbia* is apparently still more common, but it also seems that farmers are feeling more and more under pressure from the workers to accept the *gowal* system. Many farmers reported that in the harvest of 1982/83, where the average yield was considerably less than the previous year, they were at pains to press for the *ardebbia* system, but many workers would only accept *gowal*.

Wage levels based on *ardebbia* are also determined by bargaining, but after a short period into the harvest season, farmers will decide on a definite scale within which they will insist on settling wages. In this system farmers have the chance to stand together and practise collective, though individually led, pressure towards lower wages. It is evident that the *gowal* system has shaken this position and has destroyed the united stand of the farmers by bringing down harvest wage determination to the level of each individual area. It is also evident that the *gowal* system in general is more advantageous to the workers; this is why there is increasing pressure on farmers to accept it, and farmers, from their side, are trying to resist it.

A survey undertaken in 1975/76 in Habila mechanised schemes (an area of more or less similar conditions to Gedaref) contrasted the average daily wage for weeding, which is based on the *gowal* system, with that for the *dura* harvest, which is based on the *ardebbia* system.

From Table 5,3 it is obvious that the *gowal* system in weeding has resulted in better average daily wages than the *ardebbia* system in the *dura* harvest. Although the comparison concerns wage rates in two different operations, wages in both operations are based on piece rates, the working day is not fixed and the workers would normally work according to their own assessment of their working capacity which can justifiably be assumed to be the same in the two operations.

Next in importance to weeding and the *dura* harvest in respect of labour demand is the sesame harvest – although the total labour needed here may be far less. The bargaining in sesame harvesting, due to the special conditions surrounding it, may be of special interest.

The sesame harvest is undertaken in two stages and wages are determined by piece rates in both stages. The first stage is reaping of sesame stalks and tying them together in different sized bundles. Wages are set according to quantity and size of bundles (which may be either *rabta*, small *tukul* or large *tukul*). The second stage is threshing, which is normally undertaken by women, and wages are determined by the quantity of sesame sacks filled. The period in which sesame stalks are ready for cutting is similar all over the region (sesame is mainly grown in the southern areas where rains at present are relatively heavier). After this time, which extends to about 10 days, the sesame would shatter and be very difficult to collect. Therefore, at this stage the wage workers do their best to drive a good bargain. Following initial agreement, and after actually working for some days, but while there is still sesame to be harvested, the workers will stop working under any pretext and ask to be paid off. The workers, of course, know that because the season of sesame harvest is so short *wakeels* and farmers will not be able to replace them at such short notice, and will have to offer increased wages to persuade them to stay. This action by the sesame harvesters is repeated during every harvest season, bringing about a rise in wages each time.

Some farmers have reported that workers working in different groups on one farm not only coordinate their action among themselves, but also encourage workers on neighbouring farms to join them in the wage fight. It has been estimated that by the end of the sesame harvest workers may be able to come away with at least a 50% increase in wage rates.

Table 5,4 demonstrates clearly that the sesame harvest, although based on piece rates and not on *gowal* (area harvested), has resulted in the highest average daily wage, due to the particular conditions of the sesame harvest which serve to strengthen the workers' bargaining power.

TABLE 5,3

Comparison of average daily wage rates in weeding and dura harvest in the Habila area in 1975/76

Agricultural Operation	Av. daily wage according to workers' estimate (in S£)	Av. daily wage according to farmers' estimate (in S£)
1. Weeding (*gowal*)	.53	.65
2. *Dura* harvest (*ardebbia*)	.39	.42
3. Percentage of 1 over 2	136%	155%

Source: Affan, 1978: Table 16, p.20 and Table 20, p.27.

TABLE 5,4

Comparison of daily wages of dura *harvest, weeding and sesame harvest in the Habila Mechanised Farming Area in the season 1975/76*

Agricultural Operation	Index of daily wage based on dura harvest	
	According to workers' estimate	According to farmers' estimate
Dura harvest (base)	100	100
Weeding	136	155
Sesame harvest	162	191

Source: Affan, 1978; Table 16, p.20 and Table 20, p.27.

III. SEGMENTATION OF THE RURAL LABOUR MARKET[5]

Jay O'Brien (1983)[6] suggested a four-phase periodisation of the 'Formation of the Agricultural Labour Force in Sudan'. Phase I extended from 1898 (the British occupation of the country) to 1925 (when the Gezira Scheme was established). Agricultural development was limited to small-scale experimentation with cotton cultivation. Phase II, which started with the Gezira, continued to 1950. The supply of agricultural labour to the Gezira and a few pump-irrigated private cotton estates dominated all labour policy in that period. West African Moslem immigrants were encouraged by the British Administration to settle in and around the Gezira as a ready wage labour supply for the Scheme. Phase III (1950–75) and IV (1975 to the present) constitute O'Brien's main concern. This is only to be expected. The 1950s saw the development of commoditisation in general. This started to affect even the most remote areas and its active agents were merchant capital and the state. With this came the expansion of capitalist agricultural production (the rainfed mechanised farming) resulting in the separation of an increasing number of producers from their means of production.

O'Brien considers Phase III to have been characterised by the Sudanisation of the Gezira Scheme; the rapid expansion of Sudanese private investment in 'pump schemes' along the Nile (especially the White Nile) and in 'rainfed mechanised farming' schemes. Wage rates in the latter seem to be higher than in the former by about 50%. Wage differentials for O'Brien stem from the 'different cost of the social reproduction of the specific labour forces involved'. He elaborates this as follows:

99

... cotton picking wages have been relatively low because so many of the cotton pickers worked as family groups in which several members earned incomes to meet the consumption needs of the family. Conversely, wage rates in the rainfed schemes have been relatively high because the work force there has been composed principally of individuals who leave their families at home and go out in search of an income to help meet the family's consumption needs.

In areas where the traditional division of labour excludes women from some or all types of agricultural work, the availability of women for wage labour is necessarily restricted. O'Brien seems to suggest that labour recruited in rainfed mechanised farming has been drawn from such areas. Moreover, new schemes (which O'Brien takes to include the rainfed schemes) 'had to pay somewhat higher wages initially than the going rate in order to attract labour'. These higher wages, however, continued because the type of labour attracted was of 'a different type with different reproduction requirements'.

In Phase IV (1975 to the present) wage rates began to rise sharply and by a greater proportion in cotton-picking than in the sorghum and sesame harvests. There has been a tendency for wage rates in the different segments of the labour market to converge. In this phase 'the boundaries between the various segments of the labour market are breaking down [and] labour is beginning to flow across them, particularly the boundary

TABLE 5,5

Average daily wage for men and women in Gezira by crop in some selected operations in 1981/82

Crop	Operation	Men Daily Wage in S£	Women Daily Wage in S£
Dura (sorghum)	Weeding	2.10	1.50
	Harvesting	2.33	0.9
	Mean All Operations	2.17	1.20
Cotton	Harvesting	1.86	1.27
	Mean All Operations	2.18	1.60
Groundnuts	Mean All Operations	1.95	1.75

Source: ILO–UNHCR, 1984, Tables 3.12, 3.13, 3.14, pp. 120–1.

TABLE 5,6
Average daily cash wages by crop and operation in Gedaref in 1981/82

Crop	Operation	Average Daily Wage in S£
Dura	Weeding	6.02
	Harvesting	5.13
Sesame	Weeding	6.10
	Harvesting	5.05
Cotton	Harvesting	4.88
Gum arabic	Harvesting	3.76

Source: ILO–UNHCR, 1984, Table 2.17, p.54.

between cotton picking and sorghum and sesame labour markets'. Participation of women in agricultural wage labour had started to increase by the late 1970s; 'male household heads continued to harvest sorghum and sesame while their families began to go to the cotton schemes without them'. The effectiveness of centralised systems of recruitment (which O'Brien describes as a non-market mechanism) has begun to decline. 'By 1978 the management of several large irrigated schemes including the Gezira had suspended cotton-picking labour recruitment activities' and migrants were increasingly finding their own ways to the market. These changes 'reflect a fundamental restructuring of the previously highly segmented market for agricultural labour towards the formation of a truly national labour market'.

Evidence available suggests that the segmentation of the labour market still persists and there have not yet developed those signs to which O'Brien refers as evidence of the formation of a national labour market in the Sudan.

First, it is worth remembering that methodologically Tables 5,5 and 5,6 are comparable. Data were collected in the same agricultural season, using the same questionnaire and the same enumerators. Money wages in the two different regions are comparable in terms of real wages as the price of consumer goods in the two regions are, on average, more or less the same. There is nothing to suggest any difference in intensity of the working day or labour productivity in the two regions, at least not in identical operations.

A look at Tables 5,5 and 5,6 suggests that the average daily wage for harvesting gum arabic in Gedaref, which is the lowest daily wage amongst

101

the different operations, is much higher than the highest daily wage paid in the Gezira, which is for the *dura* harvest. A comparison of wage rates in identical operations such as *dura* weeding and cotton harvesting reveals that in Gedaref wages were higher in 1981/82 by 187%, 120% and 162% respectively.

Wage differentials exist not only between Gedaref and the Gezira but within the latter as well. A comparison of wage rates received by different groups of wage labourers in the Gezira during cotton-picking in 1982/83 by the author (referred to in Chapter 3) shows that the seasonal wage labourers were paid on average about 62% of the wage rates paid to the settled wage labourers (the latter group is almost ignored by O'Brien). Between two different groups of seasonal labourers – the Westerners (or 'peasant' group) and the Arabs of the Two Niles (or 'pastoralist-peasant' group) – there were also differences in wage rates. The latter were paid about 41% more than the former. In other words, while the Arabs (pastoralist-peasants) were paid 72%, the Westerners (peasants) were paid only 51% of the wage rates paid to the settled labourers of the Gezira for the same type of work and under the same working conditions. Amongst different individuals within each of the two groups of seasonal labourers differences of up to 40% have also been recorded, while amongst settled labourers in different localities in the Gezira, with the exception of a few rare cases, the rates paid were almost the same. All this suggests, contrary to O'Brien's belief, that there have been no signs of convergence of wage rates in the different labour markets in the Sudan.

The second argument that O'Brien puts in support of the formation of a national labour market is that boundaries between the different segments are breaking down as labour is moving from one segment to another. In contrast, the ILO/UNHCR (1984: 59) study concludes that the survey of seasonal workers in Gedaref

> did not substantiate the commonly held view that migrants tend to move between different jobs and areas in irrigated and mechanised farming schemes, as well as in urban areas. Ninety-seven per cent of the jobs held by the respondents in 1981, and 98 per cent of those held at the time of the interview in 1982 were in Kassala province (where Gedaref region is), with most of the remaining jobs in Gezira.

Only 3% in 1981 and 2% in 1982 of the Gedaref workers went outside Kassala searching for jobs. In the Gezira none of the 82 wage labourers interviewed in 1983 by me reported going to mechanised rainfed farming schemes to sell his/her labour power.

O'Brien also asserts that the non-market mechanisms organising the movement of seasonal wage labour have begun to break down; from the mid-1970s migrants have 'increasingly elected to finance their own travel to the scheme areas in order to negotiate the highest rates they could find'. More importantly, the centralised system of recruitment has begun to be less effective, so that 'by 1978 the management of several large irrigated schemes, including Gezira, had suspended cotton picking labour recruitment activities'. It is true that in Gedaref the role of the labour contractors had begun to decline, finally coming to an end as a result of the flow of Eritrean and Ethiopian refugees from the 1970s. However, in Gezira, as the 1983 survey shows, non-market mechanisms of labour recruitment were strongly evident (Chapter 3).

The evidence suggests that O'Brien's periodisation of the development of the Sudanese agricultural labour markets does not work. However, there are still further problems with O'Brien's methodology and arguments. He describes his third phase (1950–75) as one in which segmentation of the agricultural labour market has been the rule. Wage differentials, which for O'Brien are the clearest manifestation of that segmentation, are to be sought, as we have seen, 'in the differential cost of the social reproduction of the specific labour forces involved'. In cotton-picking (i.e. in our case the Gezira), the whole family participated and therefore contributed to the reproduction of the household, whereas in sorghum and sesame harvests (rainfed schemes) the type of labour recruited, according to O'Brien, has mainly been one which originally excluded women and therefore has had to be paid higher wages to 'ensure the reproduction of the village economy as a source of seasonal labour'.

This raises numerous problems. Although O'Brien asserts that wage rate differentials are not 'a simple reflection of any essential differences in the quality of the types of work involved', he later seems to contradict this view by mentioning groups 'who regarded heavy agricultural activity as undignified', preferring to work 'on the relatively light work of cotton-picking rather than the arduous work in the rainfed schemes'. The division of labour among such groups permitted participation by women in the labour process, allowing them to come in family groups. O'Brien clearly suggests that there exist differences of work between the cotton schemes and the rainfed mechanised schemes, but he does not show that the wage differentials discussed stem from such work differences. In sum, there are major problems with his three related arguments concerning (a) the division of labour among peasants and pastoralists embarked on wage labour in the different segments of the labour market; (b) whether or not women are excluded from the agricultural labour process; and (c) the link made between the needs of reproduction and the level of wages in the different segments.

Classification of the casual agricultural workers even at a broad estimatory level according to their areas of origin (when they are non-settled wage workers), types of household economy and degree of involvement of women in agricultural tasks in the different agricultural labour markets in the Sudan is not available at present, and could not have been available to O'Brien. His arguments regarding the different types of workers that go to rainfed mechanised schemes and to cotton schemes do not seem to be founded on any substantial evidence. It is true that the seasonal workers who come to the Gezira come more in family groups than as individuals, whereas in Gedaref (for reasons associated with the specific nature of production and labour organisation in that region) they come almost exclusively as individuals (see ILO/UNHCR, 1984). However, this does not mean that in other rainfed schemes and other cotton-producing schemes the same thing happens, nor does it mean that the remaining household members are not engaged in economic activities and therefore contributing to the household's economic viability. O'Brien's argument, as we have seen, suggests that workers in rainfed mechanised schemes receive higher wages because meeting the needs of reproduction of the household lies on the shoulders of the men. The evidence available does not support O'Brien's assertion.

In fact, seasonal labour does not go to the rainfed mechanised schemes only for sesame and sorghum harvests. It is not clear why O'Brien refers to that only. Neither, in fact, is it clear why his article is concerned only with seasonal wage labour and ignores the formation of settled wage labourers. In 1982 it was found that in Gedaref 79% of the workers who were engaged in weeding (which extends to about two months and which requires on average no fewer work days per *feddan* than that required for harvesting; see ILO/UNHCR, 1984: 47) and who came from outside the region, did not consider the Gedaref region as their current home at that time (*Ibid*, 59).

A survey of Habila mechanised farms by Affan (1978) also shows clearly that the seasonal workers there undertake the weeding operation as well. The importance of the fact that seasonal workers go weeding as well is that their labour power must then be absent from their home areas during a crucial period and would need to be provided by other household members. In fact it is also possible, though not documented, that a large segment of those workers will also stay for the sesame and *dura* harvests, as going back home and returning again, taking into account the distances involved, would not be practical. (Of the workers in Gedaref, 49% were reported to come from homes in the western part, 10% from the southern part and 9% from the central part of the country, as well as 11% from Eritrea and Ethiopia.)

Nor, in any case, is female wage labour restricted to cotton-picking. In the Affan survey, conducted in 1976, it was found that the participation of women in wage labour was as high as 30% (Affan, 1978: 25). In the same region a survey conducted by Abdalla Elhassan in 1982 (results of which appeared in Elhassan, 1985) showed that about 40% of the wage labourers were female. What this shows is that the participation of female household members in wage labour is not restricted to cotton-picking.

Even if it were true that the type of labour that goes to rainfed schemes excludes women from wage labour (and other income generating activities), would that be sufficient reason, from the point of view of employers, to pay higher wages? In other words, are wages determined directly by the level of needs of the workers?

In the last section of the next chapter it will be suggested that the explanation of wage differentials among different groups of wage labourers in Gezira and between them and the wage labourers of Gedaref is to be sought mainly in differences in class consciousness and collective organisation of different groups of workers.

CHAPTER SIX

The Process of Free Wage Labour Formation

Marx was emphatic that the historical conditions of the existence of capital *'are by no means given with the mere circulation of money and commodities'* (Marx, 1976: 272, my emphasis). The existence of the 'double-free' wage labourer is the historical precondition for the existence of capital, for the development of the capitalist mode of production.

> For the transformation of money into capital, therefore, the owner of money must find the free workers available on the commodity-market; and this worker must be free in the double sense that as a free individual he can dispose of his labour-power as his own commodity, and that, on the other hand, he has no other commodity for sale, i.e. he is rid of them, he is free of all objects needed for the realisation of his labour power. (*Ibid*: 272–3)

It is then clear that for Marx the transformation of the labour process itself into a capital–wage labour one, with the production process becoming a valorisation process, is what essentially distinguishes the capitalist mode of production from other modes of production.

However, it should not be thought that we cannot conceive of capital until the process of the double-freeing of large numbers of labourers has been totally completed. In fact, capital may start realising itself as capital (i.e. appropriating surplus value) from the very time when that process (of freeing of wage labour) is set in motion. In other words surplus value may be appropriated from not yet completely double-free wage labourers. This is characteristic in the stage of primitive capital accumulation. However, the domination of the capitalist mode of production entails that the production process is predominantly capitalist; the producers are predominantly wage labourers and the wage labourers are predominantly free in the double sense.

This chapter attempts to expose the process of freeing wage labour (and hence the development of the capitalist mode of production) in rural Sudan in two sections. In the first, the freeing of the producers from access to the means of production and the need to sell their own labour power is discussed. The second section is an investigation into the freeing of the wage labourers from non-market labour relations, an important area of study and condition of capitalist development which has largely been neglected.

I. THE NEED FOR WAGE LABOUR AND THE PROCESS OF FREEING OF THE PRODUCERS FROM ACCESS TO THE MEANS OF PRODUCTION

Notes on the Early History, 1898 to the 1920s

We can distinguish three categories of people who, during the early period of British colonial rule (1898–1956), were sources of wage labour: (1) people freed temporarily or permanently from their lands during Mahdiyya rule (1881–98) as a result of the continuous warfare or, in the northern part of the country, as a result of land pressure; (2) people of slave origin, who had been freed from their bond relations; (3) migrant labour coming mainly from countries to the west of Sudan.

The Mahdist movement originated and was more firmly established in Western Sudan. The period between the rise and fall of the Movement was a period of continuous warfare (see Holt, 1958). Many 'Westerners' served in the Mahdist armies and when defeated by the British army they scattered to different places, either as independent producers – where land was available and other conditions favourable – or as wage labourers – since a systematic demand for wage labour had already started to form. Indeed the Westerners were among the first Sudanese wage labourers, and still form the bulk of the wage labour army in the country.

Cultivable land along the Nile is limited. Being unable to depend on rainlands, owing to scarcity of rains, inhabitants of the northern region had emigrated as a matter of course to seek their living long before the coming of the British. In addition to settling in different parts of the Sudan, some settled outside it, mainly in Egypt, with which the northern part of Sudan had been in continuous contact for many centuries. For decades they have been moving around as petty traders (*gellaba*) and working in clerical posts in government service and in commercial firms all over the Sudan (Purves, 1935: 170). As Purves (*Ibid*: 171) notes further, the tribe of the Ababda of the northern Sudan 'provided at the time of the reconquest of the Sudan, the bulk of the irregular forces that served under Kitchener'. According to him, other northern tribes including Shaigia and Kababish had also been serving in the police force and Sudan Defence Force.

Anti-slavery regulations, as has been mentioned, existed as early as the time of British rule. However, as O'Brien (1980: 159) notes, effective measures were not taken until the 1920s when the need to mobilise labour for Gezira grew. One may also add that the British administration's stabilising policy (see below) sought to minimise conflicts with the indigenous people and leaders, including slave-owners. Effective steps to ban slavery could only be taken when the British felt they had established themselves firmly. However, even before the 1920s those slaves who wanted to abandon their masters according to then existing laws obviously could not be stopped. Freed slaves, who were unlikely to have any resources at hand at least for a time, would most probably go for wage labour if available. Shaaeldin (1982: 10) goes as far as considering ex-slaves as the first Sudanese wage labourers.

West African migrants coming to Sudan as settlers or on pilgrimage had been an important source of wage labour during this early phase and later when Gezira was established. Hassoun (1952) and Duffield (1983) show us that even before the establishment of the Gezira Scheme these migrants, as well as some western Sudanese, had moved to different parts of the country (urban areas, the Funj area in the central region, the Nuba Mountains in the western region and Gash Delta and Gedaref in the eastern region) as cultivators and as wage labourers.

During the early period of British rule (1898–1920s) need for wage labour was not extensive. The occupation of Sudan by the British was not initially primarily for economic reasons such as the direct appropriation of surplus from the indigenous population through state-run projects; rather, it was mainly for political-strategic ones.[1] Apart from labour needed to establish some infrastructural projects and government buildings and services, the colonial government did not demand wage labour as an employer.

Involvement of foreign capital in direct production, which had not been very much encouraged by the colonial administration for reasons associated with political stability, was very limited and in those few cases it was a failure.[2] However, during this early period foreigners were busy in trade. In their trade and in associated services (transport and storing) as well as for domestic work, those foreigners had employed wage labourers. Martin (1921: 221), for example, observed that demand for labour in Western Sudan for handling of gum arabic, a trade in which foreigners were also active, had intensified since the arrival of the railway at El Obied.

In addition to the need for wage labour in services in which indigenous people might have been engaged and in domestic labour in urban areas, wage labourers were also in demand for the *harig* cultivation, which, as has been noted, had been in existence in Gedaref since at least the earlier period of this century. Although the extent of such demand for wage labour is difficult to estimate, it seems that it was relatively small.

Although relatively low, the demand for wage labour during this early period occasionally exceeded the supply, in the form of people already freed totally or partially from the means of production. To meet the demand for some 'public works' the government sometimes needed to compel local communities to supply labour by rotation for a number of days (O'Brien, 1980: 168). O'Brien (*Ibid*: 169) and Shaaeldin (1981: 61–2) notice that such demands were extended for longer periods in the south, sometimes exceeding three months. When such methods were insufficient Egyptian convicts were occasionally put to work (Martin, 1921: 223).

Following these introductory notes on the early history of wage labour, let us now present some selected case studies from rural Sudan. These case studies represent different patterns of capitalist penetration. Geographically they are well dispersed. Gezira lies in central Sudan; Gedaref is in the eastern region; Western Savannah extends into the southern parts of the western region; the Dinka inhabit southern Sudan and the Kababish seasonally migrate to the north-western and northern regions. Our rural case studies also provide a wide range of comparisons in terms of 'release' and 'absorption' of labour power. Gezira is a case of both intensive release and absorption. Gedaref is a case of 'absorption' rather than release. Other case studies show release without absorption.

The Gezira

The Gezira Scheme undoubtedly marked the start of a systematic process of free labour formation in Sudan. This does not contradict what has been mentioned previously about freeing of producers from access to land even before the coming of the British. In fact, such processes of occasional freeing of segments of the population occurred at different times and at different places in the world before the development of the capitalist mode of production (see Hilton, 1976). However, that in itself did not create capitalism. Capitalism requires a systematic freeing of producers from land and in themselves (as free proprietors of their labour power) under the domain of capital (i.e. with a presence of accumulated money wealth striving to reproduce itself on an expanded scale in order to survive competition).

The Beginnings

As has been mentioned earlier, the colonial government spared no effort to encourage West African immigrants (and also Western Sudanese) to settle in the Gezira region even before the start of the Scheme itself. The establishment of the Scheme, on the other hand, from the beginning started a process of free labour formation in the region of Gezira itself. In the allocation of lands in the Scheme priority was given to the landowners and their nominees. Apparently many land users were not offered tenancies (or did not want to settle in the Scheme as permanent cultivators). These consisted of pastoralists and pastoralist-cultivator groups who had used mostly the central area of the Gezira away from the rivers which was not privately owned, for grazing as well as occasionally for cultivation. Not restricting themselves to the same pieces of land every time, those groups of pastoralists and pastoralist-cultivators could not claim the right to land as required by the British colonial authorities, and therefore were not offered priority in the allocation of tenancies. However, many of them might have refused the settled life anyway. What matters to us here is that these groups were forced to move away from the Scheme area to the east and the west towards the Blue and White Nile areas (the latter includes the Managil region, to the east of the 'Gezira Main' before the extension of the Scheme there), probably to share lands with people already living there. However, it seems that moving away affected the natural growth of their herds, and this, probably among other reasons, made them look for additional sources of income. They were easy to recruit as seasonal wage labourers; they needed work, and Gezira and its people were not alien to them. From the early times of the Scheme, Arabs of the Blue and White Nile areas (including Managil) have supplied Gezira with a major part of its seasonal labour (see O'Brien, 1980: 149, 207–8).

Besides those described above two other groups of people were sources of wage labour in Gezira after the establishment of the Scheme. The first group were landless people under bond relationship or who had worked as sharecroppers. The second were independent peasants who had not qualified for a tenancy at the time of tenancy distribution. Some members of these two groups may have moved outside the Scheme as independent cultivators. Some others, who had no such alternative or for some other reasons preferred to stay, had to sell their labour power in the Scheme to secure subsistence. Apparently this group was small compared to that of the migrant labourers.

With the growth of the Gezira tenant population, and with the Scheme either being unable to offer lands or becoming unattractive economically as an alternative for a growing number of Gezira local people, many started looking for alternatives in off-Scheme farming activities within the region or outside it (Chapter 3). Naturally, for a large segment of the population this involves selling labour power.

It can be concluded that the Scheme has begun a process of free labour formation in the region, though a large number of the people who have been freed from access to land did not actually work as wage labourers in the Scheme itself. From another side, in some other areas where the process of free labour formation has begun, the Gezira, by providing wage labour opportunities, may have been playing an accelerator role in that process.

Settled Wage Labour

Those among Gezira settled people who sell their labour power belong to one of the following three categories:

1. Those Gezira tenants (and their household members) who may have small holdings and/or comparatively large households, and owning hardly any assets other than their tenancies, may sell their labour power to other tenants (or to other people) at certain periods (Barnett, 1978, 1983). There is no data available regarding the frequency of wage labouring among tenants' household members.
2. The majority of the subtenants (80% of 1983 sample) reported that they were selling their labour power systematically beside working in their subtenancies. These landplot-holding wage workers are in a similar social position to the tenants who sell their labour power. Both of these two categories are obviously not totally free from access to the means of production (and hence not yet free wage labourers); they exercise control over their tenancies (or subtenancies) though this control is limited by the role of the Administration of the Scheme.
3. The third group consists of those who have no access to the means of production, except probably for some few animals kept mainly for milk (on average every household in the Gezira camps owns 4.5 animals, Tamim, 1980: 29). This group comprises only 22% of the inhabitants of labour camps interviewed in 1983. Also included here are those wage workers who live in the Gezira tenant villages (mostly non-Westerner workers). Their numbers are not known but it is commonly believed that they are far fewer in number than the Westerners of the labour camps.

We can conclude that the majority of Gezira settled wage workers are not totally free from access to the means of production.

Seasonal Wage Labour

Of the sample of Gezira seasonal labourers, 92.5% have access to land (as cultivators and/or pastoralists). Some other 2.5% have access to other

TABLE 6,1

Why do seasonal wage labourers come to the Gezira to work?

1.	Income derived from home production is generally not enough	75%
2.	Production in home areas has not been successful this year (e.g. not sufficient rains in the specific season of 1982/83)	8%
3.	Have been persuaded by government officials or sheikhs or other people to go	8%
4.	Seeking commodities and services (e.g. medical treatment) that are not available in home areas	6%
5.	Following other members of the household	3%
	Total	100%

Source: 1983 Gezira Agricultural Wage Labourers' Survey

means of production. Only 5% of the sample surveyed in 1983 were free from the means of production.

Sixty per cent of the seasonal labourers spend over six months in their original areas while most of the rest spend three to six months, and only a few spend less than three months. Apparently most of the time not spent in the home areas is spent in search and performance of wage labour elsewhere. Table 6,1 shows us that wage labouring seems to be an important aspect of the economic reproduction of the Gezira seasonal labourers. As many as 75% have declared that they more or less regularly need to supplement home produce by wage labour. Eight per cent go searching for wage labour occasionally when their home produce is not enough. For the rest (17%), who have been either persuaded by other people, or have come following their other household members or seeking commodities and services that are not available in their home area, the element of the need to wage labour is also there.

The Gezira seasonal labourers survey also manifests clearly that the need for wage labouring in order to supplement income has been growing considerably over one generation in the areas from where the seasonal labourers come. Only 10% of the seasonal labourers in the sample have had one or both parents having to resort to wage labour at a certain period in their life. This indicates that the need to wage labour in those areas may have multiplied by up to 10 times in one generation.

This increasing trend of depending on wage labour to meet part of the requirements of economic reproduction seems to be reflected in the seasonal labourers' perception of their position and future; 22.5% of them have expressed the intentions of seeking permanent positions as wage labourers if they could find them.

THE PROCESS OF FREE WAGE LABOUR FORMATION

Other Rural Areas

Gedaref

It has been estimated that in 1982/83, the number of wage workers involved in Gedaref farming was in the range of 350,000 (Chapter 4), of whom 49% had no access to land (ILO/UNHCR, 1984: 61). Reasons reported for seeking wage labour in Gedaref according to the ILO/UNHCR survey (*Ibid*: 62) have been the following: money in general, personal experiences, marriage, buying land, livestock or shops, building houses, insufficient land for needs, household member ill/died so cash shortage, travel/independence/try luck, as well as other unspecified reasons.

From among Gedaref wage labourers surveyed in 1982 only 11% reported having been born in the region (*Ibid*: 59). This indicates that the relatively fast expansion of capitalist farming in the region has not been accompanied by a proportionally fast process of separation of the producers from the land. This may be partly due to the fact that before the expansion of capitalist production the Gedaref region had been relatively underpopulated. It may also be the case that some expropriated producers have moved away. This is particularly the case of the Shukriyia pastoralist tribe, segments of which have been compelled to change their seasonal migratory cycles to move away from the region at least in some periods during the year. However, since the 1970s, with the vast spread of Mechanised Farming Schemes, pressure on the land has been growing. The result of this has been a larger need to wage labour by the small household producers in the region.

In terms of both absolute numbers and proportion of the wage labourers who are totally free from access to the means of production, the Gedaref region is the leading one among the agricultural regions of Sudan. The proportion of landless among Gedaref wage labourers (reported to be 49% in 1982) no doubt must have increased considerably with the increase in the influx of the Ethiopian and Eritrean refugees in the latter half of 1984 and 1985 as a result of the famine.

The Western Savannah

Our source in this case study is the survey conducted by Elhassan (1985)[3] in the Western Savannah region. Fifty-four per cent of the sample surveyed depended on wage labour to meet on average 22% of their total farm labour requisites while 40% and 3% of the households, respectively, had hired labour to conduct on average 58% and 95% of their farm labour. However, in the four villages surveyed, there seems to be no landless class. Wage labour is provided by landplot-holding fellow villagers. Depending on the size of plot cultivated, assets and amount of household labour available, households surveyed had different degrees of involvement in the labour market, as buyers and sellers. There is a group of households that only buys labour power (30.4%); another only selling, but not buying labour power (27.3%); another both buying and selling (21.8%); and a fourth one that neither buys nor sells (21.6%). It is the conditions of production – the occasional need to mobilise a larger number of people to undertake a certain job – that leads about 52% of the households in those villages to hire wage labour. In earlier times, before the expansion of money-commodity relations and the development of wage labour, extra household labour had been met by *nafir*.

The expansion of capitalist mechanised farming in the Habila area within the same region is reducing the land available – whether cultivated land or forest land, which is often a source of extra farming income for households in the Savannah region.

From this study it can be concluded that the internal evolution of the village economy itself, though showing a clear tendency for the households to differentiate, has not yet resulted in the creation of a landless class residing in the village as full-time wage workers. However, we do not have information as to whether or not there has been any outmigration, the result of which may have been the creation of free wage labourers realising their labour power elsewhere.

Dinka

Among the Dinka it seems that wage labour is very limited. Dinka are mainly animal breeders, although they also practise crop production. In the sample surveyed by Lako (1983) it was found that in crop production only 5% of the households resorted to wage labour, and this apparently was limited to land preparation alone. Female wage labour may also be hired for beer-making. No wage labour, according to the survey, is used in herding. However, it should not be understood from these facts that Dinka society is a fairly closed, self-reliant society. Of those interviewed by Lako, 38% reported having been involved in migration seeking employment outside the region. The ratio of those away in employment at the time of the survey is not known. However, while Dinka pastoralist-farming household production is not able to meet the requirements of realisation of labour power of all its members, Dinka communities have not yet polarised widely enough to allow the absorption of the excess labour force as wage labour within their communities. This does in fact appear explicable from the slow rate of development of the forces of production. Apart from the use of some veterinary drugs it seems that for long decades there has been no notable change in the production process. (The same slow rate of development of the forces of production is of course also the case in many other places in the Sudan.)

Kababish

In Kababish in the late 1960s, 11% of the households surveyed by Asad (1970) used wage labour in herding. Waged herders in Kababish, according to Asad, work for wages only for temporary periods, until they have saved up enough animals (as they usually get part of their wages in animals) to become independent household producers. Wage labour is also used for digging and repairing wells as well as some other casual jobs. Differentiation among Kababish is clear, not only in terms of access to political power, which has been dominated by one section of the Nurab tribe and a few individuals from other sections (section-sheikhs and other officials), but also in terms of animal wealth. However, from Asad's work we can only conclude that a permanent class of non-animal owners having to depend for their entire lives on wage labouring did not exist in the 1960s; wage labour was only a transitory phenomenon. The difficulty with Asad's work, as with that of many others, is that it has not taken adequate account of possible 'open ends' of the community studied; that is, of out-migration. Thus we remain with no knowledge of the actual extent of the process of differentiation. However, it seems that there has been a process of out-migration in Kababish. As early as the 1930s, Purves (1935: 171) observed that many Kababish worked in the police force in the northern riverain part of the country. Omer (1979: 38–44, 78–81) also notes that the settlement in Dongola of members of nomadic tribes coming from the Western Desert, which is largely inhabited by Kababish, has been going on for a long time and has especially intensified in the wake of a series of droughts. These two statements are a clear indication that Kababish have for a long time been able to move out of their community.

The Urban Sector: The Case of Industrial Workers

Differentiation among the agricultural population in Sudan has resulted in the generation of free labour in excess of what the agricultural sector could absorb. This excess free labour will tend to turn up in urban areas. In the post-colonial period the urban population has been growing faster than before.

In 26 years, from 1955/56 to 1982, the proportion of the urban population in Sudan has more than tripled, while there has been a

TABLE 6,2

Rural and urban distribution of the population in Sudan for the years 1955/56 and 1982[4]

	1955/56	1982
Urban	853,873 (8.3%)	4,697,000 (25.1%)
Rural	9,408,663 (91.7%)	14,055,000 (74.9%)
Total	10,262,536 (100%)	18,752,000 (100%)

Source: Figures for 1955/56 are from the 1955/56 Census of Sudan, Vol.3, Table 7.4 cited in Galal el Din, 1973: 15. Figures for 1982 are from the Six Year Plan Projection, Census Office, Department of Statistics cited in the Statistical Abstract, 1981: Table 7, p.16.

natural population growth of 83%. Nevertheless, the rural population still comprises three-quarters of the total population in the country.

The urban sector itself apparently has not been able to absorb all of the free labour released from both the rural and the urban sectors. This fact, coupled with an increasingly high demand for labour in the Arab oil-producing countries, especially since the oil price boom in the 1970s, where average wage rates in real terms are many times higher than in Sudan, has led to an accelerating trend of emigration of Sudanese. In 1984, the number of Sudanese migrants was estimated as 250,000 (Galalel Din, 1984: 70). The total number of Sudanese migrants comprised about 4–5% of the economically active population of the Sudan. (In 1976 estimates put economically active people as 31.5% of the total population. This percentage included 12.8% of the total female and 49% of the total male population.)

The proportion of urban workers in the total urban population is not available in the present Sudanese population statistics. According to surveys undertaken in the 1970s the total number of industrial workers in the Sudan is 123,784, of which 105,365 work in manufacturing industries where modern machinery is used (Department of Statistics 1978/79 Industrial Survey) and 17,419 work in handicrafts (Department of Statistics, 1976).[5]

A sample survey study regarding the position of the industrial workers in the process of free labour formation was undertaken by the author in 1982/83. This survey, probably the first such survey of industrial workers in the Sudan, was composed of 163 workers. All workers were selected from the capital and the central region which, according to the 1978/79 Industrial Survey undertaken by the Department of Statistics, contains 77% of the industrial workers in the Sudan. Our sample was selected from seven different types of industries including the textile, chemical, metal, beverage and food industries, and in accordance with their proportional representation in manufacturing industries. Sizes of industries have also been proportionately represented in the sample as far as possible.[6]

Separation from the Means of Production

For some industrial wage workers the process of their separation from the means of production started earlier than their own working lifetime, as their parents had already lost access to the means of production. Of the wage workers, 27.3% reported that they had resided in towns all their lives.

Let us, then, start investigating the process of the separation of the industrial workers from the means of production a generation earlier – since their parents' time.

At least 7.8% of the industrial workers (categories 5, 6 and 7 in Table 6,3) have parents who have no access to the means of production. (I say 'at least' because it is not known whether those engaged in farming and services are all self-employed or whether some of them are wage workers.) Engaging in trade and services as self-employed (which apparently in most cases means in the informal sector) may not mean attaining a level of income higher than the wages received by workers. However, this still means that most of the parents of the industrial workers had not been freed from access to the means of production.

As Table 6,4 shows, industrial wage workers have been less fortunate than their parents in terms of access to the means of production; 52.9% had no access to the means of production at any time.

Out of 161 workers, 118 (73.3%) reported being migrants, having originally resided in rural areas. The reasons for their migration are shown

TABLE 6,3

Work of parents of industrial workers in 1983[7]

1.	Farming in the original area	52.5%
2.	Services sector in towns	17.7%
3.	Trade (as self-employed either in towns or in rural areas)	10.9%
4.	Services sector in the rural areas	9.6%
5.	Employees (clerks) in towns	3.1%
6.	Workers in towns	2.8%
7.	Trade as employee	1.9%
8.	Others	1.9%
	Total of respondents	100.1% (161 workers)

Source: 1983 Own Industrial Workers' Survey

in Table 6,5. From their answers it can be concluded that it is not only non-availability of work, or non-availability of sufficient income sources, that press rural inhabitants to migrate, but also worse working conditions than in the towns, and non-availability of what have become necessary services and commodities as well as other attractions of town life. A few (25) had decided to go in search of work in the towns for the purpose of getting cash and probably with the conscious intention of coming back.

For most of the migrant workers, relations with home areas have not yet ended. Most (89.4%) reported visits to their original areas, while the rest (10.6%) would not go for a visit. Among those who do visit their original areas, 59.4% paid their last visit within the last six months, 26.7% between 6 months and 2 years ago, 5% between 2 and 5 years ago; 8.9% of the respondents had not visited their original areas for 5 years or more (at the time of the survey).

Some migrant workers expressed their attachment to their original areas in more than merely visiting them; 39% expressed a wish to go back to re-settle. However, 33.9% do not think of going back, while 27.1% do not know. Reasons given by those who want to go back to their original areas (who represent 28.2% of the total number of all the industrial workers) are given in Table 6,6. While some workers coming to towns intended from the outset to stay only temporarily (this includes category (6) in Table 6,6, but probably also other individuals), for others the reasons behind their wish to go back are mainly disappointment, both economic and social, with the towns. However, the intention to go back may not be founded on realistic expectations.

Among the 163 workers interviewed, 7 (4.3%) do have access to the means of production. They are self-employed as craftspersons, in agriculture and services. They spend on average 14 hours a week in their other jobs (actual range among the different workers is 4–24 hours a week) and earn income amounting to 34% of their average income

TABLE 6,4

Types of work of industrial workers prior to their present employment (1983)

1.	Farming as cultivators	36.5%
2.	Wage labourers in the services sector	23.1%
3.	Petty trade (informal sector)	10.6%
4.	Wage labourers in agriculture	7.7%
5.	No non-industrial work	22.1%
	Total	100%

Source: 1983 Industrial Workers' Survey

Note: About 44% of workers reported working in more than one type of work (as characterised above) before working in industry.

TABLE 6,5

Why did the industrial workers leave their original areas?

1.	Working conditions in home areas not favourable (low income etc.) compared to towns (or industry)	32.3%
2.	No work available in home areas	22.0%
3.	Living conditions had generally become difficult in home areas	14.4%
4.	Followed other household members	12.7%
5.	Life generally in towns is better	5.1%
6.	To try luck	5.1%
7.	To attend schools not available in home areas	2.5%
8.	To get some cash	2.5%
9.	Other (e.g., war in home area, to see Khartoum, etc.)	3.4%
	Total	99.9%
		(118 respondents)

Source: 1983 Industrial Workers' Survey

(ranging between 12% and 51%). Another 6 workers also reported owning various objects (e.g. plots of land, tools, etc.) which generate some irregular income which is insignificant in relation to the wages they receive. Five other workers also reported receiving money donations. These too were described as irregular and insignificant. The structure of the industrial workers' activities regarding the means of reproduction of their labour power, then, is as follows: 145 out of 163 (89%) depend exclusively on selling their labour power in order to reproduce it, 11 (6.7%) depend on that almost exclusively, while 7 (4.3%) mainly rely on it to secure subsistence.

Some workers seem not to be content with their social position, while some others seem to be dissatisfied with the specific job they do; 69 workers (42.3%) expressed their intention of leaving their present work, and one-third of these (14.1% of the total sample) expressed the wish to become self-employed (these are categories 3, 4 and 6 in Table 6,7). About one-fifth (8.6%) want to migrate to a foreign country (Arab oil-producing), which for some of them is intended as a step towards becoming self-employed (to collect enough resources to buy the means of production). It can be concluded that about one-fifth of the industrial workers seem to seek ways to 'free' themselves from wage labour, i.e. want to obtain access to the means of production. The rest seem not to conceive of, or not to realistically foresee, any possibility of finding an alternative to selling their labour power.

119

TABLE 6,6
Why do some migrant workers want to go back?

1.	Work opportunities are now better there	32.6%
2.	Family reasons (i.e. unite with other members of the household)	23.9%
3.	Town life is not as I thought it to be	15.3%
4.	Have decided to discontinue working in industry	13.0%
5.	Living in towns has become too expensive	6.5%
6.	Obtained enough cash	4.4%
7.	Other	4.4%
	Total	100%
		(46 respondents)

Source: 1983 Industrial Workers' Survey

The Paradox: Separation of Producers from Land in Conditions of Land Abundance

As has been shown above, the process of separation of agricultural producers from land (and other means of production) in Sudan, systematically begun in the 1920s, has been steadily progressing. In the early 1980s, six decades later, we have the following state of affairs. Out of about 18.8 million people, 4.7 million (25% of the total) already reside in the urban sector (Statistical Abstract, 1981: 16). The proportion of wage workers in the total urban population (or in the total number of economically active people) is not available to us. In the rural sector itself in 1983 we estimate that between 250,000 and 300,000 people are already free from access to land, and are selling their labour power in large agricultural employment areas (like the Gezira and Gedaref); 800,000 to one million people need to travel to other rural areas in search of jobs to supplement income from their own household produce; and there are an unspecified number of wage labourers at village level.[8]

The need to become wage labourers which usually entails migration, seasonally or permanently, seems from the case studies discussed above to result from one of the following conditions:

1. No access to land or other means of production in home area and hence the need to migrate in search of wage labour.
2. Access to land but land is small compared to available household labour force and hence the need to sell labour power within the same locality or to migrate seasonally to employment centres.
3. Access to land, but income derived from home production is not enough, since a shortage of household labour prevents the cultivation

TABLE 6,7

Where do dissatisfied industrial workers want to go to?

1.	To other industrial work with better conditions	31.9%
2.	To migrate to another country (oil-producing Arab countries)	20.3%
3.	To agriculture as independent cultivators	17.4%
4.	To trade or services as self-employed	13.0%
5.	To any work with better conditions	5.1%
6.	To become independent craftspersons	2.9%
7.	To original areas as industrial workers[9]	2.9%
8.	To agricultural wage labour	2.9%
9.	To retire	2.9%
10.	To clerical work	0.7%
	Total	100%

Source: 1983 Industrial Workers' Survey

of more land. Hence the need to migrate seasonally when own production season is over and before the start of the following season.

4. Access to land, but wages in area of settlement are higher than income derived from home area, and/or lifestyle in area of new settlement is more desirable, and/or other social reasons;

5. Access to land, which is not small compared to available household labour force, but some members of the household engage in wage labour locally or away as part of the household strategy in face of conditions of uncertainty of their own home produce. Possibly also some household members go away to obtain cash needed by themselves (e.g. to establish own independent household) or to explore and experience other types of life.

Among the five cases listed above, the first two have problems of access to land. Land has been lost, or has become too small for increasing needs, or has lost fertility. Expansion of capitalist farming and hence expropriation of household producers' land (or part of it), increased size of household and/or their needs (with no possibility of increasing land size), increased appropriation of surplus by circulation capital and/or the state, ecological changes or a combination of these factors are responsible for the land pressure felt on the particular locality. The question which may arise immediately is why such household producers do not move to new lands in a country which has far more arable land than is actually cultivated? (Arable land has been estimated to be 200 million feddans and the land

121

actually cultivated in the early 1980s has been estimated as less than 21 million feddans.) However, this solution is not as easy as it may look at first glance.

- Moving to new lands requires initial resources which may not be available. Resources are needed in, for example, building a house, preparation of land (clearing forest lands, ploughing), other production inputs like seeds, provision of enough food and other money resources to sustain the household up to harvest time.
- New lands may be far from market places, transport centres and roads, water resources, other services centres, etc. To secure needed material goods and services may be difficult, expensive or both.
- Size of the migrating group, at least in the initial periods, may be too small to allow such division of labour as exists in most Sudanese villages, e.g. between village merchants, housebuilders, carpenters (mainly bed-makers), tailors, *shail* financiers, beer makers, traditional healers (*fakis*) etc. A very small community is also disadvantaged in meeting other social and spiritual needs of its members.
- Purchase and sale of labour power is gaining increased importance in Sudanese villages (as a result of the increasing tendency to 'commoditise' *nafir*, and as a necessity to supplement own household income). The small size of the living unit and its distance from other employment areas is definitely a disadvantage in this respect.
- It is also worth noting that the relative abundance of land in Sudan is on the rainlands, not the riverlands. Those used to the latter may find it difficult to become used to a different type of agriculture and also a different type of social life. Moreover, risk in rain farming is higher. (This is probably one reason why migrants from northern Sudan, being used to irrigated agriculture, seek to settle in other irrigated areas, e.g. the Gezira, or in urban areas or elsewhere as retail merchants.)
- Some particular ethnic groups seem to be in an advantaged position in waged employment outside agriculture (e.g. Gezira people migrating to urban areas and to Arab oil-producing countries) which may be economically and socially (in their own view) more rewarding. Those may not think of going back into agriculture even if factors that have led to their migration cease to function.
- When the initial decision to migrate to an urban area or another agricultural area as a wage labourer has been taken with a view to collecting enough cash to establish oneself as an independent producer, the following may happen. First, migrants may never be able to collect enough money to allow them to set themselves up as independent producers. Second, as a result of migration a change

in the level of needs and tastes may occur among those migrants. Accordingly, they may do away forever with the idea of going back to establish themselves as independent producers. Third, migrants thinking of becoming independent producers would definitely need assistance from the state in finding suitable resettlement lands and the provision of some necessary services. However, the state seems to have little enthusiasm for such projects.

From the ranks of these and other migrants and those who decide to stay at home as landless and sell their labour power in their own local communities, a Sudanese free wage labour class is forming, amid conditions of apparent land abundance at the frontier.

II. ARE SUDANESE WAGE LABOURERS FREE PROPRIETORS OF THEIR LABOUR POWER?

In the previous section the continuing process of the separation of the producers from access to the means of production in Sudan has been described. However, this is only one condition for the formation of free wage labour. There is another essential condition that has been largely neglected in the studies of the formation of free wage labour and the development of the capitalist mode of production. In Marx's words this second essential condition is as follows:

> In and for itself, the exchange of commodities *implies no other relations of dependence* than those which result from its own nature. On this assumption, labour power can appear on the market as a commodity only if, and in so far as, its possessor, the individual whose labour-power it is, offers it for sale or sells it as a commodity. In order that its possessor may sell it as a commodity, he must have it at his disposal, he must be the *free proprietor* of his own labour-capacity, hence of his person. He and the owner of money meet in the market, and enter into relations with each other on a *footing of equality* as owners of commodities, with the sole difference that one is a buyer, the other a seller; both are therefore *equal in the eyes of the law* (Marx, 1976: 271, my emphasis).

Marx explicitly states that the formation of free wage labour, which is the historical precondition for the existence of capital, also demands the freeing of wage labourers from non-market relations, i.e. from non-capitalist juridical, ideological and political forms of consciousness that may undermine their becoming free proprietors of their own labour power commodity.

Neglect of this second essential condition of the formation of free wage labour lies in the economistic conception of the mode of production. The study of the process of the separation of wage labourers from non-capitalist forms of consciousness immediately evokes the study of the process of the formation of wage labour class consciousness. Separation from non-capitalist juridical, ideological and political forms is only realised in class struggle. But success in that struggle does not result in a 'vacuum' of consciousness – the outgoing forms of consciousness will be replaced by other forms. The economistic conception of the mode of production cannot accommodate a study of the changes in social forms of consciousness and of class struggle (see Chapter 1).

The aim of this section is to study to what extent the Sudanese agricultural wage labourers are becoming free proprietors of their own labour power, using evidence from the case studies of Section I.

Agricultural Wage Labourers

There have been some types of wage labour contracts in different places in Sudan which did not imply totally free contractual relations. *Zoul shahria* labourers in Gezira and *jiygols* in Dongola, as well as some wage labourers in seasonal contracts in Gedaref (more or less similar to *zoul shahria* in the Gezira) have been in dependent relations. At present such dependent relations may not exist at all in Gedaref and may be very limited in scale in other areas (e.g. Gezira and Dongola). The anti-slavery campaigns, the influx of non-attached (relatively free) wage labourers to the Gezira and Gedaref and other major employment areas from different areas and their mixing with the then dependent (attached to one employer) wage labourers, as well as probably the struggle of those employers who had no access to such dependent wage labour, and whose interest, therefore, lay in the freeing of such labourers from their attachment to one employer, have led to the disappearance of such relations of domination. It is also probable that the influx of wage labourers from outside has led to lower labour costs for existing 'dependent' labour employers and hence from their side the latter have become less keen on maintaining the dependent relationship.

However, the cases discussed above are not the only cases of wage labourers not standing with their employers on a footing of contractual equality as owners of commodities. In fact, most agricultural wage labourers are not on such a footing yet.

Some such cases will be discussed briefly.

1. *Nafir* (communal cooperative work) is increasingly losing significance and is being replaced by wage labour (amongst others, O'Brien, 1980; Elhassan, 1985). However, in many respects such wage labour

relations among villagers (who interchangingly play the role of the employee and the employer) are not to be considered as purely market relations. As O'Brien (1980: 366, 386) observes, wages paid within Um Fila village in central Sudan (a finding which probably applies to many other places) vary considerably according to the closeness of the relations between the employer and the employee and also to the latter's perception of the financial position of the former. He observes that if a villager works for a socially equal fellow-villager, employing others only occasionally in agricultural peak periods, he would ask for 30 to 50 p.t., while for a relatively well-off merchant or other employer from outside the village the wage claim could go up to 100 p.t. The underlying ideology for the lower rates of wages among fellow similar-positioned villagers is 'brotherhood'. Strangers (employers outside the village) and wealthy people (who employ people to make money) are outside the obligations of brotherhood.

2. The 'choice' to go to the Gezira by the majority of the seasonal wage labourers interviewed in 1982–83, as Table 6,8 shows, was not built essentially on a wish of owners of commodity to realise the maximum possible price of this commodity (as the nature of market relations would necessarily imply). Only 2% reported choosing to go to the Gezira because they thought wages were better than elsewhere. As many as 39% clearly stated that going to the Gezira was not their own choice in the first place – they were either following other members of the household, or the advice of the authorities or of other people, or just following the recruiters 'who have come all this way to look for labour'. Another 35% have chosen to go to the Gezira only because it is the closest employment area. Clearly this choice has not been built on comparative cost-benefit analyses, as most of those seasonal wage labourers do not know of other places or of the wages prevailing there. (This argument is to be justified in the last section of this chapter when we shall see the enormous wage differentials that exist among different seasonal agricultural employment areas.) Choosing the closest possible area apparently has socio-psychological reasons – the wish to remain as close as possible to the home area. However, this reduces considerably the notion of free proprietors of a commodity seeking ways of maximising their own interest.

3. In Gedaref, the labour market is more uniform than in the Gezira. Very few workers have ties and connections with the farmers other than the market ones. Great numbers of buyers and sellers of labour power enter the market with some awareness of the formation of the price of that commodity, and thus with an appreciation of the market limits influencing the formation of the price.

TABLE 6,8

Why do Gezira seasonal labourers go specifically to the Gezira?

1.	The closest possible area of employment	35%
2.	Chances of getting work in Gezira are better	19%
3.	Family reasons (e.g. accompanying other household members)	15%
4.	Following advice of village sheikhs or others	12%
5.	Following recruitment campaigns of Gezira tenants	6%
6.	Have become used to going to Gezira every year	6%
7.	Gezira provides services	4%
8.	Free transport has been offered	2%
9.	Wages are better in Gezira	2%
	Total	101%

Source: 1983 Survey of Agricultural Wage Labourers in Gezira
Note: Most of the respondents gave more than one reason.

Although wage workers in Gedaref have more 'free choice' than those in the Gezira, and stand on a more equal footing with their employers regarding the knowledge and possibility of influencing the wage level (Chapter 4), they are not yet totally equal with their employers in the eyes of the law. There is no agricultural labour legislation in Sudan defining and securing the rights of agricultural wage labourers (see also ILO/UNHCR, 1984), while the interests of farmers, the protection of their properties and rights, are secured in the civil laws and other specialised legislation. In the absence of agricultural labour legislation, farmers in Gedaref (and elsewhere in the Sudan) take the law into their own hands on many occasions. Normally, no contract is written when a job is being agreed on. In fact, only a moral obligation compels farmers to pay the workers at all, or to pay the total amount agreed on time. However, cases have been reported to the author (by labourers and the Labour Office) in his 1983 field survey, of farmers delaying payment, underpaying or not paying at all. Cases of unresolved disputes are numerous (see ILO/UNHCR, 1984). Also probably in other cases workers are forced to accept unfavourable compromises. This situation, of farmers not always abiding by their agreements with the wage workers, seems to arise as a result of differences in the degree of separation of the two classes from the non-capitalist, juridical-ideological form. Agreement by giving one's word is a non-capitalist form of contract. By accepting it, the wage workers show that they have not been sufficiently freed from their non-capitalist juridical-ideological forms of consciousness. By not keeping it, farmers seem no longer to be under the strong influence of such forms of consciousness.

The arguments above suggest that although at the time of price formation buyers and sellers of labour power commodity in Gedaref enter into relations with each other more or less on a footing of equality, they may not do so at the time of the realisation of the price of the commodity (wage-paying and -receiving), because they stand at different places in the process of their separation from the non-capitalist forms of consciousness and because at the legal level they are not totally equal commodity owners. Inequality with the employers in the eyes of the law is a fact for all casual agricultural labourers in the country.

Urban Wage Workers

The situation of urban, or at least industrial, wage labourers is different. Urban centres allow the meeting of great numbers of workers and employers and urban wage labourers seem to stand in relative equality with their employers regarding the knowledge and possibility of influencing wage levels within certain limits. What is more, urban workers and their employers are more or less regarded as equals at the legal level. Trade union protection legislation was passed in 1948. The Trade Disputes Act, 1960, covered all workers, whether union members or not. Besides regulating terms of service these laws have set certain procedures for resolving disputes, from direct negotiations, to referring the dispute to the Commissioner of Labour, or to the Conciliation Board (headed by a judge and comprising two conciliators representing the employer and the workers). Since 1948 trade union legislation has gone through different amendments and sometimes suspension (in connection with and as a reflection of the class struggle at a national level).

Amendments, such as those introduced in 1960 (Trade Unions Ordinance (Amendment) Act of 1960) and at different periods since 1971 were aimed at curbing the influence of trade unions and also suspension of trade union legislation (e.g. between 1958 and 1960, during the Aboud's first military rule, and between 1971 and 1973 under Numeiry's regime) and reduced the ability of the workers to stand on a footing of equality with the employers. Nevertheless, even at times of suspension of the trade union legislation, urban wage workers, as individuals rather than as groups (unions), had access to the Labour Commissioner, who could rule on disputes under the

Trade Disputes Act 1960 (which excludes agricultural workers). To what extent this access was used we do not have information. At times when trade unions were banned or restricted in some way, pressure groups in different forms (including underground unions) sprang up and at times were successful in securing some rights for urban wage workers. Such movements, however, must have been limited in scale and must not be over-stressed.[10] Not all the urban workers are in the same situation vis-à-vis equality in the eyes of the law. Trade unions are only permitted, according to the Trade Union legislation, where 50 or more wage workers are employed by the same employer (although lorry drivers have been able to compel the authorities to accept their formation of trade unions without fulfilling this condition). This means that there are a great number of urban wage workers who are not organised in unions.

Even so, generally speaking, it may be concluded that urban wage workers are in a more advanced situation than the agricultural wage workers regarding their position as free proprietors of their labour power commodity, i.e. their separation from non-market relations.

III. WAGE DETERMINATION, FREE LABOUR FORMATION AND CLASS CONSCIOUSNESS

A comprehensive study of the formation of class consciousness among Sudanese wage workers, though of great interest, is beyond the scope of this work. However, the exposition of some of the main factors that may influence that process as well as some general ideas about its actual progress are in line with some of the practical objectives of this work as set out in the Introduction.

It has been shown above that industrial wage workers do demonstrate a politically active class consciousness. Below, an attempt will be made to explain some differences in the level of class consciousness among some agricultural wage workers' groups in the two largest agricultural regions in the Sudan, the Gezira and Gedaref. This is to be viewed from their position in the process of wage determination. It should be noted here that this method is not without its limitations. Though the position of different groups of wage labourers in the process of wage determination may reveal some differences in the level of, and factors influencing, class consciousness, it is by no means a comprehensive approach. We shall also show how in practice the process of free labour formation and the process of the formation of class consciousness are inseparable.

Wage Determination, Bargaining Power and Class Consciousness:
Some Theoretical Notes

The Marxian theory of wage determination at the abstract level (which assumes a capitalist mode of production in which labour power is a commodity and in which capital is being expanded and wage labour is being reproduced) may be briefly summarised as follows.[11] As in the case of any other commodity, the value of labour power determines the price of it (i.e. wages). The quantity of labour socially necessary to produce and reproduce a commodity (that is its value) is, in the case of labour power, expressed in the average value of the basic necessities required to produce, develop, maintain and perpetuate it (in a subordinate position to capital). At a higher level of abstraction (a closed, homogeneous capitalist economy) labour power has a single price. At a lower level of abstraction Marx introduces two elements of value of labour power: the physical element – the absolutely indispensable minimum to maintain and reproduce the labour power of the workers – and the historical or social element, which is determined by the 'traditional standard of life', 'the satisfaction of certain wants springing from the social conditions in which people are placed and reared up' (Marx, 1950: 401). Marx asserts that 'this historical or social element entering into the value of labour power may be expanded or contracted or altogether extinguished, so that nothing remains but the physical limit' (*Ibid*: 401). The fixing of the actual rate of surplus value (or profit) between the limits of the physical minimum of wages and the physical maximum of the working day 'is only settled *by the continuous struggle between capital and labour*, the capitalist constantly tending to reduce wages to their physical minimum, and to extend the working day to its physical maximum, while the working man constantly presses in the opposite direction' (my emphasis – *Ibid*: 401–2). The historical or social element is therefore, for Marx, determined by the class struggle. It should also be added that even within a pure capitalist mode of production the physical limit is maintained only through aggregation; the actual price of labour power (wages) at a particular place or time may go below this limit for substantial numbers of people.

In the complex reality we then have the following. Individual capital has to continuously seek ways to maintain profitability by lowering real and relative wages, by increasing the productive powers of labour and the extent and the intensity of labour extracted, and by decreasing the value of labour power and the value of a given money wage. Sometimes, although perhaps far less frequently, capital may also attempt to decrease nominal wages. The working class, on the other hand, may strive to resist a fall in nominal and real wages and may seek ways to raise them. The success or failure in raising or lowering wages depends on the bargaining power of the two classes, and this is determined by economic, political and ideological factors or, in other words, by market relations, collective organisation and class consciousness.

The economic factors (or market relations) are largely supply and demand of different types of labour. What determines the supply side, in general, is the need to earn wages in order to reproduce labour power, and the availability or non-availability of alternatives to wage labour. The supply of a particular type of labour is determined by a number of factors such as wage levels and conditions of work. The wage labour demand side is generally determined by the amount of capital available and the possibility of enough surplus extraction ('enough' is determined by the prevailing rate of profit at a particular period). Demand for particular types of labour is determined mainly by the relative possibilities of surplus extraction (e.g. relatively more demand for the type of labour that creates relatively more surplus value).

Class consciousness is determined essentially, but not automatically, by production relations. Capitalist production relations are the way by which capital brings labour to work and the relations that arise between them in the production process in which labour is subordinate to capital. Capitalist production relations emerge and develop in different socio-economic formations with different cultural and political histories. Differences in cultural and political background may not be neutralised or nullified by newly developing production relations and class consciousness, but may, in fact, remain for some time, influencing the specific ways in which class consciousness is formed in the different socio-economic formations. Collective organisations, which themselves are products of class consciousness at a certain level, also influence the specific manner and the pace of development of class consciousness in a cumulative fashion.

Class consciousness, as a process, essentially develops through different levels or degrees. Perception of belonging to a class, which is a level or degree of class consciousness, may not be enough to create a perception of class interest, or to produce the will to advance the interests of that class.[12]

To the extent to which the production process itself is spatially fragmented, it produces fragmented classes. The perception of belonging to a certain segment or group within a class may precede the perception of belonging to the whole of that class. The perception of belonging to a whole class rather than a class-segment, coupled with the perception of class interests and the will to promote those interests, grows (albeit at varying rates in different places and over different periods of time) together with the growth of the division of labour and the interconnections between the different production units and the level and effectiveness of collective organisations. The growth of class consciousness amongst the dominant class (capitalist) precedes that of the dominated class (wage labour). Among different segments or groups within a class, class consciousness may develop unevenly. This is due to the particular experiences that different segments gain in the production process, the cultural and political background and the effectiveness of the particular form of collective organisation of that segment or group.

Elimination of Some Factors Influencing Wage Determination in the Gezira and Gedaref

The effect of the market relations of supply and demand of labour on variations of wage rates seems to be analysable in certain cases within the two regions. Demand for labour in both regions differs in different periods during the agricultural season. So does the supply of labour, especially that of the wage labourers who have access to land in their original areas. In Tables 5,5 and 5,6 above, variations in the daily wages of the workers in different operations are noticeable. As we have seen in Chapters 3 and 4, wages both in the Gezira and in Gedaref are mainly based on piece rates. The calculation of daily wages comes from relating the sum of money received and other components of wages in kind at the end of the job to the number of working days. In jobs based on piece rates the intensity and length of the working day is normally left to the wage worker. If we assume that the wage worker in this case would expend, on average, more or less the same quantity of labour in the different operations, based on his/her own working capacity, which seems to be a reasonable assumption, then the differences in wage rates for the different operations should at least in part be sought in the forces of supply and demand. In the sesame harvest in Gedaref (and also in Habila, see Chapter 4) this has clearly been shown to be the case. There seem to be no tangible differences in the conditions of supply and demand of labour generally between the regions. The two surveys carried out for an ILO/UNHCR project, from which wage differentials have been observed in this study, establish that no labour shortage existed, at least in 1982 when the surveys were undertaken (see Barnett, 1983 and Dey et al, 1983, and also the final report of ILO/UNHCR, 1984: 68, 126). The author's own observations in the two regions confirm this. Therefore, wage differentials between the two regions (indicated in Chapter 5) are to be sought in other factors affecting the bargaining power of capital and wage labour. The same would apply for wage differentials among the two different groups (seasonal and settled workers) in the Gezira. No significant differences in the conditions of supply and demand may be assumed, as wage differentials have shown up among groups working in all the different parts of the Gezira during the same period of time. Hence wage differentials are to be sought largely in differences in bargaining power.

According to current information available there seem to be no strong reasons to believe that there are any substantial differences in the bargaining power of the employers in the two regions or among different groups within them. From the point of view of supply and demand of wage labour, as suggested above, their bargaining power is the same, at least in the agricultural season that forms the basis of the data of this study. Employers have established forms of collective organisation: a Tenants' Union in the Gezira and Farmers' Associations in Gedaref. Besides the opportunity of meeting and formulating collective stands and seeking ways of promoting their interests in their collective organisations, which both Gezira tenants and Gedaref farmers enjoy, the latter may be advantaged in that most of them live in and administer their farms from the same place: Gedaref town. This, coupled with the fact that a Gedaref large farmer will probably employ many more workers than a Gezira tenant, means that the Gedaref large farmer will be able to acquire relatively more experience. On the other hand, Gezira tenants reap their comparative advantages firstly in that they have generally been acting as employers for longer periods than the more recently emerging farmers of Gedaref. Second, their Union was formed in and has been operating since a much earlier period than the Gedaref Farmers' Association (20 years earlier than the first Farmers' Association in Gedaref and 30 to 40 years earlier than the rest). Third, the Gezira Scheme's Administration, which is itself a large employer, and consequently affects the formation of wages in the Scheme, may also help in bringing together tenants living and working in different parts of the Gezira. This is possible because although the Administration is centrally controlled, it also maintains close contacts with the tenants in the different parts of the Scheme through its inspectors and by extending cash advances which serve to meet wage labour costs.

Wage Differentials and Wage Workers' Class Consciousness in the Gezira and Gedaref

It is suggested, therefore, as is apparent from the foregoing, that wage differentials, for similar agricultural operations affecting all wage labourers, are to be sought mainly in the differences in the class consciousness (and collective organisation) of the different groups of wage labourers. This will be explored through the investigation of the various factors that might lead to different experiences gained in the production process by the various groups of wage labourers and/or their different cultural and political backgrounds that might also lead to differences in their class consciousness.

It is worth remembering here that neither in the Gezira nor in Gedaref are there permanent forms of class-based collective organisations among the agricultural labourers.

Within the Gezira

Before starting to look at the case of the Gezira, it must be mentioned that the wage differentials prevailing there were not discovered for the first time in this study. Galal-el-Din and O'Brien, from separately collected observations, came to realise that there exist substantial differences in wage rates for cotton-picking in the Gezira, contrary to the ILO Report (1976) which asserts that these are almost uniform and 'appear to function almost like textbook models' (see O'Brien, 1980: 210–13). Neither Galal el Din nor O'Brien has yet analysed these differences in wage rates in association with specific groups of labourers (settled or seasonal); they have merely been conceived as individual variations with apparently no reasons having been researched.

There are a number of factors that may contribute to the enhancement of the formation of class consciousness and therefore the strengthening of bargaining power of the settled workers of the Gezira compared with the seasonal workers (and which have resulted in the latter receiving on average only 62% of the wages paid to the former in the cotton-picking season of 1982/83). The dependence of settled wage workers in Gezira on wage labour for their reproduction – in other words, the wage-labouring aspect of their lives – seems to be higher than for the seasonal wage workers. As has been mentioned, 92.5% of the seasonal workers have access to land in their original areas. Of the Gezira camp labourers, 74% have sharecropping arrangements (acting as subtenants), but the percentage may drop if other non-camp labourers (those who are mostly of non-Westerner origin who live in tenants' villages) are taken into consideration. The proportion of landless among the settled workers is therefore higher than among the seasonal workers.

Even when sharecropping, most of the settled wage labourers would need to earn wages at certain periods of the year to supplement their incomes from the subtenancy. The wage-labour aspect of the settled workers as a whole (including the landless and the category of wage labourer subtenants) is a continuous aspect of their lives throughout the whole year, while for most of the seasonal workers it is only temporary during a few months of the year. Moreover, as we have seen, the phenomenon of sharecropping in the Gezira is of recent origin and prior to this the present subtenants had had no access to land.

Coming from different scattered locations the seasonal labourers enter the labour market with little or no prior knowledge of current wage rates, especially those prevailing among the settled workers. When arriving in the Gezira most of the seasonal workers live in scattered places, in small camps built on site, consisting of a few households mostly working for the same tenant. The form of their payment, as has been mentioned, is normally in both cash and kind, while that of the settled workers is only in the form of cash. This may conceal the differences in real wage rates from seasonal workers. Even if they know about the differences in wage rates between themselves and the settled workers, or among different groups within them, it seems that because of moral considerations which fit their own ideology (giving their 'word', receiving *mal-al-diayia* and other advances) they choose to stick with the terms of their original agreement.

The situation of the settled workers is different. The majority of the settled workers live in Gezira labour camps and the rest in the tenants' villages. Not only do they learn about wage rates received by each other, they also learn about the cash advances received by the tenants from the Scheme's Administration to meet the costs of picking labour. These advances are estimated annually and paid to the tenants according to their estimated production. Settled workers, knowing the rate of advances paid to the tenants, may not agree to work for less.

Despite the sums of money advanced, it should be understood that the Administration does not actually control the picking wage rate. The rate of money advanced for cotton-picking seems to be calculated by the Scheme's Administration more or less according to the prevailing wage rates in the whole agricultural season, and also by taking into consideration other possible factors such as average yields in the particular season, the expected labour market, and supply–demand relations. The fact that the advance rates set by the Administration are not final and are subject to bargaining may be confirmed by the reactions of a considerable number of settled workers who have boycotted picking labour in the past, an action which has given rise to complaints and campaigns against them by tenants and officials (see Tamim, 1980: 17–22).

Settled labourers are also advantaged in that the majority of them live in labour camps among fellow labourers, which adds to their social experiences, psychological solidarity and ability to take collective action. The fact that most of these labour camps are inhabited by people of the same tribe or ethnic origin, however, means that their solidarity is formed on an ethnic rather than a class basis, but this still positively affects their local bargaining power.

The arguments above serve to suggest that having to depend more, or for longer periods, on wage labour for their economic reproduction, and living and working all the time in the Gezira itself amid fellow-labourers, has meant that the settled labourers become more conscious of themselves as wage labourers and have a better perception of and better possibilities to promote their interests than the seasonal labourers. This argument may also be underlined by the results of the survey of 1983, which has shown that while 74% of the settled labourers accept wages only after bargaining, only 25% of the seasonal labourers could confirm this (35% said wages were fixed on their behalf by their village sheikhs or other representatives, and they did not know whether bargaining was involved, and 40% would accept what was offered by the employer).

The Gezira and Gedaref

It seems that there is a multiplicity of factors that might have led to the differences in the bargaining power between the Gezira and Gedaref wage workers, and to the strengthening of the latter's bargaining power:

1. The process of 'free' labour formation, at least in terms of being free from any access to land, seems to be more advanced among the Gedaref wage labourers. As has been mentioned, in Gedaref, 49% have no access to land, while in the Gezira, among the seasonal labourers, only 7.5%, and among Gezira camp labourers only 26% have reported this. Thus Gedaref wage workers depend more on wage labour to meet subsistence needs and might therefore be in a position, and need, to gain more experience due to their place in the production process.

2. There are differences in the recruitment process in the two regions. While only one-third of Gezira seasonal workers are self-recruited, and among these it seems the majority would choose the same employer every year, and 60% of the settled labourers would wait for the tenants or their representatives to recruit them, in Gedaref all workers are self-recruited; even those who are on some occasions brought from their home villages by the employers will normally go to recruitment centres or other farms on other occasions looking for jobs. In Gedaref the workers choose between many employers. In Gedaref town, which is the main recruitment centre, thousands of

wage workers meet hundreds of employers. There is no such centre in the Gezira. On average, there are about 90 economically active persons in each of the 710 Gezira labour camps and each camp is a recruitment centre in itself.

3. The physical size of the average production unit in Gedaref is much larger (a standard scheme in Gedaref is 1,000 or 1,500 feddans, while a standard tenancy in the Gezira is only 40 feddans). Accordingly, the number of workers who may come together at one time is much larger in Gedaref. In fact, at certain peaks between 100 and 400 workers may come together in one scheme, while only a few workers may meet during the labour process in the Gezira.

4. In Gedaref jobs are normally offered to groups and not individuals. Those arriving as individuals or in smaller groups will be asked to form a larger group. Working groups may also be formed of wage workers of ethnically different origins. The working group bargains with the employer for the wage, and if agreed it undertakes the specific job, carries it out collectively and then divides the wage equally among its members. In the Gezira, due to their small size, the job pieces are undertaken either by individuals or by small working groups based on the household.

The arguments above suggest that the nature of the labour market and the labour process in Gedaref is more favourable to the formation of class consciousness and the consequent strengthening of the bargaining power of the wage workers than in the Gezira. There are other factors related to the cultural-political background of Gedaref wage workers which may also positively affect their bargaining power. As we have seen earlier, the Gedaref labour market is probably the most diversified agricultural labour market in Sudan in terms of the origins of the wage workers. Taking the possibilities that the Gedaref labour market offers in terms of the frequency of meetings between large numbers of workers (in Gedaref town and on farms), it can then be suggested that Gedaref workers may be able to exchange wider varieties of experience. It should also be emphasised that many of the Ethiopian and Eritrean refugees are already politicised at home and may have experienced or are closer to some forms of collective organisation than other workers, and consequently bring these experiences with them to Gedaref. In fact, many farmers in Gedaref have related the emergence during the *dura* harvest of the *gowal* system, which is generally more favourable to the workers, to the arrival of the refugees.

Forms of wage workers' collective organisation in Gedaref, though still temporary, voluntary and at a low stage of development, are more developed than in the Gezira. Among the casual workers of the Gezira at present the only form of collective organisation is the labour camp. The labour camp is a loose, primitive and basically ethnic form of collective organisation. The labour camp is used at times to act as a pressure group against individual tenants who do not fulfil their terms of contract with some members of that labour camp. This may sometimes prove to be effective, as the tenants of a particular village have very few labour camps from which to recruit labour. In Gedaref the working group itself is a form of temporary collective organisation, and sometimes a particular group works together for a long period. Cases of trans-group cooperation and common actions are not uncommon. Wage fights may involve many or all of the groups working on a farm. In the case of the sesame harvest, as has been mentioned, combined action may even be planned between working groups in different farms. However, more developed, permanent forms of collective organisation – trade unions – still seem to be far away, even in Gedaref.

CHAPTER SEVEN

Dominance of Circulation Capital: The Bottleneck of Capitalist Development

In the first chapter of this book it has been emphasised that the dominance of merchant (or largely circulation) capital is not, as Kay (1975) argues, the cause of underdevelopment, but represents, rather, a specific lower stage of the development of capitalism (a stage of primitive capital accumulation). We argued that not all fractions of merchant capital are in the same position, or capitalist production would never come into existence. In this chapter we expose these arguments empirically.

The first section gives an account of the development of private indigenous circulation capital in Sudan. In the second section we hope to show that at a national level circulation capital is still the main form of capital (i.e. occupying a wider material base than production capital) and following this and stemming from it, that some fractions of merchant capital are able to dominate all the others, including production capital. (Dominance of one fraction of capital by another necessarily entails the ability of the latter to be more privileged in the distribution of surplus.) The third section presents a detailed case study of surplus appropriation and distribution among different fractions of circulation capital in a prominent agricultural region. In the fourth and final section we expose some indicators of the deepening economic crisis in the 1970s and early 1980s in Sudan as a result of the dominance of some fractions of circulation capital. We will also investigate whether that dominance is being challenged.

I. THE DEVELOPMENT OF PRIVATE INDIGENOUS CIRCULATION CAPITAL

Private Merchant Capital

As has been mentioned in Chapter 2, trade within the country and with neighbouring countries was in existence prior to British rule. However, we maintained that the incorporation of the Sudanese socio-economic formation into a wider one and the systemic penetration of capital (the introduction and intensification of the process of commoditisation) started with British rule. Both Shaaeldin (1981) and Taisier Ali (1982) have shown the subordinate position of indigenous traders to foreign trading companies and expatriate traders during the colonial period. Export–import trade was monopolised by foreign trading companies such as Sudan Mercantile, Gellately & Hankey, and Mitchell Cotts. Wholesale trade and retail trade in urban centres and rural towns was largely dominated by expatriate traders – mainly Indians, Syrians, Armenians and Greeks. Barbour mentions that these expatriate traders and business persons 'keep very close together, lending one another money, employing compatriots, keeping business among friends, and doing all they can to avoid allowing one of their number to descend into extreme poverty. For the most part these communities have brought no capital into Sudan from outside' (Barbour, 1961: 271). These expatriates mostly played an intermediary role; distributing imported commodities from, and purchasing local products for, the big export–import companies. Sudanese local traders known as *gellaba*, mainly originating from northern Sudan, were largely restricted to small retail trade at village and rural town level as well as itinerant traders. They also served as purchasers of local products for export companies via expatriate traders.

The colonial government restricted the movement of *gellaba* traders in certain zones. The Closed District legislation of 1929 prohibited entry into the southern region (and some other places in Sudan) by Sudanese traders coming from elsewhere. These measures had been taken, according to the official declarations of the colonial officers, to protect the tribesmen from exploitation by 'clever *gellaba*'. T. Ali (1982: 85) who documents this also points out that the anti-*gellaba* laws were not intended to prevent the tribespeople's exploitation by others. He explains that this step was merely meant to be a shift of benefits from *gellaba* to the traditional (or 'customary') leaders who had been given extended powers of jurisdiction and taxation. Traditional leaders, during the period of Closed District legislation (up to 1946), were clearly the close allies of the colonial regime. However, it should also be mentioned that the colonial government had itself been competing with *gellaba* over the limited surplus of the household producers. The traditional leaders were in fact tax agents for the government, the chief beneficiary; the government took 85% of the collected taxes, allowing 15% for the traditional leaders.

T. Ali (*Ibid*: 86) also explains that

> the only group of indigenous merchants that were able to survive in an independent manner and with a great measure of success were

139

those engaged in border trade. Prominent in this category were the cattle merchants who traditionally sold livestock to Egypt and Saudi Arabia and who were rarely obstructed in their activities by colonial policy.

Indigenous livestock traders operating in the earlier period of colonial rule, according to Mahmoud (1979: 101), were still leading export traders in 1975.

The independence of the country in 1956 brought a profound change in the position of indigenous merchant capital. Conditions for such change had been partially forming during the latter period of colonial rule. Money capital had been accumulating gradually in the hands of Sudanese traders. Unlike the capital of most of the foreign firms and expatriate traders, apparently this money capital had been staying within the boundaries of the national economy. The Gezira Scheme, with the surplus produced there, played a significant role in the expansion of trade channels. *Gellaba* had been making progress in incorporating even the most remote areas in money–commodity relations. *Gellaba* activities had included not only trade but also finance. The period of the Second World War had been decisive for many small local traders in breaking the barrier of the small size of their money capital. Many stories are told in Khartoum about leading merchants at the time making their money from war-time profits, from scarcity of goods and black-marketeering. During the private pump schemes boom which started in the early 1950s, some Sudanese had succeeded in breaking the monopoly of export–import companies over bank finance (see below). The larger part of the surplus appropriated there (in the form of commercial profit and financial interest) had been diverted to investment in urban trade. Traditional leaders, accumulating money wealth from their position as tax collectors and other privileges, and their sons, had also started to move to investments in trade. Immediately after the Second World War, Henderson says:

> until recently the Sudanese played a comparatively minor part in what may be called the big business of the country. The native firms are now beginning to acquire the outside contacts and knowledge of world markets which will enable them to take an increasing share in commerce. (Henderson, 1946: 24)

Notwithstanding all these quantitative changes in the position of local merchant capital its further decisive push could not have been attained without the change in the political sphere – the coming of the first independent government. The target, which was not easy to reach without state intervention, was the breaking of the monopoly of foreign firms over export–import trade and over bank finance.

In 1960 the first Sudanese commercial bank (named as that) was started. Although its share of deposits, amounting to 12% of the total deposits of banks in Sudan in its early period (Mahmoud, 1979: 97), was not very significant, it signalled a change in the prospects of local merchant capital. In 1962 legislation was promulgated prohibiting the giving of trade licences to foreigners (Shaaeldin, 1981: 114). In 1965, the French-owned Crédit Lyonnais became a partnership between the government (through the Bank of Sudan) and Crédit Lyonnais in Paris and was renamed El Nilein Bank (A. Abdalla, 1982: 31).

These steps, together with the growing campaign directed against foreign capital and expatriate traders, especially during and after the October 1964 popular uprising, led many expatriates to leave their businesses. Sudanese moved in to replace them. Among the first prominent Sudanese trading firms (mainly family-based) to engage significantly in export–import trade were El-Sheik Mustafa El-Amin, Osman Saleh & Sons, El-Berir, El-Berbari (mainly based in Port Sudan), Aboul Ella and Abdel Monem Mohammed. However, foreign export–import firms remained the leading firms until 1970.

The blow to foreign circulation capital came in May 1970 (on the first anniversary of Numeiry's rule). All commercial banks were nationalised. Twenty-two major foreign commercial firms and 35 foreign insurance companies faced the same fate. The government also took over cotton-marketing. Foreign firms 'were accused of monopolising export–import trade', of being 'tools of imperialist exploitation and channels of foreign intervention' and of 'dominating the Sudanese economy, the smuggling of profits and corruption by taking advantage of the weak officials of the state and banks' (*Middle East Economic Digest*, May 1970, cited in Shaaeldin, 1981: 181–2). The arena of Sudanese internal and external trade became open only to Sudanese private and state capital.

From the early 1970s Sudanese private circulation capital seriously started consolidating its economic and political power and domain. This was not only due to the removal of foreign firms from Sudanese trade, as in fact a new (probably less militant) rival came – the state with its merchant (and financial) activities. It was also because the period of the 1970s witnessed an unprecedented inflow of foreign resources to finance imports (see Section II below). The period of the 1970s also witnessed a large increase in internal agricultural produce directed towards the market (mechanised farming). As a result, commodity circulation started to grow relatively fast; hundreds of large Sudanese trading companies came into being.

Private Financial Capital

The oldest form of money-lending (outside the personal level) known in Sudan is *shail*. *Shail* has been described and its extent in rural Sudan discussed earlier. The share of *shail* in total financing and in surplus distribution is not easy to estimate. Besides *shail* there are two further important moments or stages in the development of indigenous private financial capital in the Sudan. The first, which was temporary, was during the private pump schemes' boom and the second started in the 1970s when private indigenous banks came into being.

Financiers of Private Pump Schemes

The fast expansion of private pump schemes during the 1950s and up to the mid-1960s has been largely attributed to the increase of cotton prices internationally after the Korean War (see among others, Adam, 1971 and Osman, 1958). Besides benefiting cotton production, this expansion has also been seen as creating a class of political supporters of the colonial state, and, later, as an obvious support to the class base of the post-colonial state (T. Ali, 1983; Shaaeldin, 1981). However, there is another major factor which has not been considered. It seems that a large part of the needed merchant and financial capital was provided by foreign bank capital and foreign cotton exporters. However, indigenous capital also seems to have been very actively participating during that period. Moreover, to manage 2,283 schemes, as there were in 1964/65, 85% of which were under 500 feddans (Shaaeldin, 1981: 109), would not have been possible without the participation of local entrepreneurs, since foreign residents in Sudan during the colonial period were relatively few compared to the population. It is suggested that the boom of private pump schemes can be looked at also from the angle of the development of the process of Sudanese primitive capital accumulation. On one hand, there was the availability of large numbers of tenants (90,000 in 1964/65) who had been separated from access to their own private lands and were therefore prepared to take up tenancies within the pump schemes. On the other hand, there was a rising class of privileged indigenous people who had accumulated money wealth from circulation and/or who had access to finance sources and to the state apparatus. This latter was necessary, since 77.4% of the land occupied by the schemes was government land (Census of Pump Schemes, 1965, cited in *Ibid*: 110); even in private land pump schemes a licence had to be obtained from the government.

According to a Census of Pump Schemes in 1964/65 by the Department of Statistics (cited in Shaaeldin, 1981), land cultivated in all pump schemes

TABLE 7,1

Percentage distribution of pump schemes according to size of land in 1964/65

Scheme-size (in feddans)	Percentage of total number of schemes	Percentage of total land cultivated
Under 500	85	13
500 – 10,000	14	45
Over 10,000	1	42

Source: Pump Schemes Survey, cited in Shaaeldin, 1981: 109

was 1.2 million feddans. Land under cotton increased from 20,000 feddans in 1949/50 to 198,000 feddans in 1958/59. Since the decline of cotton prices in 1956/57, the expansion in cotton cultivation almost came to a halt, reaching its maximum of 217,000 feddans in 1966/67.

The concentration of land in pump schemes is quite obvious in Table 7, 1. About 23 large scheme holders (licensees as they were called) of over 10,000 feddans each already existed in 1964/65. Licensees of land ranging in size between 500 and 10,000 feddans numbered about 320, while about 1,940 licensees had land of less than 500 feddans each. As has been mentioned, licensees distributed the land in small amounts to tenants whose job was to provide labour. Licensees provided irrigation (pumps) and credit. After deduction of several costs (e.g. transporting and ginning of cotton) licensees were entitled to 60% of the cotton proceeds. (Tenants were to take 40% of cotton proceeds as well as the full product of the rest of their tenancy sown to subsistence crops.)

Osman (1958) mentions that almost all licensees at least at certain stages needed finance. According to him, there were three types of licensee. The first consisted of a small number who provided their fixed capital and who would need finance for ginning, transporting and selling of cotton. Financiers would charge a commission of 2% to 6% of the gross value of the cotton. The second type provided only a proportion of the capital costs of constructing the scheme, while financiers provided the rest. These licensees were under an obligation to sell their cotton through the financiers; terms of finance and of distribution of cotton proceeds varied. The third type were those who would only provide licences (as the number of licences to be given to any person was officially limited) and financiers would provide the capital. Osman says that 'to be eligible for a licence, that is, to be a man of some influence in one of the areas of the Province, was sufficient to guarantee a 50 per cent share in the net profits of a scheme' (*Ibid*: 45).

Financiers, according to Osman, were few in number, were both

Sudanese and non-Sudanese, and were not specialised financiers, i.e. had other occupations. The Sudanese financiers were mostly themselves large licensees. Foreign financiers were largely agents of foreign cotton importers. Osman stresses that

> commercial banks are the ultimate source of funds which finance pump schemes in the country, the financiers only acting as intermediaries between the banks and the scheme owners. Owing to their strong financial standing, the financiers are able to borrow at relatively low interest rates, and re-lend these funds to pump scheme owners at higher rates. (*Ibid*: 46)

The period of the private pump scheme boom witnessed the establishment of new foreign banks in the country. Besides the already existing National Bank of Egypt (1901), Barclays Bank DCO (1913), and the Ottoman Bank (1949 – later renamed National and Grindlay), there appeared Crédit Lyonnais (1953), Banque Misr (1953), the Arab Bank (1956) and in 1958 the Commercial Bank of Ethiopia (A. Abdalla, 1982: 30–1). In the latter half of the 1950s with the fall in cotton prices, foreign banks, according to Shaaeldin (1981: 126), started to become hesitant to finance cotton. Hence the then recently formed first Sudanese parliament endorsed a Bill in 1957 to establish a state bank (the Sudanese Agricultural Bank).

It is apparently during this period that the Sudanese were able to break the monopoly of foreign export firms and traders over bank finance. Being reluctant to engage directly in medium- and long-term credit, the foreign bank capital had to resort to the Sudanese and other foreigners as intermediaries. M.H. Awad writes:

> most of the finance came from the (foreign) commercial banks, especially Barclays DCO, but as the commercial banks operating in the Sudan were reluctant to undertake medium- and long-term investments in land, they preferred to lend to intermediaries who, in turn, dealt with the licences. Among the (intermediary) financiers were Dairat al Mahdi, Aboul Ella Agricultural Company, Abdel Monem Mohamed Company, Osman Salih & Sons, Rye Evans Ltd, Khuri Bros, Contomicholos & Sons, the Middle East Agricultural Company and Shushine Company. (cited in T. Ali, 1982: 83)

Among the prominent financiers enlisted for private pump schemes, four were Sudanese family-based companies. These companies were also large scheme leaseholders. After the 'nationalisation' of the private pump schemes these companies were among the most prominent, if not the most prominent, Sudanese indigenous enterprises. The private pump schemes were taken over by the government, beginning in the latter half of the 1960s, with the consent of their holders. The decline of cotton prices lowered the profits of the scheme holders, who became greatly indebted to the banks, especially to the newly established SAB. The government was urged to intervene to safeguard the interest of the rising indigenous bourgeoisie. Generous compensation was paid to the scheme holders (Shaaeldin, 1981 and T. Ali, 1982).

Private, Local and Joint Venture Banks

Experiences gained from pump schemes' finance, as well as competition with foreign firms over bank finance and export–import trade, caused some leading indigenous merchants and other businesspersons to think of establishing an indigenous commercial bank. The Sudan Commercial Bank (SCB) was established in 1960 with capital of one million Sudanese pounds. As has been mentioned earlier, its deposits in its early periods constituted about 12% of the total deposits. When banks were nationalised in 1970, SCB was also included. Shareholders decided to transfer their money into an alternative financial institution. The 1970 slogans directed against foreign and private banks evaporated quickly. In 1975 the Sudanese Investments Bank was established with a paid-up capital of £S7.5 million. In 1980/81 its total advances amounted to £S27.1 million (MFNE, Economic Survey, 1980/81: 155–6).

A new system of banking entered the Sudan in 1978 with the Faysal Islamic Bank (FIB). The authorised share capital of £S6 million was very soon oversubscribed and was raised to £S10 million. The shares were divided between Saudis, Sudanese and other Muslims in the ratio of 4:4:2. Its major difference from other banks (despite the 'non-interest-rated, Islamic way of banking' slogans that it used) was that it entered into partnership with its clients (mainly in foreign trade). The FIB was granted tax-free operations. Its equity (which included both paid-up shares and reinvested profits) increased in three years from 1979 to 1982, by 350%. Total commercial banks' equity for the same period grew by 70%. Its total deposits over the same period increased almost tenfold. Corresponding increases in total commercial banks' deposits increased by less than 1.5 times (Brown and Shaaeldin, 1982).

Soon after the spearheading performance of FIB (due mainly to its privileged position as a non-tax-paying institution) five locally initiated applications were made to establish Islamic banks. The idea was definitely not well received and was resisted by FIB and its political partner the Moslem Brothers who had by then a major role to play in Numeiry's policy formulation. However, the applications were also backed by Sudanese and foreign influential business and political circles. By early 1985, five had been granted permission: the Sudan Islamic Bank, Al-Tadamun Islamic

Bank, Al-Baraka Islamic Bank, the Western Sudan Islamic Bank and the Development Cooperative Islamic Bank, each with its own business group supporters, and often backed by political office holders.[1] (All but the last are joint-venture: private, local and foreign.) Other commercial local and joint-venture banks were also established. By early 1985 these were the International Sudanese Bank, the Sudanese Ahali Bank, the National Development Bank and the Blue Nile Bank. Similarly, each of these banks has a group of businesspersons providing initial backing.

Since the mid-1970s and especially from the early 1980s we can therefore talk of a new era in the history of Sudanese private circulation capital. Money capital concentrated in the hands of rapidly enriched merchants during the 1970s and backed by the state (see Section II below) started to move into banking and to establish a tendency to centralisation of finance capital not seen previously. Most of the business institutions in Sudan up to that period had been individually or family-based. This new trend towards centralisation of capital apparently signals the start of a period of freeing Sudanese capital from its 'patriarchal' limitations.

II. DOMINANCE OF CIRCULATION CAPITAL: SOME MACRO-INDICATORS

The Scope of Movement

In the process of transformation to capitalism productive capital at first owns a smaller segment of the production process, while the major part is still under non-capitalist production relations.

In Sudan, agriculture still provides the major source of livelihood for most of the population. (The contribution of agriculture in the GDP was 4–5 times as much as that of industry between the years 1973/74 and 1980/81 – MFNE Economic Survey, 1980/81: 13.) However, in the early 1980s, 71.3% of the land under cultivation was estimated to be outside the direct control of productive capital.

In addition to the stages listed in Table 7,2 the pastoralist sector, which provides a living for 10.7% of the population (Sudan Guide 1984/85: 7), is largely non-capitalist (i.e. governed by the logic of household production relations).

We can then conclude that the vast majority of the rural population live under non-capitalist production relations, i.e. outside the direct control of productive capital. Circulation capital, however, has been penetrating almost everywhere in rural Sudan, as has been shown in the previous chapters. The scope of movement of circulation capital (especially merchant capital) is hence much wider than that of productive capital in Sudan.

TABLE 7,2

Estimates of total area of cultivated land under three different stages of capitalist development in the early 1980s in Sudan

	Stage of Development	Area of Land Cultivated	
1.	Household production (a lower stage of transition)	10,500,000	50.8%
2.	Transitional	4,250,000	20.5%
3.	Capitalist	5,934,000	28.7%
	Total	20,684,000	100.0%

Source: (1) and (2) adapted from World Bank Report, Vol. II (1979).[2]
(3) from Chapter 4 in this book.

Use of Foreign Funds

Paradoxically, while the recession of the Sudanese economy was in evidence – GDP registering a negative real growth between 77/8 and 84/5 (Brown, 1984: 39 and Arab Monetary Fund, 1985: 2) – circulation capital flourished greatly, as large foreign funds had been entering the country since the early 1970s (and especially in the period 1978–82). Sources of these funds were transfers of Sudanese working abroad and loans from different sources received by the Government of Sudan.

Based on a field survey and other sources Galal el Din (1985: 7) estimated the number of Sudanese working abroad in the first half of the 1980s as 250,000. Transfers of Sudanese working abroad, as Table 7,3 shows, is equivalent to almost three times the total earnings of recorded exports. However this source of income goes mainly to expand the consumption and not the production capacity of the country. According to Galal el Din's surveys (Galal el Din, 1986/b), in 1979 32% of the remittances went as investments in agriculture, industry and services (the latter alone was about 23%) and in 1983/84 the recorded percentage was 23 only.

Table 7,4 shows loans taken by the Government of Sudan in different years. The increasing importance of Sudan in the geopolitics of the region since 1971, as it became an opponent of the Ethiopian and Libyan regimes and the only member of the Arab League backing Egypt after Egypt's peace agreement with Israel, has led some Western countries and international organisations, as well as Arab regimes (headed by Saudi Arabia), to pour greater amounts of funds into the country. Up to 1978, two billion US$ in loans were extended to Sudan. By the end of 1984 outstanding debts exceeded seven billion US$. However, with the inability of the regime to service its debts, which are in fact larger than its total export earnings (World Bank, Vol. 1, 1985), the influx of foreign loans since 1982 has started to decrease (Brown, 1984: 38). The negative rate of growth of the GDP between 1977/78 and 1983/84 clearly suggests that those foreign funds have not been directed to expand the production capacity of the country. Foreign loans have been largely spent on militarisation, the regime's internal security, and current budget expenditure, and may well have been subject to misappropriation by the ruling elite and the leading class element in their social base, the merchants. In short, those funds, as is the case with remittances from migrants, have created an unprecedentedly high demand for goods not produced at home, while home production capacity has not been increased. A World Bank Report (1985, Vol. II: 28) states that

> The erroneous Government policies during periods of high capital inflows eventually led to excessive levels of consumption. A recent study indicated that in 1975 a structural shift in the consumption function (a lowering of the marginal propensity to save) occurred. This can be partly explained by the weakening tax effort that should not have accompanied the higher capital inflows. Estimates indicate that every pound of foreign inflows was coupled with tax revenue declines of 0.25 pounds. This coupled with an abnormally high direct effect of capital inflows on consumption resulted in *increase in consumption that surpassed the size of the capital inflows*. Of the six countries researched, Sudan had by far the worst record in implementing policies that should have accompanied aid flows.[3] (my emphasis)

Increase in consumption of different social groups was not equal. Elsewhere, the World Bank Report (1985, Vol. I: 54) goes on to say,

> Although it is not possible to distinguish between the different causes

TABLE 7,3

Sudan's exports and imports (1984) and transfers of Sudanese working abroad (1983/84) (in million US$)

| Total exports | 384 | Transfers (money and kind) | 1,040 |
| Total imports | 701 | % of exports/transfers | 37% |

Source: Bank of Sudan, 1985: 4 and Galal el Din, 1985: 17.

Note: Total exports and imports are according to official records. Actual imports and exports (that is including unofficial) may well exceed the recorded.

of shifts in income, it is apparent that not all economic groups could defend themselves equally well against the combined effects of economic stagnation, inflationary pressures, and price control. The losers were, by and large, *wage earners, farmers in the rainfed sector, industrial producers*, savers and money lenders. The gainers were tenants of irrigated land, traders, holders of real assets and borrowers. The tenants in the irrigated schemes represent a relatively small part of national income. Initially, they improved their financial position, but from 1981 onwards, could only maintain it. There is, however, a widespread opinion that the *traders benefitted most*, in particular those making use of the existing scarcities or those involved in the extensive parallel markets or illicit foreign trade. These broad impressions are confirmed by the mission's estimations of various rates of return in the economy. (my emphasis)

Profitability

The results of a study financed by the UNDP/IBRD Planning Assistance and Training Project (Abdus Sattar, 1982) can be used to compare the profitability of agricultural capital and size of surplus of household production with the profitability of merchant capital in some of the main agricultural crops in the country.

In Table 7,5 'border values'[4] were calculated from trade statistics for 1980/81 – FOB.[5] Sorghum was an exception, as the calculated unit price was found to be lower than the unit price at which export contracts were approved by the government. So, instead, the minimum export price approved by the government was adopted (Abdus Sattar, 1982: 29). The two exchange rates of Sudanese pounds used in Table 7,5 refer to two different bank rates applied in the year 1981. However, the 'free' market (often called black market) exchange rate was lower than the ones used in Table 7,5. One £S is estimated to be equivalent to US$ .95–1.05 in 1981 (see Galal el Din, 1986/a: 38 and 1986/b: 25). In 1981 exporters were allowed to keep 75% of their export earnings in foreign currency to be used in importation of different goods, and the government would exchange the rest in Sudanese pounds. Prices of imported goods would be calculated by private importers according to the 'free' market value of the foreign currency and not according to the central bank's exchange rate. The earnings of exporters (and the government's central bank) should then be viewed according to the 'free' market exchange rate.

Table 7,6 compares the profitability of circulation capital calculated as an average of the bank rates used in Table 7,5 and as an average of the 'free' market exchange rate. We can observe the following from Table 7,6:

- Using the 'free' market exchange rate, profitability of circulation capital is higher than the amount the producers realised as profit/surplus. An exception is groundnuts grown in the 'traditional rainfed' areas (i.e. household production areas).

- Profit realised by circulation capital in both types of cotton is higher even if we use the bank exchange rate.

- There are some reasons to believe that border prices (at least for crops exported by private business) are underestimated in the trade statistics, and hence that the profit margin of exporters is higher than Table 7,6 suggests. Private exporters have reasons to lower their declared selling prices as they can then evade part of the taxes and export duties levied, they can keep the difference between the amount realised and that declared outside the country, and they can also lessen the amount (25%) of this foreign currency to be exchanged at the central bank's declared exchange rate.

As Table 7,6 showed that circulation capital was more privileged than the agricultural producers in the distribution of surplus, Table 7,7 goes to confirm the same between circulation (and investments in other non-productive areas such as residential construction) and industry. Commodity trading comes first on the list with nominal average profits of 50% per annum, followed by residential construction (45–50%) and foreign exchange assets (31%). Foreign exchange speculation is a relatively new area of activity in the Sudanese economy, becoming especially active from 1978 with the series of devaluations of the Sudanese pound and the high inflows of foreign resources.

TABLE 7,4

Outstanding foreign debts of Sudan in selected years (in US$ millions)

End of Year	Outstanding Foreign Debts
1974	602
1978	2000
1983	6351
1984	7174

Source: 1974, 1978: Brown, 1984: 38
1983: World Bank, Vol. I, 1985: 145
1984: Bank of Sudan, cited in Arab Monetary Fund, 1985: 43

TABLE 7.5

Border value and total costs of some of the main crops in 1980/81

Product	Border Value of One Feddan Produce (in $)	Border Value of One Feddan Produce in Sudanese Pounds (1 L.S. = $1.25)	Border Value of One Feddan Produce in Sudanese Pounds (1 L.S. = $1.11)	Total Costs FOB in Sudanese Pounds
Cotton - long staple (Gezira)	279.84	223.87	251.86	230.18
Cotton - medium staple (Gezira)	294.32	235.46	264.89	234.30
Sorghum (Gedaref)	72.02	57.62	64.82	53.64
Sesame (Gedaref)	40.83	33.66	36.75	52.47
Groundnuts (Gezira)	135.45	108.36	121.91	110.43
Groundnuts ("Traditional Rainfed")	73.18	58.54	65.86	42.55

Source: Abdus Sattar, 1982, Tables 4.01 (p. 32), 4.02 (p. 33), 4.06 (p. 37), 4.08 (p. 39), 4.10 (p. 41).

TABLE 7.6

A comparison of profitability/surplus of producers with profitability of circulation capital in some of the main crops in 1980/81

Product	Producers Profitability/ Surplus (in percent)	Profitability of Circulation Capital (1)* (in percent)	Profitability of Circulation Capital (2)* (in percent)
Cotton – long staple (Gezira)	-25	3	22
Cotton – medium staple (Gezira)	-23	7	26
Sorghum (Gedaref)	29	14	34
Sesame (Gedaref)	-28	-33	-22
Groundnuts (Gezira)	8	4	23
Groundnuts ("Traditional Rainfed")	121	46	72

Source: Compiled from Table 7,5, and Abdus Sattar, 1982, Table 1.03 (p. 8).
(1)* Calculated as an average of the two exchange rates used in Table 7,5.
(2)* Calculated as an average of the 'free' market exchange rate in 1981.

TABLE 7.7

Rates of returns to alternative private non-agricultural activities, 1983–84 (average % per annum)

	Nominal	Real
Foreign Exchange Assets		
– Holdings in cash (a) legal	31	6–7
(b) illegal	33–36	8–12
– Holdings in deposits (a) legal	36–40	11–15
(b) illegal	38–45	13–20
Time deposits in domestic currency	13–15	negative
Commodity Trading		
– Intermediate inputs and spare parts	50–100	25–75
– Machinery	40	15
– Estimated average	50	25
Residential Construction	45–50	20–25
Industrial plants	13–15	negative

Source: World Bank Report 1985, Vol. II, Table 14, p. 31 – based on mission estimates.

The nominal return on industrial investment is 13–15% (which makes the real return negative by 10–12%, considering inflation rate of 25% as estimated in the calculations of the cited report). The report explains continuity of operation of some industries as follows: 'many industrialists, particularly those with large fixed investments, are continuing production because of large losses in fixed capital that would be increased if they completely close down' (World Bank Report, 1985, Vol. II: 32).

Dominance Enhanced by the State

The wider material base of merchant capital is also reflected in and enhanced by the political level. Circulation capital in general and more specifically the international export–import fraction of it seems to be the *dominant fraction* in the power bloc. This is best reflected in the economic policies of the state and in other means available to the state apparatus. Before examining these it is important to show that the state as a capitalist entrepreneur is mainly active in circulation – and especially in foreign trade.

The state's overall involvement in direct production in the Sudan is limited. State capital investment in industry is relatively high, but the proportion of the industrial sector's contribution to total GDP is low. In the year 1980, the industrial sector contribution to GDP was 8.02%, while the agricultural sector contributed 34.9% (MFNE Economic Survey, 1980/81: 13).

The state investment in industry is mainly concentrated in the sugar and textile industries. It also invests in the cement, leather, oil and beverage industries. However, with the sharp deterioration of the balance of payments in the country since the late 1970s the industrial sector has been showing stagnation or even decline in absolute terms. The state investment in agricultural production is limited to six farms within the MFS areas and a few others. The state farms within the MFS areas were meant to be experimental farms. However they never seriously fulfilled this role. Attempts to expand them were resisted. Since 1978/79 their size has been showing a continuous decline. Other farms are those associated with the state sugar factories on which sugar cane is grown. As Table 7,8 shows, state capital involved in agricultural production is negligible. The state's role in agriculture, as has been mentioned earlier, is mainly confined to land and machinery hiring and provision of irrigation and credit. In other words, the state assumes the role of land-owner and circulation capital. The state played such a role with regard to about 19% of the cultivated lands in the Sudan. However, the state's role as circulation capital within the agricultural sector is only a small proportion of its activities in the field of circulation.

TABLE 7,8

*Estimates of the contribution of state and non-state
enterprises to total agricultural and industrial production
and to GDP for the year 1980*

	Percentage Contribution in Agricultural Production	Percentage Contribution in Industrial Production	Percentage of the Total Agricultural and Industrial Contribution in the GDP
State Enterprises (farms or factories)	0.9	20–35	1.9–3.1
Non-State Enterprises (private capitalist and household production)	99.1	80–65	41.0–39.8
Total	100	100	42.9

Source: Own estimates based on First National Economic Conference Report on Main Industries in Sudan, 1982; MFC Agricultural Statistics, 1979 and MFNE Economic Survey, 1980/81.

Table 7,9 shows that as far as revenue is concerned the state as a capitalist enterprise in production is much less important than in circulation. State revenues from its involvement in foreign trade and from its financial institutions, as the details in the sources of Table 7,9 show, are greater than revenues from its activities in the Gezira (and other similar schemes) as a circulation capitalist.

Table 7,9 shows further that the role of the state enterprises as a source of revenue has been declining during the selected years. Percentage contribution of the revenues from the state enterprises in its total revenue for four-year intervals is as follows: 1970/1 to 1973/4: 18.9%; 1974/5 to 1977/8: 10.8%; and 1978/9 to 1981/2: 5.8%.

The Privileged Position of Export–Import Merchant Capital: Some Indicators

The fact that the state as a capitalist entrepreneur is mainly active in trade and especially foreign trade and that state resources, as we have seen in terms of use of foreign loans, are not directed essentially to production or associated services, may be indicative of a bias towards trade, and especially foreign trade. However, this may need to be demonstrated even further. It will first be shown why the state moved into foreign trade. Then, two economic policy issues will be picked up briefly: bank credit distribution and price control.

The State and Foreign Trade

Foreign firms backed by finance of foreign banks largely dominated the export–import trade until 1970 (see Shaaeldin, 1981, and T. Ali, 1982). The nationalisation of the banking system, as well as of those foreign firms, in 1970, by Numeiry's regime, was a significant step towards changing control from foreign to national. Although this analysis is restricted to the post-1970 situation, it should be understood that the dominance of the export–import fraction of capital is not recent; what is recent is only that this fraction is now basically national. The nationalisation of the banking system and foreign firms operating in external trade has not only been in the interests of already established national capital. It has also been largely initiated by, and in the interest of, rising aspirations of the high-ranking bureaucracy whose military branch initiated the takeover of power in 1969. This bureaucracy aspired to use the state apparatus in order to join as individuals the ranks of the primitive capital accumulators. In fact, the steps taken in 1970 support this argument. The state, besides nationalising the banks, formed state companies in place of

TABLE 7.9

Role of the state enterprises as sources of revenue from 1970/71 to 1981/82

In ES Millions

Year	(1) Revenue of the State Enterprises in Circulation	(2) Revenue of the State Enterprises in Production	(3) (1 + 2) Revenue from all State Capitalist Enterprises	(4) Total State revenue from all Sources	(5) (3 ÷ 4) Percentage Contribution of State Revenue as Capitalist Enterprise in its Total Revenue
1970/71	37.5	n.a.	37.5	164.5	22.8%
1971/72	26.9	n.a.	26.9	163.7	16.4%
1972/73	38.9	n.a.	28.9	176.2	16.4%
1973/74	35.9	1.7	37.6	209.5	20.0%
1974/75	14.1	0.1	14.2	287.8	4.9%
1975/76	34.5	0.1	34.6	332.0	10.4%
1976/77	58.2	-	58.2	388.4	15.0%
1977/78	59.1	1.0	60.1	465.3	12.9%
1978/79	39.9	2.4	42.3	580.7	7.3%
1979/80	63.2	1.4	64.6	717.1	9.0%
1980/81	n.a. separately		33.7	906.4	3.7%
1981/82	n.a. separately		28.5	873.3	3.3%

Sources: Compiled from 1970/71 to 1979/80 MFNE Economic Survey, 1980/81, Appendix 4/1, p. 211.
1980/81 to 1981/82 Sudan Guide, 1982/83, p. 34.

Notes: Under (1) the following sources have been entered: Gezira Scheme, State Bank's Profits, Commercial Corporations, Sudan Development Corporation (a financial institution).
Under (2) Industrial Corporations and those categorised as Other Corporations have been entered.

TABLE 7,10

Commercial bank advances to private borrowers in some selected years (in £S thousands)

Year	Short-Term Advances					Medium and Long Term Loans	Total Advances
	Exports	Imports	Industrial Enterprises	Other Business Enterprises	Others	Capital Investments and Others	
1975	67,708 (36%)	14,603 (8%)	59,456 (32%)	21,063 (11%)	12,029 (7%)	11,212 (6%)	186,071 (100%)
1978	93,080 (27%)	39,193 (11%)	106,979 (31%)	28,613 (8%)	23,246 (7%)	52,117 (15%)	343,228 (99%)
1981	162,084 (21%)	125,172 (16%)	227,101 (29%)	63,023 (8%)	33,782 (4%)	166,364 (21%)	777,526 (99%)
1982	298,195 (26%)	204,300 (18%)	268,256 (24%)	84,080 (7%)	48,689 (4%)	243,017 (21%)	1,142,527 (100%)

Source: Reports of the Bank of Sudan; 1977, 1978 and 1983 – Vols. 23/4.
Note: Percentages in brackets refer to share in the total advances.

the foreign firms previously working in external trade. This step had two rationales behind it. National capital was not yet fully prepared to take over the place of either foreign banks or, to the full extent, of foreign trading firms. The state bureaucracy, through their position at the apex of the political system, the financial system and foreign trade, could thus secure for themselves as individuals, by different methods of corruption (e.g. commissions, bribery, falsification of books and documents) some of the surplus appropriated by the state banks and firms, and also access to credit. Indeed besides state companies formed, after changing their names, to replace the foreign ones, new specialised state and state–private joint-venture companies were formed, and secured a monopoly of the external trade in certain items. These were the Cotton Marketing Corporation, the Oil Seeds Company, the Sugar Corporation, the Petroleum Public Company, the Gum Arabic Company, the Sudan Coffee Company and the Sudan Tea Company. Foreign trade has thus been divided between the state and the national private sector, in other words, between the state bureaucracy and national private exporters and importers.

Bank Credit Distribution

The privileged position of export–import capital is reflected, among other things, in the distribution of bank advances in Sudan.

Among all other fractions of capital, as Table 7,10 shows, export–import capital has been privileged regarding its share in the banks' advances. In 1975, 1978, 1981 and 1982, its share was 44%, 38%, 37%, and 44% of the total advances. Exports' share is larger than imports' because in the latter private capital is much more active and depends largely on finance from export earnings (i.e. the advance transaction for both exports and imports in this case appears on the exports side as it would be the first reason for getting the credit) and also on finance by migrant Sudanese.[6] (Also, a considerable proportion of imports come through non-legal channels i.e. smuggling.)

Apart from industrial capital, which is to be dealt with in a moment, all other fractions of capital, including finance capital and other types of advances such as personal loans, were offered between 24% and 32% of the total advances. Agriculture, which contributes more than any other sector in Sudan's GDP, was offered less than 1% of the total advances in the years 1980, 1981 and 1982 (its share was 0.6%, 0.2% and 0.3% respectively) and it appears on our table among the 'Others' advances. The Sudan Agricultural Bank (SAB), which was founded to finance agriculture, in 1975 and 1980 extended credit worth £S4.4 and £S4.8 million (Statistical Abstract, 1981: 188), which compared to other banks' advances is negligible.

Bank advances to industrial enterprises on any scale are a recent

159

phenomenon which first appeared in the 1970s. It should not be deduced from the share given to industrial enterprises, ranging from 32% to 31% to 29% to 24% in the years 1975, 1978, 1981 and 1982 respectively, that banks contribute effectively to industrial expansion. In fact, the real nature of those advances is commercial rather than productive. They are short-term loans, that is for less than one year, and in fact may extend only for a few weeks or months. They finance operational needs, e.g. wages and raw materials, and are not intended to increase the productive capacity of industry. No medium- or long-term advances are being extended, either to industry or to agriculture (if we disregard the tiny amount of funds lent by the SAB and that by the Industrial Bank when it existed). In fact, advances to industrial enterprises represent a wholesale deal by the commercial banks (finance capital) on behalf of merchant capital. With the shortages in foreign currency, import-substitute industries in Sudan were granted some protection (i.e. the restriction of imports of certain items) and a higher share in the banks' short-term advances, with the condition that a factory-gate price control system was to be applied. The ILO Report (1976: 452) came to the conclusion, with regard to this price control system, that 'whereas ex-factory price control is relatively easy to apply, the control weakens at subsequent stages of distribution, permitting traders to appropriate much of the margin between the ex-factory, controlled price and the market clearing retail price'.

Table 7,11 shows clearly that control of the ex-factory price in the last five listed commodities (from 6 to 10) has been to the benefit of merchant capital, as no control is applied at the retail level. The same situation exists for other non-industrial products (from 1 to 5 in Table 7,11) where control apparently is only meant to be effective on the producers. On this issue the ILO Report (*Ibid*: 453) commented that 'opportunities to make easy profits in the commerce sector have drawn in resources (especially entrepreneurial talent) from the production sectors, and slowed the development of the latter'.

Price Control

Tightening control over the markets and ensuring that rival capital is not able to penetrate the citadel is the way in which some fractions of capital (or groups within it) may be able to appropriate a larger share in the surplus thus establishing domination. Domination which leads to a monopolistic or semi-monopolistic position may be created through economic means, through the concentration and centralisation of capital, and forcing rival capitalists out of the specific sphere of activity. However, it can also be created through political means, by enforcing a monopolistic position by legislation, by other, mainly corrupt, methods of securing the

TABLE 7,11

Controlled and actual retail prices for selected commodities
(February 1975) (in £S)

	Commodity	Unit	Controlled Price	Actual Price	Excess of Actual over Controlled
1	Fish	kilo	0.24-0.36	0.80 & above	233.3%-122.2% & above
2	Mutton	kilo	0.38	0.70	84.2%
3	Veal	kilo	0.30	0.50	66.7%
4	Beef	kilo	0.27	0.45	66.6%
5	Sorghum	ruba	0.21	0.41	95.2%
6	Butter oil	kilo	0.40	0.66	65.0%
7	Cheese	kilo	0.70	0.80	14.3%
8	Cotton seed oil	lb	0.09	0.12	33.3%
9	Cement	ton	19-22	50 & above	163.2%-127.3% & above
10	Air cooler	unit	108.8	164	51.0%

Source: ILO, 1976:452.

backing of the authorities or by political manipulation. All these methods are operative in the Sudan.

As we have seen, the state has secured for its capital, through legislation, a monopoly over the trade of some commodities. The same has been granted for the Military Economic Board.[7] Private export–import capital is securing a semi-monopolistic position by collaboration with the state bureaucracy (with whom they share the surplus) through a system of export and import licensing. To engage in export or import of any commodity, a capitalist enterprise needs to get a licence from the Ministry of Commerce. Issuing a licence is subject to some regulations. Among those, the financial ability of the applicant as well as a record of trading in the same commodity seems to be of primary importance (for detailed treatment of criteria of allocation of different types of licences see Rabih, 1979). From the beginning, many potential rivals are then kept away from competition. The citadel is strengthened by the influence of the bureaucrats, who make the final decisions as to the number and nature of the available quota of licences. It is this mixture of legislation and corruption which keeps the export–import trade in relatively few hands. This yields a monopolistic position, and hence the ability to appropriate a larger profit rate than the prevailing one. Shaaeldin (1981: 105) cites a case of seven leading export merchants dominating the livestock market. Five exporters exported 70% of the live animals, while two others monopolised the export of 90% of the frozen meat.

III. CIRCULATION CAPITAL AND SURPLUS DISTRIBUTION AND USE IN GEDAREF

The Crop Trade in Gedaref

This case study is not in a position to use any quantitative measures to compare differences in rates of profits of agricultural and circulation capital, and the different segments inside the latter and the proportion of surplus that is ploughed back into production. However, it endeavours to show some general tendencies and to contribute to understanding of the mechanisms involved.

The development of MFS in Gedaref has resulted in the production and circulation of an unprecedentedly large amount of crops in the region, which has made it the leading production and commercial centre of *dura* in the Sudan. In the first three years of mechanised farming the total cultivated land expanded from 214,000 to 403,000 to 886,000 feddans, resulting in more or less similar proportionate increases in marketable output. Local merchant capital, with relatively small accumulated money capital, was not prepared to match this relatively large expansion of marketable output. Larger merchant capital from outside the region came in, and was able to control the market for a number of years.

Basic information below on the history of the crop trade and involvement of Farmers' Associations has been provided by Ahmed Elfadil, who has been in the leadership of the Farmers' Association since the establishment of the first such Association in Gedaref in 1962.

Two large merchants dominated the crop market up to the mid-1960s. Apparently these two merchants had won the backing of the government in those days and were offered tenders to supply *dura* to other areas in the Sudan. Local merchants and farmers had a common interest in breaking this monopoly. Farmers, mainly large ones, began to organise themselves in groupings until they formed the first Farmers' Association, the North West Gedaref Farmers' Association (NWGFA), in 1962. Its leadership was dominated mainly by farmers (a number of whom were merchants too) who had connections with the then illegal three main political parties – Umma, the Nationalist Unionist Party and the People's Democratic Party. One of the main objectives of the NWGFA was to form a marketing organ run by itself, which could market for its members should they wish it. It was a clear step to break the authority-backed two merchants' control over the market. In 1964 this became easy, with the change in the political leadership of the country by the overthrow of the First Military regime (1958–64) and the taking of power by the political parties to which most of the members of the Farmers' Association's leadership belonged. In fact, the first president of the NWGFA became a minister. In 1966, government tenders to supply *dura* were offered to the Association. For example, it supplied the Gezira with 51,000 tons of *dura*, which was about 14% of the total product in that year. Personal communication from Ahmed Elfadil, the then president of NWGFA). The backing of the state secured the break up of control of the market by the 'two' merchants and at the same time paved the way for the emergence and growth of some other local ones. Standing on its feet a few years later, the local merchant capital changed tactics and decided to end its alliance with the farmers by ending the marketing role of the Association. It succeeded. At present in none of the constitutions of the Farmers' Associations is there any clause that refers to such a role.

The origins of the crop trade capital circulating in Gedaref can be traced in the following: (a) agricultural capital – farmers accumulating money in agriculture and transferring part of it to circulation; (b) 'general' merchant capital in Gedaref – consumer goods merchants, animal and crop merchants who were in existence before the expansion of MFS; (c) bank capital – mainly coming from outside the region; and (d) merchant capital coming from outside the region, mainly from Khartoum and Port Sudan.

A considerable proportion of crop merchants in Gedaref have accumulated their original capital from within the region itself, rather than having come to the region as already relatively established merchants. A few non-Gedaref-based crop merchants began to appear in the 1980s, after the large increase in *dura* exports and the high profit rates attainable in it. *Dura* exports as a percentage of the total exports of Sudan increased from 1.7% in 1978/79 to 11.8% in 1979/80 to 14.7% in 1980/81 and to 16.5% in 1981/82 (Bank of Sudan, 23/29, 1983: 29).

Crop merchants in Gedaref may be divided into three groups according to the size and profile of their merchant activities and sources of finance.

Large merchants monopolise the trade in crops directed to outside the region, which, in recent years, went mainly for export through export companies. According to the estimate of my informants (including members of this group of merchants) there were between ten and twelve large merchants in 1982/83 handling 80–90% of the crops leaving the region. Most of the marketed crops produced do go outside the region, as most of the region's inhabitants are dependent on agriculture, and consequently the internal demand for agricultural products is small.

Abdel Aziz (1979: 305), who conducted a survey 5–6 years earlier than the present research, established that 'there are only five big wholesalers of *dura* in Gedaref region'. The difference in the two estimates may be due to differences in sources used for the estimation, or in definition of 'large merchant', or they may indicate a change in the composition of the top crop merchants in the region.

Large crop merchants have permanent agents buying for them directly from Gedaref and other crop markets or from other smaller crop merchants and brokers. They may also buy from large farmers in bulk in which case, as in other bulk purchases, large crop merchants may be involved personally. They also personally organise the sale of their crops mainly to export companies and also sometimes to each other. They may also sell small quantities in the local market, not necessarily for other large merchants, through brokers mainly for market 'manoeuvring' purposes or in anticipation of a sudden change in the market.

A considerable proportion of the working capital in the hands of large merchants comes from the commercial banks, which are well represented in Gedaref town. Some bank managers interviewed said that the quantity of money capital available to this group of merchants from their own sources is more than the proportion provided by bank capital. Three large merchants interviewed, however, claimed the opposite. Many of the members of the group of large merchants, probably with the exception of those who have come from outside the region, are either engaged now or were engaged in the past in agricultural production.

Medium-sized merchants largely depend on their own money sources as they may get only a little finance from commercial banks. They market their commodities mainly in Gedaref, where they sell for the most part to larger merchants. Sometimes some of them act as agents for merchants based outside Gedaref. Most of them, apparently, engage in production, as large farmers, and/or may have other businesses, trading in consumer goods or services, or hotels and restaurants. Several of them also finance small farmers and *bildat* cultivators through crop mortgage (*shail*). *Shail* finance, due to its extremely high profits, seems to be a source of the original merchant capital of many merchants, including the present large ones. Some of the medium-sized merchants originally accumulated their money capital by playing a broker role. Brokers have an important role in the commercial business of Gedaref. Trade 'contacts' are often made through them. The sale and purchase of a significant proportion of the *dura* crop and of sesame – as most of the crop is sold for the first time in the crop market by auction – is facilitated by brokers. The sale and purchase of secondhand machinery and vehicles and of properties, land and machine leases are also within the circle of their activities. Actually, brokers are the only third-party means of communication between the large numbers of buyers and sellers in Gedaref, where no local press, radio, or other mass media or specialised agencies are available. In their dealings, especially in crop purchase, medium-sized merchants may cut out the brokerage commission by involving themselves directly. Medium-sized merchants are not necessarily based in Gedaref town. Some of them buy outside Gedaref town directly from producers or small merchants.

Small merchants are scattered all over the region, where they mostly buy from small farmers and *bildat* cultivators whose produce is insufficient to warrant hiring transport to take it into Gedaref town. Also some of them get a significant quantity of their crops through *shail* trade. Some of the brokers in Gedaref town are also small merchants, buying small quantities at a time (probably a few sacks) when the price is relatively low (e.g. when small farmers are anxious to sell quickly in order to pay off transport costs and labourers' wages). Small merchants usually have other jobs as well, either cultivating their own holdings or working as *wakeels*, or engaging in retail trade or in provision of services. They exclusively sell in the local markets, mostly working for other merchants. They do not normally receive any finance from banks.

Farmers, the other party in the crop markets, differ in their selling strategies, mostly according to their size and financial position. During the harvest season crop prices normally go down, because of the law of supply and demand, probably reinforced by the collusion of large merchants. Relatively well-off farmers may not sell all of their crops immediately after harvest, aiming to attain a higher price later. They use rented stores, which are owned by individuals and banks, and/or they may also use customary storage methods, digging large holes and preparing them in a special way to keep the grain undamaged. (These types of stores are known locally as *matamir*.) Other farmers may store part of their crops only as a form of accumulated wealth. When the need arises for cash either before or during the following cultivation season, they sell their stored crops. For this group of farmers, timing is probably more important than price changes in their decision to sell. However, even among the other group of farmers who withhold part of their crops for opportunities of better prices, the majority would need to sell all or a major part of their crops before the beginning of the following agricultural season to meet the expenses of preparation for the season, such as the maintenance of machinery, and the purchase of stocks of petrol and foodstuffs for the workers.

The majority of the small farmers and *bildat* cultivators, however, sell all or the larger part of their crops immediately after harvest to pay off their debts to financiers, and the wages of harvest labour. Some of the farmers sell all or part of their crops on site; this is probably more frequent among small producers who may not have the cash for transporting their crops. Crops bought by small or medium-sized merchants will most probably be taken for reselling in the Gedaref crop markets, unless the merchants are trying to evade payment of tax. Frequently, however, this is the intention. Tax regulations state that it is the duty of the buyer to pay all taxes either in the crop market or before handling it in any other way, such as transporting it outside the region, or processing it. The margin that is saved by tax evasion is not insignificant, as will be shown below. Some merchants (or owners of oil mills in the case of sesame crop) may attempt to evade tax payments by buying on site and transporting away the crops, avoiding tax collectors, and if necessary bribing them. Sometimes both local taxes and export duties, if not just the latter, are evaded by smuggling crops through the border to Ethiopia. However, due to war conditions this has become of diminishing importance. The smuggling trade is especially active during periods when the export of *dura* is banned; such measures are introduced by the government from time to time. Abdel Aziz (1979: 312) mentions that the reason for the smuggling trade is that *dura* and sesame prices are higher on the Ethiopian side of the border than on the Sudanese side.

Surplus Distribution and Use

The Dominant Position of Large Merchant Capital in the Crop Trade in Gedaref

In Gedaref it seems that the degree of concentration and centralisation of merchant capital is at present higher than that of agricultural capital. As has been mentioned earlier, the top ten to twelve crop merchants in Gedaref in 1983 almost monopolised the exporting of crops outside the region though not internationally, and indeed the bulk of Gedaref production is actually oriented to markets outside the region. On the other hand, the top agricultural capitalists in the region, each cultivating over 10,000 feddans, number about 28, cultivating about 19% of the land in Gedaref in 1982/83. The concentration and centralisation of merchant capital has been largely enhanced by financial capital coming from outside the region. Large merchants in particular are able to command enormous amounts of financial capital from different sources at any one time – from different commercial banks, of which there were seven in 1983 and from export firms for which some of them act as agents in specific transactions. In this way a kind of centralisation is being formed, though not a 'permanent' one, as it may last only for a specific period which may or may not be renewable. From their position at the summit of the commercial hierarchy in Gedaref, as will be shown below, they are able to attain an above average rate of profit. Therefore they are able to accumulate (concentrate) their capital comparatively faster, provided profits are not directed for investment elsewhere, and there are reasons to believe that they are not, as will be discussed below.

Apparently large crop merchants in Gedaref exercise great control over the markets in Gedaref. There are indications that a certain form of collusion takes place among the larger crop merchants of Gedaref. Abdel Aziz (1979: 308) observed that 'a few large Gedaref merchants dominate the internal *dura* trade and have an incentive to increase profits by collusion as they are all well known to one another socially and in some cases related'. Many farmers and other people interviewed, including some merchants, have asserted that at certain times during harvest, when most of the farmers sell their crops, large crop merchants may co-ordinate their purchasing strategy with the aim of pushing down prices. Interestingly enough, one of the large crop merchants interviewed by the author did not deny such collusion. However, he claimed that he did not think that this was particularly influential in price determination. Collusion among large merchants may take different forms. According to my informants, large crop merchants sometimes fix a maximum price for crops in the Gedaref crop market which is not exceeded by any of them. Sometimes they distribute the entire market among themselves by allocating a certain day to each (or a few) individuals. Accordingly, one may not be outbidden by the others on that particular day. It has also been mentioned that sometimes when they want to drive away a particular large competitor (usually a 'new' large merchant coming in from outside) they raise the price of the crops deliberately for a time. Thus, thinking that crop prices are rising the new competitor may hastily buy large quantities. Shortly afterwards, of course, prices go down again.

In accordance with this collusion, large crop merchants in Gedaref buy crops below their value by even more than the margin which would allow merchant capital generally to attain the average rate of profit prevailing in the region. Large merchants also enjoy economies of scale, which means they are in a better position in the prediction of market formation and the ability to afford more risk-taking.

Merchant Capital: Use of Surplus Appropriated

The question that may next be raised is whether the surplus appropriated by merchant capital (or at least part of it) is thrown back into production or is all kept locked in circulation. Again, different segments of merchant capital apparently act differently.

Surplus appropriated by merchant capital engaged in export of crops may not find its way back to Gedaref. Whether part of the surplus appropriated by export companies is thrown back into production elsewhere is of less concern to us here. Some export companies may finance some of the large crop merchants who have regular dealings with it, but in this case, of course, capital only changes hands temporarily, and within the circulation sphere.

Large merchants apparently retain most of their profits in circulation. The following reasons may underlie this tendency. (1) Large merchants need to maintain their position on the top of the hierarchy of merchant capital in Gedaref. (2) They need to lessen their dependence on bank credit as the interest rate has become relatively high, as we shall see below. (3) They need large financial resources available to be able to face the new competition from merchant capital coming from elsewhere in the country, and to be able to face the new challenge offered by export companies which have been trying to bring to an end their mediatory role (personal communication – the Secretary of the Chamber of Commerce in Gedaref).

All the three large crop traders, who are at the same time 'super-large' farmers, who have been interviewed have stated clearly that crop trade is affording them relatively higher profits than agriculture. The fact that they have grown as farmers and that their agricultural activities do not hamper their merchant activities, in both time and resources, makes them continue to reinvest in agriculture. Most of the large crop merchants also invest in urban estate and in transport (fleets of trucks and lorries). Both types of investment attract revenue as well as act as a guarantee for their credit demands from banks. Investment in transport is also useful in making them self-sufficient in the transport of their own commodities, especially during the peak harvest season when it is either difficult or more expensive to get transport.

As has been mentioned earlier, apparently a significant number of both medium-sized and small crop merchants engage in agricultural production as well, though it is not possible to determine how significant that is. It has also been mentioned that there are no reasons to believe that these two categories of crop merchants may be able to realise profit rates above the average in Gedaref. If this is the case it seems logical to think that since investments in agriculture generally bring a more or less similar rate of profit, there will always be incentive to plough back part of it into the surplus attained in circulation. This is especially the case because for investment in agriculture in Gedaref there has been a wider scope than for investment in circulation. Competition in circulation seems to be much stiffer than in agriculture. Moreover, the proportion of the merchants' capital that is freed from circulation by the beginning of the following agricultural season is higher in the case of medium and small merchants' capital than in the cases of large ones. Merchants in their different categories buy most of their stocks during the harvest season (which starts in November with sesame and extends from December to March with *dura*). Merchants store their crops and sell them gradually according to the market formation (demand and price). There are two types of storage places: open air stores, which are the most common types, and sealed stores which are more expensive. Most of the medium and small merchants mainly have access to the first type only, which are usable up to the beginning of the rainy season only, which may start in May. Before this time all open-air stores have to be emptied, and therefore in the case of most of the medium and small merchants, the larger part of their capital is freed from its crop-commodity form and may then be available for investment elsewhere.

Financial Capital: Share in the Surplus

Financial capital is also appropriating part of the surplus in the form of interest received over loans extended. Two main financial institutions exist in Gedaref: banks and *shail* financiers.

The Agricultural Bank of the Sudan (ABS) and the commercial banks extend credit for different purposes. The ABS extends credit mainly for large farmers who cultivate in the demarcated areas, and who it considers creditworthy. Two different types of loans are given: medium-term loans are meant to finance the purchase of agricultural machinery, short-term loans to finance part of the seasonal running costs. The average interest rate charged was 14% in 1982/83. Funds available to the ABS through the government are not regular, especially for medium-term loans. Funds available depend largely on the availability of foreign sources (grants from abroad) rather than being an integral part of the bank's budget. Its contribution in the credit business is relatively small, ranging from a minimum of £S88,110 to a maximum of £S2,058,312 between the years 1969/70 and 1979/80 (ABS – Gedaref Office), but it is the only bank that directly finances agricultural production.

Commercial banks, as has been mentioned earlier, contribute significantly to the financing of crop trade in Gedaref. They mainly finance large merchants associated with export, that is, who have dealings with export companies. Large crop merchants by banks' standards are creditworthy and the type of trade in which they are engaged is known to the banks to be of very little risk and of a high rate of profit. It is not a declared policy, from the side of the banks, not to finance other creditworthy groups of merchants, but that has developed as a practice. Moreover, probably only merchants making the highest profits can afford to pay an interest rate of up to 21.5%, the rate in 1982/83.

One bank that operates differently in form but not in direction of business from the other commercial banks is the Faysal Islamic Bank's branch in Gedaref. In order to avoid directly charging a fixed rate of interest, which Islam prohibits, it enters into partnership arrangements with merchant capital. The Bank pays up to a maximum of 80% of the deal and leaves the management of it to the merchant who is to consult the Bank in the marketing affairs. From the profits attained, normally 30–35% goes to the merchant as management fees and the rest is divided between the two partners according to the proportion of contributed capital. The Faysal Islamic Bank finances exclusively large crop merchants who supply export companies. The Bank may also finance farmers for machinery purchase on a very limited scale. Unable to go round a fixed rate of interest this time the Bank fixes a rate of interest (under a different name; 'service charge') of 8% if loans are to be repaid in one year. It charges 15% to 19% of the original amount once only if the loan is to be repaid in instalments of 2 or 3 years respectively. The Faysal Islamic Bank is exempted from taxes by the government. For other commercial banks tax amounted to 60% in 1982/83. Although claiming to charge a lower rate of interest, the Faysal Islamic Bank achieves a higher net profit than other commercial banks. Apparently this Bank has been expanding its activities quite considerably during its few years of operation in Gedaref. The total amount of credit given to merchants in Gedaref by banks is considered as 'confidential'. Nevertheless, some of my informants have asserted that in 1982 and 1983 the Faysal Islamic Bank extended more credit than any other commercial bank in Gedaref. (This has also been asserted by a regional governor in his report to the President of the Republic – see *ALAYAM*, 5 December 1984.)

Shail finance (crop mortgage) is the main credit source for small farmers and *bildat* cultivators, as well as for some large farmers who lack the banks' defined 'creditworthiness'. There is no fixed rate of interest on *shail* transactions. This depends on individual cases, but the rate normally rises the earlier the credit is demanded and the more needy the borrower is. *Shail* financiers ask for much higher interest rates than do banks. Large farmers who have reported entering into *shail* arrangements during the last two years said they paid up to 50% interest for credits extending over a period of 2–5 months, while small farmers and *bildat* cultivators have reported paying interest ranging from 50% to as high as 300% for the same period.

The State's Share in the Surplus

The government also appropriates a considerable part of the surplus in the form of indirect production taxes, which are to be paid by purchasers, and which are paid on a fixed rate per weight unit of crops. On average for the two seasons 1981/82 and 1982/83, these taxes (locally called *ushur* and *gibana*) amounted to 12–16% for *dura* and 13–14% for sesame based on the Gedaref Crop Market's prices. Taxes collected in 1981/82 were estimated by crop market officials to be about £S38 million. (This amounted to 10.7% of the total indirect taxes and 4.4% of the total central government revenue in Sudan in that year – see Sudan Guide, 1982/83: 34.) The government also receives export tax, annual land fees and machinery and vehicle tax. Services provided by the government seem to be minimal. Most of the farmers and merchants interviewed have asserted that what they get back in the form of services may be only a small proportion of what they pay.

IV. DOMINANCE OF CIRCULATION CAPITAL: THE CRISIS AND THE CHALLENGE

Some Indicators of the Economic Crisis

Sudan's economy, as described by experts in many international journals, and of course by Sudanese people themselves, has been entering a crisis, which started in the early 1970s and has deepened since the late 1970s. GDP in real terms has been showing stagnation and even a negative rate of growth. Industry in the early 1980s was utilising only 15–25% of its capacity (Sudanese Industries Union, 1982: 3). The contribution of agriculture and industry to the GDP from 1973/74 to 1980/81 showed a downward trend (MFNE, Economic Survey, 1980/81: 3). The declining value of the Sudanese pound, the rate of inflation and the external public debts reached an unprecedented level, making Sudan one of the worst economies in the world.

Tables 7,12 and 7,13 clearly manifest the economic crisis. The deterioration of the economy is reflected in the per capita GDP. Using the GDP deflator and the CPI, different but largely consistent trends emerge. In the 1960s per capita GDP was higher than in the first half of the 1970s. The rise in the per capita GDP from 1973 was halved in 1978, when an almost continuous decline began. According to the CPI-deflated per capita GDP, in the 1980s the Sudanese were on average poorer than they had ever been in the previous twenty years, with the exception of 1973.

Averages (like the per capita GDP) conceal the real differences among the different groups or subgroups they represent. In Section II above it was stated that among those who suffer the most as a result of the deteriorating performance of the economy are the wage-earners. This is clearly manifested in Table 7,13. The standard of living of wage-earners, as represented in Table 7,13, has been on the decline since 1970 (and since 1961 for the upper category: grade (4)) regardless of the three pay adjustments (in July 1974, July 1978 and December 1983). The 'best' group among those selected in December 1983 enjoyed only 26% of the real basic salary of 1970. In five and a half years (from July 1978 to December 1983) the selected groups lost 62–67% of their real basic salary. In short, the real income of wage-earners is far worse than the average represented in Table 7,12.

Taking the US dollar as a measure, the Sudanese pound in December 1984 equalled only 9.4% of its value in June 1978 (Table 7,14). The compound annual rate of increase of the US dollar compared to the Sudanese pound was 44%. The Consumer Price Index in Table 7,13 shows that inflation has been consistent and more or less identical to the deterioration of the value of the Sudanese pound from 1978 to 1983.

The inflow of large quantities of foreign funds not directed to increasing

TABLE 7,12
Sudan's per capita GDP, 1960–1983
(Index: 1970 = 100)

Year (at June)	Per capita GDP (using the SDP deflator)	Per capita GDP (deflated by the CPI)*
1960	110.8	–
1965	109.0	106.0
1970	100.0	100.0
1971	102.8	106.7
1972	97.9	109.4
1973	87.8	93.2
1974	93.6	101.7
1975	102.8	99.7
1976	118.0	114.9
1977	139.1	125.0
1978	142.2	121.4
1979	124.2	104.0
1980	121.1	99.8
1981	121.3	98.0
1982	123.2	97.8
1983	118.3	94.1

Source: World Bank (1985), Vol. III, Appendix, Table A.1.1, pp. 11–12
* CPI = Consumer Price Index.

the productive capacity of the country (Section II above) is one of the major reasons behind the deteriorating performance of the economy and the high rate of inflation. Deterioration in the terms of trade, especially the rise in the price of petroleum products, affected the balance of payments negatively and also enhanced inflation. However, the outflow of money capital has also created a continuous high demand for foreign currencies, and hence also increased the inflationary tendency.[8] This will be discussed in more detail.

There has been an outflow of Sudanese private capital from Sudan for a long time. This process intensified from the 1970s and was especially remarkable from the early 1980s. It is very difficult to document this trend in quantitative terms since the outflow takes illegal channels. A. Ali (1986: App. 3) estimates this illegal outflow of capital as equivalent to 90% of migrants' transfers. Certainly among the circles of Sudanese businesspersons and Sudanese bureaucrats, stories of Sudanese owning millions abroad are quite common. However, there are more objective reasons to believe that funds held abroad are substantial.

TABLE 7,13

Indices of real basic salaries for selected salary grades of Civil Servants, June 1961 – December 1983

Grade	June 1961	June 1965	June 1970	June 1974	July* 1974	June 1978	July* 1978	November 1983	December* 1983
Deputy Undersecretary (4)	114	108	100	65	78	46	50	18	19
University Graduate (9)	103	98	100	65	67	39	55	16	18
Secondary School Graduate (14)	99	96	100	65	71	42	60	18	20
Unskilled Worker (18)	-	-	100	65	78	46	71	21	26
Consumer Price Index	72	76	100	155	157	266	290	967	1005

* Salary adjustment.

Source: World Bank (1985), Vol. III, Table 1.1, p. 3.

Note: Special allowances are not included in the pay. The World Bank Report (*Ibid:* 9) says the results are qualitatively unaffected when allowances are included.

TABLE 7,14
Change in value of Sudanese Pound (free market rate)

	1 US$ in £S		Annual Compound Increase of US$
June 1978	0.5	June 1978–June 1983	31%
June 1983	1.95	June 1983–Dec. 1984	95%
Dec. 1984	5.3	June 1978–Dec. 1984	44%

Source: Own Estimates[9]

1. Numeiry's regime since its establishment was never in any large degree a stable one. Merchants and bureaucrats especially enriched during that period would definitely make contingency plans for a change in the regime and hence would try to keep their wealth outside the country.

2. After years of inflow of foreign funds largely remaining in circulation, and the stagnation and even reduction in the GDP and foreign loan inflow, funds accumulated in circulation must sooner or later grow beyond the need of the internal circulation. Investment in production being undesirable, those funds would seek refuge elsewhere.

3. In connection with, and as a reflection of, the crisis, Numeiry's imposition of the Islamic *Sharia* law in the second half of 1983 aggravated the general state of disruption and instability. It appears that it led to an increase in the outflow of Sudanese money capital. Table 7,14 shows that between June 1983 (three months before *Sharia* law) and December 1984, the annual compound rate of increase in the U.S. dollar compared to the Sudanese pound reached 95%, while from June 1978 to June 1983 the comparable percentage was 31. This high demand for foreign exchange has been caused neither by a proportionately higher demand for imported goods nor by any equivalent rise in the price of such goods. It was the Sudanese money capital seeking refuge abroad which largely created this high demand for foreign exchange, resulting in pushing up its value to such an extent.

What we can learn from this experience is that it is not only foreign capital that may tend to transfer its profits outside the country – in fact, foreign capital in Sudan represents only a tiny proportion of the total. National capital also seeks outside refuge at times of crisis, such as a falling rate of profit, anticipation of that fall, or fear of some political changes.

Dominance of Merchant Capital: Is It Challenged?

The surplus appropriated by circulation capital and by the state from agriculture, it has been suggested, is largely locked up in circulation, or is even transferred abroad. Even in the areas where the production process is capitalist, e.g. in Gedaref, it has been claimed that export–import and large merchant capital have an upper hand in the appropriation of surplus value, and are on the whole not investing back their profits in agriculture. Surplus appropriated from agriculture is only marginally invested in production elsewhere. Industry, as has been mentioned, contributes only about 8% of GDP. It has been estimated that in the total investments in industry in the early 1980s, the combined share of Sudanese state and foreign capital (which is largely Arab state capital) amounted to between 55% and 75%, leaving only 25% to 45% to indigenous private capital. Clearly, Sudanese indigenous private capital is not showing great interest in investment in industry.

The position of Sudanese private circulation capital, large merchant capital in particular, has been greatly enhanced by the large influx of foreign funds (loans, grants and remittances from Sudanese working abroad) from the early 1970s, and by the nationalisation of foreign banks and foreign export–import firms in 1970. It can be suggested that the political influence of merchant capital, which has apparently always been effective, has also increased with the enlargement of the material base of merchant capital. This statement can be justified by the fact that the state, through its economic policies, as we have seen, e.g. the export–import system, the licensing system, price policy, and state bank advances, has apparently not challenged the dominance of merchant capital – in fact, it has been enhancing this dominance.

However, let us examine briefly to what extent productive capital has become aware of its conflict of interests with merchant capital in a specific area, Gedaref. The outcome, in a specific area, of confrontation between two fractions of capital, e.g. productive and merchant – a confrontation naturally limited in extent by the 'banding together' of capital in its struggle with the opposing classes – is influenced by the following factors: (1) the degree of concentration and centralisation of each of the two fractions of capital and hence their ability to pose an economic threat to opponents; (2) the degree of organisation and self-consciousness of each of the two fractions of capital at the local level; (3) the position of the two fractions of capital in relation to political power at the national level, and thus the role played by political and bureaucratic authorities both at the national and local level. This last point has been discussed above; large merchant capital is in a favourable position regarding access to the political and bureaucratic powers. The first two factors will be discussed briefly.

As has been mentioned in Chapter 7, the concentration and centralisation of capital in circulation generally, and in trade especially, has been growing faster than that in agriculture in Gedaref. Ten to twelve large merchants control about 80–90% of the crop trade with areas outside Gedaref, though not with foreign markets. The position of large merchants has been greatly enhanced by the support of bank finance and by the export–import companies for which Gedaref's large local merchant capital serves as an agent. The 'super-large' farmers (a term used to denote farmers cultivating 10,000 feddans or more), who could be more effective than other farmers in challenging merchant capital, are apparently not doing so. First, a number of the 'super-large' farmers are also merchants themselves. Second, 'super-large' farmers are less subject to the control of large merchants, as they may not need to sell their crops immediately after harvest, when prices are normally at their lowest. Being under less financial constraint than other farmers, they are in a position to store a large part of their produce until the market price goes up.

Both farmers and merchants have their own organisations. Interviews undertaken in Gedaref in 1983 indicated that there seem to be no confrontations between the Farmers' Associations and the Chamber of Commerce. However, there seemed to be discontent among some of the farmers interviewed with the role of crop merchants. Some asserted that merchants appropriated the larger portion of profit for less effort. Some others did not see any serious conflicts between themselves and merchants, and some even attributed a positive role to the latter – for example they mentioned the opening up of trade with Saudi Arabia, which, during the late 1970s to early 1980s, created a large rise in demand. Other farmers expressed the view that it was the will of God that dictated the market, and they accepted that with no complaint.

What we can conclude from the Gedaref case is that there was a limited consciousness among some farmers about the conflict of their interest with that of the merchants, but that the situation up to the early 1980s had not yet developed into open confrontation.

The major conflict that appears on the political surface is between different subfractions of circulation capital, such as Islamic banks and their associated merchant groups, and non-Islamic banks. This type of conflict is on the level of surplus distribution within the sphere of circulation. It is not the type of conflict that is likely to result in a major change in capital form and structure (i.e. between circulation and production) or the development of the forces of production.

A Concluding Note

It is merchant capital which is the immediate enemy of development in Sudan; it is not foreign capital or international organisations such as the IMF and World Bank, as is continually being claimed by many political circles (generally left), academics and others. It is my contention here that the strategy of mobilising the masses through slogans directed against foreign capital, or the IMF or World Bank, is not appropriate. First, the quantity of foreign as compared to national capital is tiny. Second, in the post-colonial period foreign capital is not imposing its existence through outside forces. Its influence is only mediated through its alliance with internal dominant classes and is therefore part of the internal class struggle. The immediate enemies are to be considered as those social internal classes whose own development is inversely related to the development of society as a whole in the specific period. In the present period the development of merchant capital, and especially of large and export–import subfractions of it, appears to be impeding the development of the forces of production in Sudan.

There is no one specific recipe by which the dominance of merchant capital can be ended. Class struggle is too variable and many-sided for all its different specific issues to be dealt with in any single work. However, a central factor in the termination of the dominance of merchant capital is democracy.

NOTES

CHAPTER TWO

1. Total land cultivated in Sudan in the late 1970s was estimated to be 18 million feddans (AOAD, 1978: 27). Total land irrigated and total land under pumps were estimated to be 4,165,000 and 1,423,000 feddans respectively during the same period (World Bank Report, Vol. II, 1979: 3). Proportion of cropping intensity, which has been taken as an indicator of difference in productivity of different lands, between irrigated land and rainlands was estimated to be 73:40 (AOAD, 1978: 22).

2. All land under Mechanised Farming Schemes is considered to be tractorised. Most of the irrigated land has also been so considered. However, some other areas which do not enter into either of these two categories also use tractors, for example, household producers in the vicinity of Mechanised Farming areas (see case studies of Western Savannah and Gedaref). Also in the so-called 'Modernisation Projects', e.g. the Nuba Mountain Agricultural Production Corporation, tractors are used (in 1979 30,000 feddans had been brought into the project – World Bank Report, Vol. III, 1979: 10). It is assumed here that the tractorised areas outside the irrigated land and MFC are equal to the non-tractorised land in the irrigated areas. For estimates of the distribution of lands according to those categories see Note 3 in Chapter 3.

3. Unlike its policy in some other colonies, and due to its 'stabilisation policy' and fear of uprisings like the Mahdist movement (see below), the British administration tended to avoid levying heavy taxes and sometimes avoided them altogether; it also largely avoided the use of coercive labour (see M. Abdelrahim, 1969; MacMichael, 1954). In fact in some cases Egyptian convicts were brought to undertake some 'public works' to avoid resorting to local coercive labour (see Martin, 1921: 223).

   The Mahdist movement was led by Mohammed Ahmed El-Mahdi (the last name, which means 'divinely-guided leader', was ascribed to him). It was a national movement which led to the ending of Turko-Egyptian rule (1820–1881) and lasted until the British army conquered El-Mahdi's successor in 1898. (For details of the movement see Holt, 1958.)

CHAPTER THREE

1. The concession was granted first to an American entrepreneur called Leigh Hunt. He set up a company in England called Sudan Experimental Plantation Syndicate Ltd. His intention, according to Tracey (1948: 760), was to settle Black Americans on the lands there. The project was a failure and the company was handed over to a new one, the Sudan Plantation Syndicate.

2. This scheme was offered by the colonial government to Abdel Rahman and Ahmed Elfadil Mahdi, son of the renowned El Mahdi. In their schemes the El Mahdi family used the direct labour of their followers which was rarely remunerated other than by daily food rations.

3. The World Bank Report, Vol. II (1979: 105) estimated total land under irrigation in the late 1970s to be 4,165,000 feddans. Adding to that the expansion in the 1980s of the Rahad Scheme in central Sudan, we get a total of about 4,315,000 feddans under irrigation in the early 1980s. Subtracting from this sum an estimate of lands on which other production relations than those described as 'transitional pattern' prevail, we remain with about 4,250,000 feddans. Land under cultivation by the Mechanised Farming Schemes has been estimated to be about 5,934,000 feddans in

1982/83 (Chapter 4). The third category of land used by the World Bank Report is the 'traditional' one. This has been estimated to be about 10–11 million feddans. In my calculations, I took it to be 10.5 million feddans. Total land cultivated could then be estimated as 20,749,000 feddans. The AOAD (1978: 27) estimate of total land cultivated in the mid-1970s is 18 million feddans. So, 20.8 millions in the early 1980s may also seem to be reasonable.

Agricultural crop intensity of the irrigated areas has been estimated to be 1.825 times that of the rainlands (*Ibid*: 22). This is taken here as the main criterion for differences in output, as no significant differences in the production techniques or other factors could be traced between the two types of land.

Estimates of the number of tenants have been built on data available, and mentioned above, on number of tenants in Gezira and Pump Schemes (in the Gezira 100,000 tenants in 2 million feddans, in Pump Schemes, 90,000 tenants in 1.7 million feddans) and an estimate for the rest of the land under what has been characterised as transition to capitalism.

4. In estimating the total labour requisite (in an operation, or for all operations in one crop, etc) and within this the contribution of the different forms of labour, the different surveys in the Gezira seem to adopt one or both of the following two methods: (1) estimating the person days by multiplying the number of persons involved in a certain agricultural operation by the number of days that operation is estimated to take; (2) estimating the person days by dividing the total wages paid for a certain operation by a sum estimated to be the average payment for a working day. Several problems are posed by these two methods. In the first, the number of persons involved may not take into account the differences in the length and intensity of the working day, as neither the members of the tenant's household nor the wage labourers (who are mostly contracted on a piece rate system at present, and, when contracted on a daily basis, the whole day or only part of it – i.e. *dahawiya* (morning hours) or *douhriya* (late morning to afternoon) – may be contracted as well) are restricted to a specific length of working day. Also of course, intensity of work among individuals varies. (Among certain groups there are also some variations in labour intensity, see amongst others A. Abdelhamid, 1965; Culwick, 1955.) The second method of estimation is also problematic as it does not allow for differences in wages in different parts of the Gezira, in different operations and among different individuals. What is more, information upon which estimates are made is normally derived from the tenants, who generally do not keep records, and it therefore depends on the tenants' memory or other subjective judgements, or on the interviewer's (or researcher's) own estimates.

5. Thl was estimated to have carried out 16,175,160 person days in 1979/80 (Barnett, 1983: 38). If we assume 250 working days a year per person, then 64,702 economically active persons were fully engaged in farm labour in that year. Comparing this to the number of registered tenants, 102,247 (SGB Economic Survey, 1981: 53), we arrive at the actual number of labour units fully available for each tenant household.

6. Interviews were held by Taha Al Jack Taha during the field survey of T. Barnett's report on 'The Labour Market in the Irrigated Areas of the Sudan' in 1982. Tenants were selected from four blocks in the Gezira and the report considers the sample to be fairly representative of Gezira Scheme tenants. In the summary of interviews, information was provided as to the size of land cultivated, different crops and the number of people engaged in carrying out each operation and their distribution according to thl and non-thl (sharecropping and wage labour). From this information, the table was constructed. Persons who contributed in each operation were taken to have contributed the same amount of labour. Working days in each operation were calculated using data provided in the SGB Economic Survey for 1980/81. After calculating the contribution of thl and non-thl in every single case, the major source of labour was determined. Naturally, results of such estimates should be treated with some caution.

7. The proportion of watering labour to the total labour required in all operations per feddan per crop has been calculated using different tables in the SGB Economic Survey (1981). These proportions were then used to determine the average person days of

180

watering using data in Euroconsult Report (1982, Vol. 1, 15) assuming an average landholding of 12 feddans (5 cotton, 2 groundnuts, 3 dura and 2 wheat – an estimate based on the actual distribution of the total land cultivated among the different crops in Gezira in 1980/81, as given by SGB, 1981).

8. *Samad* is an agricultural assistant, *Khafir* means guard; both are employed by the Sudan Gezira Board.

CHAPTER FOUR

1. Anti-slave-trade rules had been enacted by Gordon, the last Governor of Sudan during Turko-Egyptian rule. Those rules were reactivated during the early period of British rule (1898–1955). However, as O'Brien (1980: 164–5) shows, slavery as an institution had not been seriously challenged before the early 1920s when a greater demand for wage labour arose on account of the soon-to-be-established Gezira Scheme.

2. Personal communication from Mirghani Mahgoub, the first Sudanese Agricultural Inspector in charge of the Gedaref area.

3. During my field trip to Gedaref I met two former tenants of the Gezira; one is at present cultivating *bildat* land and working as a casual labourer in Gedaref, and the other is a large farmer cultivating over 1,000 feddans.

4. Demarcated allotted land amounted to 55% of all land cultivated in 1982/83. According to the MFC most of this demarcated land (over 90%) had been offered to large farmers. MFC officials estimate that nearly half of the other 45% (non-demarcated) of cultivated land is in the hands of large farmers.

5. Information was provided by Wagdi Mahgoub, a friend and farmer in Gedaref. The author is grateful to Wagdi.

6. Information has been obtained from some of the MFC officials and some other individuals with a long history in Gedaref. The average land holding of super-large farmers has been estimated at 20,000 feddans. The number of super-large farmers has been counted according to information commonly confirmed by the different sources. This should be treated with caution; however, it indicates a clear trend. Between the years 1979/80 and 1982/83 on average the number of super-large farmers was 28; figures for each year separately are not available.

7. No estimate of the number of casual agricultural workers is available. I have been able to estimate the average person days needed per feddan in 1982/83 to be about 7 days; normally this may range between 6 and 10 days depending on rains (quantity of weeding) and yields (harvest labour). Accordingly, Gedaref needed about 21,000,000 person days in 1982/83. Most of the workers, as has been shown in the study cited above, come in particular seasons (weeding and/or harvest) from outside the region. In the harvest season 1982/83 workers interviewed claimed to work (or expected to work) for about 30–90 days in the entire agricultural season; weeding may require about 45 days, the dura and sesame harvest about 85 days. Taking an average of 60 days as a rough estimate, the total number of casual workers may be estimated to be about 350,000.

   Similarly there is no data on the number of tractors and lorries operating in Gedaref. From a 1977 estimate of the average number of tractors in the Sudan, it was claimed there was one tractor for every 1,500 cultivated feddans (Zein al Abdin, 1977). On this basis there would have been 2,000 tractors operating in Gedaref, bearing in mind the fact that MFS are more tractorised than what is called the 'traditional sector' and less tractorised than irrigated areas. Also that not all the 3,000,000 feddans cultivated in Gedaref in 1981/82 and 1982/83 were prepared by tractor. This estimate is also more or less compatible with data I have collected. The number of harvesters and lorries, according to estimates made from the field survey, is approximately $\frac{1}{4}$ to $\frac{1}{3}$ and $\frac{1}{3}$ to $\frac{1}{2}$ of the number of tractors respectively. Each of these mechanised units would need three persons when in full operation. Drivers and assistants operating harvesters are mostly engaged in operating tractors as well. Consequently, the number of workers engaged in operating tractors, harvesters and lorries may be estimated to have been 8–9,000 (2.3–2.6%) in 1982/83.

CHAPTER FIVE

1. Shahida Albaz conducted a field survey in Gezira in 1975/76 and Tony Barnett conducted a field survey in 1982.
2. For the year 1955/56 the Western Sudanese/West African settlers' proportion has been derived from the 1955/56 Population Census, while the relevant ratio for 1983 came from the 1983 survey (see note 4, below). Caution has been invited regarding these proportions for two reasons. First, the three proportions have been derived from different sources, which have no one unified method of estimation. Second, and more important, some of those claiming western Sudanese origin in 1955/56 and 1983 may in fact have a West African origin. Some West Africans having acquired, or hoping to acquire, Sudanese nationality may not be willing to reveal their non-Sudanese origin, as they may forfeit their chances of getting certain facilities given to Sudanese only, e.g. permanent employment in government projects, access to land, etc.
3. *Tulba* labour is a contract made by the Scheme's field inspectors on behalf of those tenants who are considered to be delaying or neglecting a certain operation in cotton production. Wage labourers are contracted to carry out these specific operations and the money, which is paid by the Administration, is deducted from the tenants involved.
4. Among 47 settled workers in the sample, 32 have reported living in labour camps. Five of the latter have not engaged in wage labouring in the Scheme in 1982/83, but have depended on sharecropping arrangements. Twenty out of the rest have engaged in sharecropping as well as wage labouring.
5. This section is based on a paper by the author (1985/86) in the *Review of African Political Economy* (*ROAPE*), 34, 1985.
6. All quotations from O'Brien are taken from his article in *ROAPE*, 26, pp. 15–34.

CHAPTER SIX

1. The British had economic, political and strategic interests in Egypt, which is at the meeting point of important trade routes. To secure these interests the occupation of Sudan seemed to be imperative, especially after the rising of the Mahdist national movement in the Sudan. They also wanted to halt the progress of rival colonial powers (see amongst others, Abdel Rahim, 1969).
2. One of the main cornerstones of the British colonial policy. One main objective of its occupation of Sudan (see note 1 above) was to provide political stability, which the planners of that policy thought would be reduced considerably by actions of foreign capital engaged in direct production, entailing subjugation of the local people. Apparently the experiences of the Mahdist movement had made the British cautious in this respect. However, this policy had often been described by colonial apologetics (e.g. Gaitskell, 1959) as a 'genuine move' towards 'elimination of exploitation of the people' by land companies, etc.
3. The author is grateful to Elhassan who made his survey available to the author prior to completion of his (1985) work.
4. The comparison is correct only if usage of 'urban' and 'rural' is similar in the two sources. However, it is unknown to the author whether this is the case.
5. In the Handicrafts Survey of 1970/71 (Department of Statistics, 1976) the total number of people working (wage labourers plus owners) was 36,441. No separate estimate of wage labourers is given. The total number of handicraft shops was 19,022. It has been assumed here that every handicraft shop owner works in his shop, and this number was then subtracted.
6. The 1970/71 and the 1978/79 Industrial Surveys were used for determining the actual weight of different types and sizes of industries, although with the latter the difficulties

were that categorisation used was mainly according to firms employing under 10, 10–25 and over 25 workers. However, this has been considered inadequate here and an alternative categorisation was used. (This is because the actual sub-categorisation within the over 25 workers' firms was great. In fact, firms employing over 100 workers are quite numerous, and firms employing over 500 or even over 1,000 workers were not uncommon.)

7. Parents' work may not necessarily mean that both parents had done the same job. In fact, only 30.4% of the respondents had parents doing the same work. 57% had only one of their parents engaging in work while the other (mostly women) was undertaking domestic work (which apparently might include some productive work as well but not as a primary job). 2.5% of the respondents had parents each doing a different job (other than domestic work). On working out the table, I have considered only one full unit per two parents; if only one is working this is, therefore, represented by the same weight as that of two doing the same job, and when the parents are engaged in different types of work each is attributed 0.5 of a unit. (Multiple answers are always calculated in this work as a fraction of one unit.)

8. It was estimated earlier that the number of wage labourers in Gedaref in the season 1982/83 was in the range of 300,000, half of whom were landless. In other large agricultural employment areas like the Gezira and other so-called mechanised farming areas, there might be roughly 100,000–150,000 such landless wage workers. Similarly, at a rough estimate, there might be 800,000 to one million land-plot-holding wage labourers in the whole of the Sudan (this has been built on the number of seasonal labourers in Gedaref and the Gezira as have been estimated in Chapters 3 and 4 as well as working out estimates for other large agricultural employment areas where seasonal migrant labour is needed, depending on areas cultivated and degree of need to resort to wage labour). O'Brien (1983: 16) gives an estimate of 1.5–2 million seasonal labourers in Sudan, which is higher than the one given here.

Studies on the extent of local wage labour in different localities characterised by household production are very limited and hence there is a difficulty in even hazarding guesses, as has been done for other areas.

9. There are two; one is from Eritrea and the second is from Juba (a major town in Southern Sudan).

10. For the early history of the trade union movement in Sudan see Fawzi, 1957 and Taha, 1970. See also Warburg, 1978 for a general discussion of the role of the trade union movement and the Communist Party of Sudan. For a record of the class struggle of urban wage workers and the role of the CPS, see its publications (CPS, 1965 and 1967) as well as its organ *El-Midan*.

11. For a more detailed treatment see Abdelkarim, 1986.

12. The concept of class consciousness as levels or degrees is derived from Miliband, 1971.

CHAPTER SEVEN

1. For example, the Sudan Islamic Bank is backed by the El Mirghani family (leaders of a religious sect, and of a main political party, banned during Numeiry's time).

2. The World Bank Report (1979) uses a different categorisation: irrigated, traditional and mechanised agriculture. With some modifications these categories could be identical to the ones used in this book. Most of the irrigated land is actually under what I called transitional production relations. In the late 1970s land under irrigation was estimated at 4,165,000 feddans (Vol. II: 105). Adding to that expansion in the early 1980s (Rahad Scheme), and subtracting an estimate of lands on which other production relations than those described as 'transitional' prevail, we remain with about 4,250,000 feddans. 'Traditional' agriculture has been estimated by the World Bank Report to be about 10–11 million feddans. In my calculations I take it to be 10.5 million feddans.

3. The six countries researched are: Sudan, Costa Rica, Senegal, Bolivia, Thailand and Malawi. Note that the World Bank Report takes the size of capital inflows as those officially received, i.e. migrants' transfers that have not gone through the official channels have not been considered.

4. 'Border value' is the value/price of a product at the borders, i.e. at the port of export (i.e. ready for export). It is different from C.I.F. in that it includes freight cost only partially – not to the consumption point but only to the port of export.

5. FOB (Free On Board) means the manufacturer's price of a product, which does not include the cost of transporting the product to the consumer. It differs from C.I.F. (Cost, Insurance, Freight) which refers to a price that includes insurance and freight as well as the manufacturer's cost.

6. Merchants would get most of their hard currency from non-bank channels, which have been coming largely from transfers of migrant Sudanese (see Galel el Din, 1986/a).

7. The Military Economic Board was established in 1982 and was granted operation in almost every field of the economy, although its activities remained mainly in commerce. After the overthrow of Numerey in April 1985 most of its activities were frozen.

8. For more details on the deterioration of the economy and inflation, see among others A. Ali (1985).

9. There is no official register of the 'free' market exchange rates. Figures cited depend on the author's own diary. Figures, however, are very close to estimates of Galal el Din (1986/a and 1986/b).

CITED WORKS

ARC Report (1975) *Problems of Mechanized Crop Production in the Gedaref Region*. A report by the Agricultural Research Council (ARC), Khartoum.

Abdalla, A. (1982) *The Political Economy of Banking in the Sudan: 1970–1977*. Discussion Paper, DSRC, University of Khartoum.

Abdel Aziz, O.E. (1979) 'Production and Marketing of Dura and Sesame in the Central Rainlands of the Sudan', PhD Thesis, University of Leeds.

Abdelhamid, A. (1965) 'Agricultural Labour in Gezira Scheme'. Unpublished report, Sudan Gezira Board, Sudan.

Abdelkarim, A. (1985/a) 'The Development of Sharecropping Arrangements in Sudan Gezira: Who is Benefitting?', *Peasant Studies*, Vol. 13, No. 1, 25–37.

Abdelkarim, A. (1985/b) 'The Segmented Agricultural Labour Market in Sudan', *Review of African Political Economy*, 34, 46–53.

Abdelkarim, A. (1986) 'Toward The Political Economy of Wage Determination: A Case Study of Sudanese Agricultural Labour Markets', *Research in Political Economy*, Vol. 9.

Abdel Rahim, A.W. (1963) 'Economic History of the Sudan', MA Dissertation, University of Manchester.

Abdel Rahim, M. (1969) *Imperialism and Nationalism in the Sudan*. Oxford University Press, London.

Acharya, S.N. (1979) *Incentives for Resource Allocation: A Case Study of the Sudan*. World Bank Working Paper No. 367. Washington D. C.

Adam, F.H. (1971) *Economic Appraisal of Agrarian Reforms in the Private Cotton States*. Working Paper, Department of Rural Economy, University of Khartoum, Khartoum.

Adam, F.H. (1978) 'Evolution of the Gezira pattern of development within the context of the history of Sudanese agricultural relations', *Sudan Journal of Development Research*, Vol. 2, No. 1.

Affan, K.O. (1978) *Output Equipment and Income Distribution in Mechanical Farms*. Economic and Social Research Council, Research Report No. 2, Khartoum.

Affan, K.O. (1982) 'Effects on Aggregate Peasant Labour Supply of Rural–Rural Migration to Mechanical Farming – a Case Study of Southern Kordofan-Sudan', PhD Thesis, University of Sussex.

Ahmed, S.A. (1977) 'The Integration of Agricultural Credit and Marketing in the Gezira-Scheme of Sudan', Unpublished PhD Thesis, University of London.

Al-Arifi, S.A. (1975) 'Landlordism among small farmers: the case of the Gezira Tenants in the Sudan', *Sudan Journal of Economic and Social Studies*, Vol. 1, No. 2.

Alavi, H. (1975) 'India and the Colonial Mode of Production', *The Socialist Register*, pp. 160–97.

Al-Ayam: 5/12/84, Khartoum.

Ali, A.A.G. (ed.) (1985) *The Sudan Economy in Disarray*, published by Ali Abdel Gadir Ali, Khartoum.

Ali, A.A.G. (1986) *Exploratory notes on transfers and development finance* (in Arabic). Paper presented to a meeting on 'Transfers of Arabs Working Abroad', held at the Arab Planning Institute, Kuwait, 5–7 April 1986.

Ali, T.M.A. (1982) 'The Cultivation of Hunger: Towards the Political Economy of Agricultural Development in the Sudan 1956–1964', PhD Thesis, University of Toronto.

Ali, T.M.A. (1983) 'The Road to Jouda', *Review of African Political Economy*, No. 26, 4–14.

Amin, M.A. (1970) 'Ancient Trade and Trade Routes between Egypt and Sudan, 4000 to 7000 BC', *Sudan Notes and Records*.

AOAD (1978) *A Study of the Problems of the Conflicts of Interests between the Nomadic Pastoralists and the Sedentary Cultivators in Khasm el-Girba, Gezira and Ruhad Schemes in the Sudan Democratic Republic* (in Arabic), Khartoum by the Arab Organisation for Agricultural Development in the Arab League.

Arab Monetary Fund (1985) *Economic Report on the Democratic Republic of Sudan* (in Arabic), Abu Dhabi.

Asad, T. (1966) 'A note on the history of the Kababish tribe', *Sudan Notes and Records*, 47, 79–87.

Asad, T. (1970) *The Kabibish Arabs: Power, Authority and Consent in a Nomadic Tribe*, Hurst, London.

Banaji, J. (1973) 'Backward Capitalism, primitive accumulation and modes of production', *Journal of Contemporary Asia*, Vol. 3, 393–413.

Banaji, J. (1977) 'Modes of production in a Marxist conception of history', *Capital and Class*, 1–44.

Bank of Sudan (1977) *Annual Report*, Bank of Sudan, Khartoum.

Bank of Sudan (1978) *Annual Report*, Bank of Sudan, Khartoum.

Bank of Sudan (1983) *Economic and Financial Statistical Review*, Vol. 23, Nos. 2 and 4, Bank of Sudan, Khartoum.

Bank of Sudan (1985) *Annual Statistical Abstract of Foreign Trade – 1984*, Vol. 17, No. 4, Khartoum (in Arabic).

Barbour, K.M. (1961) *The Republic of the Sudan: A Regional Geography*. University of London Press, London.

Barnett, T. (1977) *Gezira Scheme: An Illusion of Development*. Frank Cass, London.

Barnett, T. (1983) 'The Labour Market in the Irrigated Areas of the Sudan', a draft report submitted to the ILO/UNHCR. Published in *The Labour Market in the Sudan*, ILO/UNHCR, Geneva, 1984.

Beshai, Adel. A. (1976) *Export Performance and Development in Sudan 1900–1966*. Ithaca Press, London.

Bolton, A.R.C. (1948) 'Land Tenure in Agricultural Land in the Sudan', in Tothill (ed) (1948).

Brenner, R. (1977) 'The Origins of Capitalist Development: a Critique of Neo-Smithian Marxism', *New Left Review*, No. 104, 25–92.

Brown, R. (1984) *Sudan's Balance of Payment Crisis and the Role of the IMF since 1978*. Paper presented to Sudan Research Workshop, 3–5 July, 1984. ISS, The Hague.

Brown, R. and Shaaeldin, E. (1982) *Towards an Understanding of Islamic Banking in Sudan: The City of Fuisal Islamic Bank*. Discussion Paper, Development Studies Research Center (DSRC), University of Khartoum.

CPS (1965) *People's Revolution*. Published by the Communist Party of the Sudan, Khartoum (in Arabic).

CPS (1967) *Marxism and Problems of the Sudanese Revolution*. Published by the Communist Party of the Sudan, Khartoum (in Arabic).

Culwick, G. B. (1955) *A Study of the human factors in the Gezira Scheme, 1951/55*. Manuscript Sudan Gezira Board, Archive Center, Bib. No. 460/18.

Cunnison, I. (1966) *Baggara Arabs: Power and Lineage in a Sudanese Nomadic Tribe*. Clarendon Press, Oxford.

Department of Agricultural Economics (1979) *Agricultural Statistical Bulletin* (no number given), Khartoum.

Department of Statistics (1976) *Handicrafts Survey of 1970/71*, Khartoum.

Department of Statistics (1978/79) *Industrial Survey* (appearing in four volumes in different years), Khartoum.

Dey, J., Elbagir, I. and Wagner, A. (1984) 'The Rural Labour Market in the Rainfed Farming Areas of Eastern Sudan', in *The Labour Markets in the Sudan*, ILO/UNHCR, Geneva.

Dey, J., Elbagir, I. and Wagner, A. (1983) *The Rural Labour Market in the Rainfed Farming Areas of Eastern Sudan*. A report presented to the ILO/UNHCR Project on 'Income Generating Activities for the Refugees in the Sudan', Khartoum, February 1983.

CITED WORKS

Duffield, M. (1981) *Maiuro: Capitalism and Rural Life in Sudan*. Ithaca Press, London.

Duffield, M. (1983) 'West African Settlers in Northern Sudan', *Review of African Political Economy*, 26, 45–59.

Elhassan, A.M. (1985) 'The State and the Development of Capitalism in Agriculture in the Sudan', PhD Thesis, University of East Anglia.

Euroconsult Report (1982) *Gezira Rehabilitation and Modernisation Project*, Vols. I and II (place of publication unknown).

Fawzi, S. (1957) *The Labour Movement in the Sudan 1946–1955*. Oxford University Press, London.

First National Economic Conference (1982) *Report on Main Industries in the Sudan*, Khartoum, December 1982.

Foster-Carter, A. (1978) 'The Modes of Production Controversy', *The New Left Review*, 107, 47–77.

Funno-Tchuiquua, B. (1978) 'De facto wage earners in the Gezira Scheme (Sudan)', *African Development*, 3(1), 25–50.

Gaitskell, A. (1959) *Gezira Scheme: A Story of Development in Sudan*. Faber & Faber, London.

Galal el Din, M.E. (1973) 'Internal Migration in the Sudan Since World War II', PhD Thesis, University of London.

Galal el Din, M.E. (1985) Transfers of Sudanese Working Abroad. Paper presented in a seminar in the Development Research and Studies Center, University of Khartoum – later published by them (in Arabic).

Galal el Din, M.E. (1986a) External Economic Relations and Possibilities of Self Reliance – Sudan Case Study. Paper presented in the Arab Planning Institute, Kuwait, 15 February.

Galal el Din, M.E. (1986b) Transfers of Sudanese Working in the Oil Countries. Paper presented to a conference on 'Transfers of Arabs Working Abroad', the Arab Planning Institute, 5–7 April (in Arabic).

Haaland, G. (ed) (1980) *Problems of Savannah Development: The Sudan Case*. Occasional Paper No. 19, Department of Social Anthropology, University of Bergen.

Haaland, G. (1980a) 'Problems of Savannah Development', in Haaland, G. (ed) (1980).

Haaland, G. (1980b) 'Social Organisation and Ecological Pressure in Southern Darfur', in Haaland, G. (ed) (1980).

Harriss, J. (1979) *The Mode of Production Controversy – Theories and Problems of the Debate*. Discussion Paper No. 60, School of Development Studies, University of East Anglia.

Hakem, O. (1976) *Revision of agricultural production relations in the Sudan*. A report by the Department of Agricultural Economics, Ministry of Agriculture, Khartoum, Sudan (in Arabic).

Hassoun, I.A. (1952) '"Western" migration and settlement in the Gezira', *Sudan Notes and Records*, 33, 60–103, Khartoum.

Henderson, K.D. (1946) *Survey of the Anglo-Egyptian Sudan 1898–1944*. Longmans and Green, London.

Hewison, J. (1948) 'Northern Province Agriculture', in Tothill (ed) *Agriculture in the Sudan*. Oxford University Press, London.

Hilton, R. (ed) (1976) *The Transition from Feudalism to Capitalism*. New Left Books, London.

Holt, P.M. (1958) *The Mahdist State in the Sudan 1888–1898*. Oxford University Press, London.

ILO (1976) *Growth, Employment and Equity – a comprehensive strategy for the Sudan*. ILO, Geneva.

ILO/UNHCR (1984) *Labour Markets in Sudan*. ILO, Geneva.

Industrial Survey 1970/71 (1976) A Report by the Department of Statistics, Khartoum.

Kay, G. (1975) *Development and Underdevelopment: A Marxist Analysis*. St Martin's Press, London.

Kursany, I. (1982) 'The Impact of the Development of Capitalism on the Past and Future of Pre-Capitalist Agriculture in Sudan', PhD Thesis, University of Leeds.

187

Laclau, E. (1971) 'Feudalism and Capitalism in Latin America', *New Left Review*, 67, 19–39.

Laing, R.G. (1953) *Mechanisation in Agriculture in the Rainland of the Anglo-Egyptian Sudan 1948–51*. Report of the Sudan Survey Department, Khartoum.

Lako, G.T. (1983) 'Jonglei Canal Project and its Impact on the Development of the Southern Sudan and on the Life of the Dinka People', PhD Thesis, University of Manchester.

Lange, O. (1963) *Political Economy*, Oxford University Press.

Leinhardt, G. (1967) 'Western Dinka', in Middleton, J. and Tait, D., *Tribes without Rulers: Studies in African Segmentary Systems*. Routledge & Kegan Paul, London.

Luxemburg, R. (1963) *The Accumulation of Capital*. Routledge and Kegan Paul, London.

Mackinnon, E. (ed.) (1948) 'Blue Nile Province', in Tothill (ed) *Agriculture in Sudan*, Oxford University Press.

MacMichael, H. (1954) *The Sudan*, Benn, London.

Mahmoud, F.B. (1979) 'Origins and Development of the Capitalist Class – A Socio-political Analysis', PhD Thesis, University of Hull.

Martin, P. F. (1921) *The Sudan in Evolution*. Constable, London.

Marx, K. (1950) 'Wages, Price and Profit', in Marx & Engels, *Selected Works*, Volume 1, Foreign Languages Publishing House, Moscow.

Marx, K. (1976) *Capital (Volume 1): A Critique of Political Economy*. Penguin Books and New Left Books, London.

MFC *Agricultural Statistical Bulletin* (1979). An Occasional Bulletin of the Mechanized Farming Corporation.

Miliband, R. (1971) 'Barnava: a case of bourgeois class consciousness', in Meszaros, I. (ed), *Aspects of History and Class Consciousness*. Routledge and Kegan Paul, London.

MFNE – Ministry of Finance and National Economy (undated), Economic Survey 1980, Khartoum.

Mustafa, M.A. (1980) 'A comparison of sedentary cultivation and nomadic pastoralists and their market integration in the Radoam area of Southern Darfur', in Haaland, G. (ed) (1980).

O'Brien, J. (1980) 'Agricultural labour force and development in the Sudan'. Unpublished PhD Thesis, University of Connecticut.

O'Brien, J. (1983) 'Formation of the Agricultural Labour Force', *Review of African Political Economy*, No. 26, 15–34.

O'Fahey, R.S. (1980) *State and Society in Dar Fur*. Hurst, London.

O'Fahey, R.S. and Spaulding, J. L. (1974) *Kingdoms of the Sudan*. Methuen, London.

Omer, E.A.B. (1979) 'Local Traders and Agricultural Development in Dongola Area: A Study in Rural Capitalism from Northern Sudan', PhD Thesis, University of Hull.

Osman, O.M. (1958) 'Some Economic Aspects of Private Pump Schemes in the Blue Nile Province'. *Sudan Notes and Records*.

Preobrazhensky, E. (1967) *The New Economics*. Clarendon Press, Oxford.

Purves, W.D.C.L. (1935) 'Some Aspects of the Northern Province', in Hamilton, J.A. de C. (ed) *The Anglo Egyptian Sudan*. Faber & Faber, London.

Rabih, S.U. (1979) 'Commercial Policy and Effects on Manufacturing Industry', PhD Thesis, University of London.

SGB (1981) *Field Crops Economic Survey of 1980/81*, Sudan Gezira Board, Barakat, Sudan. (1982) *Study of Cost of Production and Comparative Advantages of Crops under Different Farming Systems in Sudan 1980/81*. UNPD/IBRD Planning Assistance and Training Project, Ministry of Finance and Economic Planning, Khartoum, Sudan

Sattar, A. (1982) *Study of Cost of Production and Comparative Advantages of Crops under Different Farming Systems in Sudan 1980/81*. UNPD/IBRD Planning Assistance and Training Project, Ministry of Finance and Economic Planning, Khartoum, Sudan.

Shaaeldin, E. (1981) 'The Development of Peripheral Capitalism in the Sudan', PhD Thesis, State University of New York.

Shaaeldin, E. (1982) *The Mechanisms of Proletarianisation in the Sudan*. DSRC Seminar Series 6, University of Khartoum.

CITED WORKS

Shaw, J.D. (1961?) 'Labour problems in the Gezira Scheme'. A manuscript, Sudan Gezira Board, Archive Center.

Simpson, G.A. and Simpson, M. (1978) 'Alternative Strategies for Agricultural Development in the Central Rainlands of the Sudan', *Rural Development Studies No. 3*, University of Leeds.

Smith, A. (1976) *The Wealth of Nations*. Clarendon Press, Oxford.

Sorbo (1977) *How to Survive Development: The Story of New Halfa*. DSRC Monograph No. 6, University of Khartoum.

Spaulding, J.L. (1979) 'Farmers, Herdsmen and the State in Rainlands of Sennar', *Journal of African History*, 20,3.

Statistical Abstract 1981 (undated), an irregular statistical bulletin, Department of Statistics, Khartoum, Sudan.

Sudan Guide (1982/83) Planning and Management Consultancy, Khartoum, Sudan.

Sudan Guide (1984/85) Planning and Management Consultancy, Khartoum, Sudan.

Sudanese Industries Union (1982) *The Views of the Industries Union on the Economic Policies*. Paper presented to the First Economic Conference, Khartoum (in Arabic).

Taha, A.E. (1970) 'The Sudanese Labour Movement: A Study of Labour Unionism in a Developing Society', PhD Thesis, University of California, Los Angeles.

Tamim, O.A. (1980) *Labour Camps in Gezira*. A report of Sudan Gezira Board's Department of Social Research (in Arabic).

The Guardian (1/10/1984) London.

Tothill, J.D. (1948) *Agriculture in the Sudan*. Oxford University Press, London.

Tracey, C. (1948) 'A Note on Zeidab Project', in Tothill (ed) (1948).

Warburg, G. (1978) *Islam, Nationalism and Communism in a Traditional Society*. Frank Cass, London.

Wolpe, H. (1980) 'Introduction', in Wolpe, H. (ed) *The Articulation of Modes of Production*. Routledge and Kegan Paul, London.

World Bank (1979) *Sudan – Agricultural Sector Survey, Vol. I, II and III*. Report No. 1836a-SU-W.B, Washington D. C.

World Bank (1985) *Sudan – Prospects for Rehabilitation of the Sudanese Economy, Vol. I, II & III*. Report No. 5496-SU, World Bank, Washington, D.C.

Zein al Abdin, O. (1977) *Problems of Mechanisation of Agriculture in the Gedaref Area*. Paper presented to the 2nd Conference of Mechanical Farming, Gedaref, Sudan.

NEWSPAPERS, PAMPHLETS AND ADDRESSES

Al-Ayam: 5/12/84 – Khartoum.

CPS (1973) 'On the Programme', issued by the Communist Party of Sudan.

CPS (1977) 'Issues and Duties of Foreign Policy', a pamphlet issued by the Communist Party of Sudan.

Gezira newspaper: 26/1/80.

The Guardian: 10/1/84.

'Military Economic Board', an undated prospectus, MEB (Sudan) Office, London.

President of the Sudanese Chamber of Commerce address to the Second Conference of the Sudanese Business Association – December 1982.

Sudanow: March 1980, SGB.

The Times: 18/2/85.

INDEX

190

Printed in the United States
by Baker & Taylor Publisher Services